Exploring Python

Timothy A. Budd
Oregon State University

 **Higher Education**

Boston   Burr Ridge, IL   Dubuque, IA   New York   San Francisco   St. Louis
Bangkok   Bogotá   Caracas   Kuala Lumpur   Lisbon   London   Madrid   Mexico City
Milan   Montreal   New Delhi   Santiago   Seoul   Singapore   Sydney   Taipei   Toronto

The *McGraw·Hill* Companies

 **Higher Education**

EXPLORING PYTHON

Some ancillaries, including electronic and print components, may not be available to customers outside the United States.

This book is printed on acid-free paper.

1 2 3 4 5 6 7 8 9 0 DOC/DOC 0 9

ISBN 978–0–07–352337–8
MHID 0–07–352337–2

Global Publisher: *Raghothaman Srinivasan*
Director of Development: *Kristine Tibbetts*
Senior Marketing Manager: *Curt Reynolds*
Project Manager: *Joyce Watters*
Senior Production Supervisor: *Laura Fuller*
Associate Design Coordinator: *Brenda A. Rolwes*
Cover Designer: *Studio Montage, St. Louis, Missouri*
(USE) Cover Image: © *Brand X Pictures/PunchStock*
Senior Photo Research Coordinator: *John C. Leland*
Compositor: *Lachina Publishing Services*
Typeface: *10/12 Times Roman*
Printer: *R. R. Donnelley Crawfordsville, IN*

Library of Congress Cataloging-in-Publication Data

Budd, Timothy.
  Exploring Python / Timothy A. Budd. — 1st ed.
     p. cm.
  Includes index.
  ISBN 978–0–07–352337–8 — ISBN 0–07–352337–2 (hard copy : alk. paper) 1. Python (Computer program language) I. Title.
  QA76.73.P98B84 2010
  005.13'3—dc22
                              2008051611

www.mhhe.com

CONTENTS

PREFACE

TO THE STUDENT: WHY PYTHON?

With so many other programming languages available, why should you learn to program in Python? Your reason could be simply that you signed up for a beginning programming class, and this is what was offered. But because Python is powerful, Python is easy, Python is fun, and Python is educational, it's a great place to start. Python also lets you do some very interesting things.

If you look at the case studies toward the end of the book, you will realize that programming in Python can be a versatile skill. Tasks such as writing your own blog, automatically solving Sudoku puzzles, reading your iTunes database, or writing a wiki take no more than a page or two of Python code. This is a considerably smaller amount of coding than is required by the equivalent programs in almost any other programming language.

Is it easy? Let's say it is eas*ier*. Computer programming in any language takes skill, organization, logic, and patience. Python is no different in this regard. What makes Python attractive is that you can begin writing code quickly and easily. Your first Python program can be as simple as 2 + 3:

```
>>> 2 + 3
5
```

Thereafter, the path to learning how to create your own complex applications is, hopefully, at least clearly laid out, even if it will take some effort on your part.

Active Learning

This book follows a teaching methodology called *active learning*. Rather than treating you, the student, as a passive repository into which knowledge is poured, active learning seeks to engage you as a fully equal partner in the process of learning. Rather than simply telling you how some feature works, this text suggests experiments that you can perform to discover the answer on your own.

This approach has several benefits. First, it makes you use a different part of your brain than you'd use if you were simply reading. Second, it gives you a greater sense of ownership of the knowledge. Third, experimentation is often the fun part of programming. Last, by encouraging you to experiment in the discovery of simple information, I hope to instill habits that you will continue to carry with you throughout your programming career. When it's all put together, active learning helps you more easily retain and use the information you have learned.

What Is Python?

For those looking for buzz words, Python is a *high-level, interpreted, reflective, dynamically typed, open-source, multi-paradigm, general-purpose programming language*. I could explain each of these terms in detail, but in the end the result would still not convey what makes Python programming different from other languages. Python offers no special tools or features that let you do things that you cannot do with other languages, but its elegant design and combination of features make Python a pleasure to use.

Python is sometimes described as a *scripting language*, because thousands of working programmers use the language daily in this fashion. They use Python as a quick and easy tool to glue together software applications and components written in many different languages. But even this categorization is far too narrow, and Python can justly be described as a general-purpose language that you can use for almost any programming task.

This is not to say that Python is the *only* programming language you will ever need to learn. A working computer scientist should know how to use many different tools, and that means he or she should have an appreciation of many different types of language. For example, because Python is interpreted, the resulting programs are often not as fast as those written in lower-level languages, such as C or C++. On the other hand, Python programs are much easier to write than they would be in C.

There is a trade-off in using Python: Is less time in execution of the final program worth spending more time in development and debugging? For the beginning student, and in fact for the vast majority of computer programmers, the answer is clearly no. (Another way to express this trade-off is to ask, "Whose time is more important, your time or the computer's?") Low-level languages such as C have their place, but only for the small group of computer programs for which ultimate execution time *is* critically important. You may eventually work on such systems, but not in your first programming course.

Another important category of programming languages are those tied to a specific application. A good example is the language PHP (www.php.org), a programming language used to create interactive web pages. A general-purpose language such as Python cannot hope to be as easy to use in this application area. But PHP is extremely clumsy to use for purposes other than web pages. If, or when, you start extensive work in such an application area, you will want to learn how to use the tools found in Python.

Bottom line, Python is an excellent place to start—and to stay, for many of your programming tasks. But you should not assume that it is the last language you will ever need or learn. Fortunately, most languages share many common features. Having a solid foundation in one language (such as Python) makes it much easier to learn a second (or third, or fourth) language. Appendix B provides hints as to how you should approach the task of learning a new language.

History of Python

Python was designed by Guido van Rossum while he was working at the CWI (the *Centrum voor Wiskunde en Informatica*—literally "Center for Wisdom and Informatics"), a world-class research lab in the Netherlands. The CWI group with which he was associated designed a programming language called ABC. I was fortunate to spend a year with this group in 1985. ABC was clearly intended as a pedagogical tool for teaching programming, and a great deal of work went into developing both the language and associated teaching materials.[1]

The ABC language offered a number of features that were impressive for the time: a tightly integrated development environment, interactive execution, high-level data types (lists, dictionaries, tuples, and strings), dynamic memory management, strong typing without declaration statements, and more. The idea to use indentation for nesting and eliminating the brackets or BEGIN/END keywords found in most other languages was taken directly from ABC—so was the idea of dynamic typing. Software development in ABC was both rapid and enjoyable, and it was totally unlike almost any other competing language. (The one exception might be Smalltalk, which was just becoming well known in 1985. Indeed, during my time at the CWI, I was writing a book on Smalltalk, and part of the work I performed during that year was to explain to my colleagues in the ABC group the basic ideas of object-oriented programming, which I myself was only just beginning to understand).

Guido started designing Python around 1990. For those familiar with the earlier language, the heritage of ABC in Python is clear. Guido discarded some of the annoying features of ABC and kept all the best ideas, recasting them in the form of a more general-purpose language. By then, the mechanisms of object-oriented programming were well understood, and the language included all the latest features. He added a number of features not found in ABC, such as a system for modularization and including libraries of useful utilities. Python was released to the world in 1991, and it very quickly attracted a loyal following. Python's design turned out to be general enough to address a much wider range of applications than ABC. (To be fair, the designers of ABC were focused on teaching, and they never intended the language to be general-purpose.) The features that programmers appreciated in 1990 are still available today: ease of use, rapid software development, and the right set of data types that help you quickly address most common programming problems.

Python, Monty

The name, by the way, owes nothing to the reptile and everything to the 1970s BBC comedy series *Monty Python's Flying Circus*. Many diehard Python programmers enjoy making sly references to this series in their examples. You don't need to watch *Monty Python's Life of Brian, The Meaning of Life, And Now for Something Completely Different,* or *Monty Python and the Holy Grail*—or even *Spamalot*—to become a Python programmer, but it can't hurt.

---

[1] See the Wikipedia entry on ABC for further discussion of this language. The Wikipedia entry for Python has a much more complete history of the language. Another Wikipedia entry explains the concepts of active learning. See www.wikipedia.org.

TO THE INSTRUCTOR

This section begins with the same question used at the start of the preface to the students. Why is Python a better programming language for a first course than C, C++, Java, C#, Delphi, Ada, or Eiffel, just to name a few alternatives? The answer, as I suggested earlier, is that students will find that Python provides a much easier entrance into the world of programming, yet it is complete enough to provide a comprehensive introduction to all the important ideas in programming—plus it's fun to use.

The fact that Python can be used in both an interactive and textual style makes the barrier for the beginning student extremely low. This is not true for other languages. To write even the simplest Java program, for example, the instructor must explain (or worse, not explain and leave as a magic incantation) ideas such as classes, functions, standard input, static variables, arrays, strings, and more. In contrast, the first Python program can be as simple as 2 + 3:

```
>>> 2 + 3
5
```

The positive influence of interactive execution for the beginning student cannot be overstated. It permits (and the conscientious instructor should encourage) an exploratory and active approach to learning. To find out how something works, try it out! This empowers the student to take control of his or her own voyage of discovery, instead of simply playing the role of a passive container into which the instructor (or the book) pours information. I have discussed this *active learning* approach in my earlier remarks for the student.

The fact that programs are easy to write in Python should not be an excuse for thinking that the language is just a toy. It is a credit to the good design skills of Guido van Rossum and countless others that simple ideas are simple to express, and complex ideas can also be illustrated with simple examples. In what other language might an introductory textbook include examples of creating a blog, a wiki, or an XML parser?

Python is also an excellent vehicle for teaching computer science. All the basic concepts of programming (ideas such as values, variables, types, statements, conditionals, loops, functions, recursion, classes, and inheritance, to name a few) can be found in Python. The student gaining experience with these topics in this language is therefore in an excellent position to learn other languages more easily at a later time. Appendix B offers some general hints on how to go about learning a second, or third, programming language. These hints work for the student coming to Python with experience in a different language as well as students to whom this book is directed—those learning Python as their first language.

ORGANIZATION OF THIS BOOK

The first 11 chapters of this book present a more-or-less conventional introduction to programming. Students learn about variables, types, statements, conditionals, loops, functions, recursion, classes, and inheritance. What makes my approach different from that found in many other books is an attitude of exploration. Basic ideas are explained, and then the reader is led through a process of experimentation that helps them find and test the limits of their understanding. By making the learning process active, rather than simply a matter of absorption, the reader can engage in a wider range of cognitive operations, and this hopefully makes the material both more enjoyable to learn and easier to remember.

The next few chapters represent a series of case studies that explore the use of Python in a number of representative programming tasks, such as the creation of a blog, a Sudoku solver, a wiki, reading an iTunes database as an example of parsing XML, and more. These are intended to illustrate good Python programming style and to open the reader's mind to the range of problems that can be addressed using the language.

The case study chapters should be examined only after the students have examined the first 11 chapters, as they assume a familiarity with that material. After the first 11 chapters, the organization is much less linear. Instructors should feel free to present the latter material in any order, or pick and choose chapters as fits their needs.

Although the basic syntax of Python is covered in the first chapters and in Appendix A, the book cannot be considered a substitute for a reference manual. Much of the power of Python derives not from the basic language syntax, but from the wide range of libraries that have been developed to address problems in different domains. Fortunately, excellent reference material can be found at the web site www.python.org. Similarly, the scope of this book is purposely limited. Programs are generally restricted to no more than two pages in length. Readers interested in larger examples are encouraged to look at the much more comprehensive, encyclopedic, and *heavy* book *Programming Python*, by Mark Lutz (published by O'Reilly).

ADVANCED PACKAGES AND LIBRARIES

A huge amount of exciting and fun activities are available right now in the Python universe. Unfortunately, most of them require that the programmer download and install at least auxiliary libraries, if not complete applications. Examples include the integration of OpenGL and Python for 3-D visualization, game development systems such as PyGames, visual development environments such as Alice, and much, much more.

For a number of reasons, I have resisted discussing these topics in this book. First, I doubt that many students encountering programming for the first time using Python will have the ability, even after a term or two of experience with Python, to install such systems on their own. Second, the speed at which changes are occurring in this arena is phenomenal. Almost anything I could say in print would likely be obsolete, or even wrong, by the time the book appears on the bookstore shelves. On the positive side, if I am successful in my goal of encouraging students to embrace the ideas of active learning, then by the time they are finished with this book, they should have not only the knowledge, but also the self-confidence, to find information on the Internet on their own (and the Internet is now where the most reliable and up-to-date information is to be found). Try Googling the phrase "Python OpenGL" or whatever topic you want to explore. To those students, I say Good hunting, and have fun!

ACKNOWLEDGEMENTS

I wish to acknowledge the helpful comments I received from many readers, including Guido van Rossum (Google), Paolo Bucci (The Ohio State University), Pai H. Chou (University of California–Irvine), Paul Hewitt (University of Toledo), Stanley Reksc (Binghamton University), Robert H. Sloan (University of Illinois–Chicago), Zhi-Li Zhang (University of Minnesota), and a number of unnamed reviewers. Unfortunately, all remaining errors are entirely my own responsibility.

PART 1

Basic Features of Python

Exploring Python

Almost everybody has used a computer. If you have used a bank ATM, you have used a computer. If you listen to music on an iPod, you have used a computer. If you have a cell phone, you have used a computer. Nowadays, even your credit card can have a computer embedded in it.

© PictureNet/Blend Images/Corbis

The fact that the computer can be used in such a wide variety of different applications is astounding. But the computer is really just an extremely fast calculating machine—it performs a great many simple tasks with extreme rapidity. Before the computer could be used in any of these simple applications, somebody had to specify the exact instructions required to perform the task. This process is termed *programming*.

A computer does not understand natural languages, such as English. You cannot tell the computer "Play for me again that tune you played last Tuesday afternoon around

4 PM." Instead, instructions for a computer must be presented in a very structured form, termed a *programming language*. A great many programming languages are in common use. In this book you will learn one of these, a language named Python.

INTERACTIVE EXECUTION

Unlike many computer languages, Python allows the user to work in an interactive fashion, much like you'd use a calculator. You type an expression, and immediately the expression is executed and the result printed. If you start the Python system, you should first see a line containing version and copyright information. This will be immediately followed by a line beginning with three right arrows, as shown next:

```
Python 2.3.5 (#1, Mar 20 2005, 20:38:20)
[GCC 3.3 20030304 (Apple Computer, Inc. build 1809)] on
darwin
Type "help," "copyright," "credits" or "license" for more
information.
>>>
```

The three right arrows are the *expression prompt* telling you that the Python system is waiting for you to type an expression. The window in which the output is displayed and input is gathered is termed the *console*. Try entering a simple mathematical expression, such as 2 + 3. After you press enter/return, you should see the result printed, followed by a new expression prompt:

```
>>> 2 + 3
5
>>>
```

You can try various other expressions to get used to this style of operation. (A whole section on the range of operations that Python supports will be presented shortly.) You halt interactive execution by pressing control-D or ctrl-Z. (That is, press z while holding down the ctrl key. It's control-D on Macintosh and Unix machines and ctrl-Z on Windows machines). Try halting execution and restarting the Python system until you feel comfortable with the process. If you haven't made one already, try making a purposeful mistake. For example, try typing **2 plus three**:

```
>>> 2 plus three
```

The Python system doesn't know what to make of this statement. Therefore, it produces an error message—a text message that hopefully should tell you what it does not understand. Afterward the system resets itself and issues a new prompt and waits for you to continue.

```
>>> 2 plus three
File "<stdin>", line 1
2 plus three
^
SyntaxError: invalid syntax
>>>
```

Mistakes Are Opportunities for Learning

This book strongly advocates a style of instruction termed *active learning*, in which you, the student, participate in a discovery process by which you uncover important information on your own, rather than simply being told a series of facts. Making mistakes is (and always has been) an important part of the learning process. Mistakes help you uncover boundary cases, discover the limits of what Python can and cannot do, and explore the meaning of new ideas. You cannot seriously damage your computer by using the Python system, so you should feel free to experiment.

Almost all Python expressions are typed on a single line. You can see this if you type a binary operation and forget to fill in the right side:

```
>>> 2 +
File "<stdin>", line 1
2 +
  ^

SyntaxError: invalid syntax
```

An exception to this rule occurs when expressions are typed in parentheses. Each opening parenthesis must be matched to a closing parenthesis. If the closing parenthesis is not found, a *continuation prompt* is shown. Normally this continuation prompt looks like an ellipsis (. . .):

```
>>> (2 +
. . .
```

The continuation prompt is telling you that you need to type the rest of the expression. Type in the rest of the expression, press enter/return, and the expression will be evaluated:

```
>>> (2 +
. . . 3)
5
```

If you are faced with a three dot prompt and don't know what to do, you can simply enter right parentheses until you get back to the top-level prompt.

Comments

Any text that appears after a hash mark (#) is termed a *comment*. Comments are ignored by the Python system and are used purely to communicate information to a human reader. Here's an example:

```
>>> 2 + 3 # print two plus three
5
```

In interactive input, a line consisting entirely of comments will produce a continuation prompt. You can simply press return to proceed.

```
>>> # nothing at all
...
>>>
```

While legal, comments are not common in interactive input. However, they are common when Python statements are gathered together in a file to form a program. This style of use is described in the next chapter.

Types

Think of the information that is printed on your driver's license: your name, age, date of birth, a driver license number issued by the state, probably an indication whether or not you need corrective lenses, and so on. Notice that this information comes in a variety of forms. Your age is a *number*. Your name is a *string*. Whether or not you need lenses is a true/false value. In programming languages, we call these different forms of information *types*. The Python language has several built-in types.

The type you have been using up to this point is termed an *integer*. Integers are the counting numbers you are accustomed to from mathematics, both positive and negative. Some programming languages place an upper bound on the size of integers you can use. Python does not. Integers can be as large as you can type.

```
>>> 9999999999999999999999999999999999 + 1
10000000000000000000000000000000000
>>>
```

On some systems, you might see the capital letter *L* following the output, indicating that the result is *long*. The integer type does not include fractional numbers, which in programming languages are termed *floating-point numbers*. A floating-point number (or simply a *float*) has a decimal point and a fractional part. Arithmetic operations work with either integer or floating-point:

```
>>> 2.4 + 3.7
6.0999999999999996
```

Notice that floating-point numbers are subject to a phenomenon called *rounding error*. Computations that would be precise when performed in base 10 arithmetic might not be precise when performed in the internal computer arithmetic. Floating-point numbers can also be written in *scientific notation*. This format is written as a number followed by the letter *e* (or *E*, either works) and an integer. The integer represents a power of 10—that is, $2.3e3$ represents the value $2.3 * 10^3$, which is equal to $2.3 * 1000$, or 2300.0.

```
>>> 2.3e3
2300.0
>>> 2.3e47 + 5.2e46
2.8199999999999998e+47
>>> 1.0 + 2.3e47
2.2999999999999999e+47
```

The last example illustrates the fact that adding a very small number to a very large one will have a negligible effect, as only the most significant values are kept.

Often you can ignore the distinction between integer and floating-point and simply think of a value as being a number. However, the distinction is important in one common situation, although this is an area where the definition of Python is in transition. For versions of Python prior to version 3, and for most other programming languages, the division operator—the slash (/)—works differently for integers and floating-point values. For integers, the result is the integer part of the quotient; any remainders are simply thrown away:

```
>>> 5 / 2
2
```

For floating-point numbers, the result is floating point:

```
>>> 5.0 / 2.0
2.5
```

When one argument is integer and the other is float, the integer is converted into float and the result is float:

```
>>> 5.0 / 2
2.5
>>> 5 / 2.0
2.5
```

This will change in Python version 3. After that point, a single slash division will return a true division—that is, the value *5/2* will be equal to *2.5*. A new operator, written as two slashes, will be used to produce integer division.

Language Evolution

If you have read or attended a play by Shakespeare, you know that the English language has changed over time, as many words or phrases that were common in Shakespeare's era now sound odd to our modern ears. The same is true for computer languages, only changes have occurred at a vastly faster pace. All computer languages are modified and evolve over time. Sometimes new features are added to make a certain class of problems easier to solve. Sometimes things are changed to make the language more uniform or easier to understand. For example, the designer of the language has decided that in the future the division operator should have a single uniform meaning, rather than meaning one thing for integer values and another for floating values. As you go through your career in computing, you will undoubtedly learn many other programming languages, and you should be careful to pay close attention to transformations such as this. Usually major changes in a common programming language will be announced many years in advance, with opportunities for you to adapt to the new features at your own pace.

Another common type is a *string*. Strings can use either single or double quotation marks, which is useful when a string must include a quotation mark:

```
>>> "hello"
'hello'
>>> 'hi there'
'hi there'
>>> "don't do that"
"don't do that"
>>> 'I said: "stop right now"'
'I said: "stop right now"'
```

Try creating several different string expressions, using both forms of quotation mark.

The *Boolean* type represents a true or false value. The most common way to produce a Boolean value is with a relational operator:

```
>>> 17 < 21
True
>>> (2/3) < (3/5)
False
```

The names `True` and `False` represent Boolean constants. In addition, logical operators (and, or, not) work with Boolean valued expressions as they do in standard logic.

```
>>> True and False
False
>>> True or False
True
```

Python has a number of other built-in types. These include complex numbers (using, curiously, the letter *J* instead of the letter *I* to represent the square root of *-1*), lists, tuples, dictionaries, functions, and classes. We won't use complex numbers in this book, but the others will be examined in later chapters.

Names (Variables)

Computers are used to manipulate information—often lots of information. To help keep track of things, a name can be associated with a value. A name is attached to a value by means of an *assignment statement*, or simply an *assignment*. The text to the

George Boole (1815–1864)

The name *Boolean* is used in honor of George Boole, an English mathematician and philosopher who explored the use of logical (that is, true/false) values in symbolic computations.

What Is a Name?

A programming language will have strict rules for what can be used as a name. In Python, a name must begin with a letter or underscore and can include any number of letters, digits, or underscores. A name cannot begin with a digit, and it cannot include any characters other than letters, digits, or the underscore character. In particular, spaces are not allowed as part of a name. Legal name examples are `x`, `c3p0`, and `TaxForm1040`. Illegal names are `3c`, `4$x`, and `two bad`.

left of the assignment is the name, and the text to the right is the value that will be remembered for the name:

```
>>> name = 'fred'
>>> count = 7
```

After an assignment, if you use the name, the value stored for the name is remembered:

```
>>> name
'fred'
>>> count + 2
9
```

You can change the value associated with a name simply by assigning the name a new value:

```
>>> name = 'sally'
>>> name
'sally'
```

Notice that types are a property of values, not of names. A name can be given a different type simply by assigning it a new value:

```
>>> name = 5.0/2
>>> name
2.5
```

A named value is often termed a *variable* (since it represents a quantity that can change over time—that is, can vary). You should at this point stop reading and experiment with the Python interpreter, creating and using several variable names, until you are comfortable with this idea. Variables are useful when you want to use a value more than once or when you want to break a complicated computation into several smaller parts.

You need to learn how to select good names. Names are a fundamental part of computer programming—or, indeed, of all science. Names are attached to many different features. In addition to variables, you will eventually use names for functions, programs, modules, and other objects. Names are helpful for people, not computers. The computer could not care less if you name a variable `X3WkG` or `exchangeRate`, but the latter will likely convey much more contextual information to another human being than the former. You should strive to make names convey your intent. This means selecting names that are short, easy to understand, and evocative of the purpose of the values they represent.

In line with our assertion that names influence they way you think about values and operations, do not call the = operator *equals*, as that confuses the concept with the mathematical notation of equality, which uses a different operator. Instead, the symbol should be read as *gets*. So if you are reading aloud the statement name = 'sally' you would say "the variable name gets the value sally." If you want to represent the mathematical idea of equals, which is asking whether a variable is or is not holding a particular value, you must use the == operator:

```
>>> name == 'sally'
True
>>> name == 'name'
False
```

This brings us to a discussion of operators.

Operators

Each of the built-in types brings with it a set of *operators*. The following are the binary operators recognized by Python. (*Binary operators* appear between their two arguments, as in 2+4).

```
+ − * ** / % << >> & | ^ < > <= >= == != <>
```

Some of these operators, such as +, will undoubtedly be familiar to you. Others, such as >>, are almost certainly not familiar. Can you guess the meaning of some of the unfamiliar operators? What do you think is the meaning of the >= operator? Experiment with a few values to test your hypothesis. Not all operators can be used with all types, and sometimes operators have surprising meanings. You may be familiar with the * symbol to represent multiplication—for example *7 * 3* represents the value 21. Try typing **'abc' * 3**. What do you think the result represents? How do you think this value is tied to the idea of "multiplication"? The exercises at the end of this chapter will lead you through an exploration of the operations provided by Python.

The following can be used as *unary* operators, meaning they are written before their argument (the expression -x, for example, returns the arithmetic inverse of the value stored in the variable x).

```
+ − ~
```

You might remember from a mathematics class that in a string of computations, multiplications are performed first, and then additions are performed in order of their appearance. This is termed *precedence*. The order in which operators are evaluated can be controlled using parentheses. Using the idea of precedence, explain why the following two expressions produce different results.

```
>>> 5 + 2 * 3
```

So Many New Symbols, So Little Time

Hopefully you will recognize at least four or five of the standard operator symbols. The symbols + and − are used for addition and subtraction, just as in regular math. The symbols < and > are used to represent less-than and greater-than, respectively. It is only a small step to get used to * as the multiplication symbol, rather than the × mark more commonly found in mathematics textbooks. The slash symbol (/) used for division can be thought of as a printed representation of the line separating the top and bottom of a fraction; that is, ¼ is now written as *1 / 4*. You might guess that <= is a two character representation of ≤, and you would be right. But what about the others? Don't worry if at the moment you don't have a clue, as each will be explained eventually.

One operator that will soon be used in several examples is the percent sign (`%`). You might at first think that `%` represents the division operation, since it looks superficially similar to the ÷ symbol you used in grade school. But the slash operator is used for division. When used with integer arguments, the `%` operator is called the *remainder* operator and computes the value remaining after an integer division. For example, `17 % 3` returns 2, as there are five 3s (that is, 15) in 17, and 2 left over.

```
>>> (5 + 2) * 3
21
```

In mathematics, the term *associativity* applies when two operators with the same precedence are used one after another. For example, does the sequence *9 − 5 − 2* evaluate to *6*, which would be the same as *9 − (5 − 2)*, or to *2*, which is the same result as *(9 − 5) − 2*? Try it and see. What about *12 / 2 * 3*? What does the latter expression tell you about the precedence of the multiplication and division operators?

Python has precedence and associativity rules for all operations. When in doubt about these rules, you should use *explicit parentheses*.

A few binary operations have a text name but are otherwise used in the same way as binary or unary operators. The most common examples are the logical operations and, or, and not.

```
>>> (3 < 7) and (4 < 5)
True
>>> (3 < 2) or (6 > 4)
True
>>> not (3 < 7)
False
```

Another operator with a text name is in. This can be used (among other purposes) to determine whether a character value is found in a string. It returns True if the argument to the left of the operator is found in the argument to the right, and False otherwise.

```
>>> 'a' in 'abc'
True
```

```
>>> 'z' in 'abc'
False
```

Does the in operation work if the argument on the left is larger than a single character? Try it and see. What is the meaning in this situation?

Functions

Not all operators use the binary operator syntax. An alternative syntax is termed the *function call* notation. In this notation, the name of the operation is given first, followed by a list of the arguments surrounded by parentheses. For example, the abs operation returns the absolute value of the argument:

```
>>> abs(-3)
3
```

Just as the parentheses in an arithmetic expression indicate that the enclosed expression needs to be evaluated first, the arguments to a function are first calculated, and then the function is applied:

```
>>> abs(2-3 * 7) # first calculate 2-3*7, which is -19
19
```

Here, the function len returns the number of characters (that is, the length) of a string:

```
>>> len('abc')
3
>>> len('ha' * 4)
8
```

The function call syntax is more flexible than the operator syntax, because a function can take more than two arguments. Most operations defined using this syntax have a fixed number of arguments. However, a few can take any number of arguments. An example of the function call syntax is the min function, which returns the smallest of the arguments, regardless of how many are given:

```
>>> min(2, 3)
2
>>> min(5, 6, 2.2, 17)
2.2
```

An important class of functions is used to convert values from one type to another. The function int, for example, can be used to convert a *string* into an *integer*. The function str goes the other way, converting a *value* (such as a number) into a *string*:

```
>>> int("42")
42
>>> int("42") + 2
44
>>> "42" + "2"
'422'
```

```
>>> str(42+2)
'44'
>>> str(42+2) + "2"
'442'
```

The `int` function can also be used to convert a floating-point value into an integer. For example, suppose you live in a state where the sales tax rate is 8.7 percent. How much will you pay for an item marked $10.52?

```
>>> 8.7 * 10.52
91.523999999999987
```

Since fractional pennies are not part of US currency, you can convert the amount in cents using the `int` function:

```
>>> int(8.7 * 10.52)
91
```

Most states, however, don't simply truncate the fractional cent amount, but instead round to the nearest cent. Python has a function that will do this, but for a floating-point argument it returns a floating-point result:

```
>>> round(8.7 * 10.52)
92.0
```

You can combine `round` and `int` to return a value that is both rounded and an integer:

```
>>> int(round(8.7 * 10.52))
92
```

Notice how one function (`round`) is called inside the argument list for another (the function `int`). Just as before, the argument to `int` will be computed. But to do so, the function named `round` must be computed first. It is common to *nest* function calls one inside another in this fashion. They are evaluated from the inside out—first the innermost function, then the next level, and so on.

The function `eval` takes a string, interprets it as an expression, and returns the result:

```
>>> eval ("42+2")
44
```

The function `type` returns a somewhat cryptic value that nevertheless can be used to determine the type of its argument:

```
>>> type(42)
<type 'int'>
>>> type(2.5)
<type 'float'>
>>> type(999999999999999999)
<type 'long'>
```

Try using the `type` function with several different argument values.

An extremely useful function is `raw_input`. This function takes as argument a prompt. It prints the prompt, waits for the user to respond, and returns as a string the value typed.

```
>>> name = raw _ input("what is your name?:") # user types, e.g. fred
fred
>>> name
'fred'
```

You can combine `raw_input` and `eval` to make a simple calculator:

```
>>> expr = raw _ input("type an expression:")
2 + 3
>>> 'answer is'
'answer is'
>>> eval(expr)
5
```

If you completed the exploration of operators suggested earlier in the chapter, you know that the + operator can be used to concatenate two strings and that the `str` function can be used to convert a value into a string. Combining these provides a better way to produce *multipart* output. Instead of the previous two-part output, this could have been written as follows:

```
>>> 'answer is' + str(eval(expr))
'answer is 5'
```

Print Statement

An even simpler way to produce multipart output is to use a *print* statement. The print statement takes a series of values separated by commas. Each value is converted into a string (by implicitly invoking the `str` function) and then printed. Additionally, quotation marks are removed from printed strings.

```
>>> print 'answer is,' eval(expr)
answer is 5
```

The print statement also formats numbers in a slightly different way than those in a simple expression. For example, it produces fewer digits for floating values:

```
>>> 1.0/3
0.33333333333333331
>>> print 1.0/3
0.333333333333
```

Finally, the print statement recognizes a few commands that can be used to format input. These are termed *escape characters* and are written as a character following a backslash. The most common is the newline character, written \n. This moves the output on to a new line. The tab character, \t, moves the output to the next tab stop. (To print a literal backslash character you use two slashes, \\.)

```
>>> print "one\ntwo\tthree"
one
two three
```

Escape characters can also be used to embed a quotation mark within a quoted string:

```
>>> print 'don\'t do that'
don't do that
```

The print statement, as well as other Python statements, is discussed in more detail in the next chapter. Escape characters are also described in Appendix A. Experiment with the print statement and various different types of expressions.

Input from the User

The combination of `eval` and `raw_input` occurs so frequently that Python provides this combination as a standard function named `input`. Use `input` if you are reading a number, and use `raw_input` if you want the response stored as a string.

```
>>> x = input("type a number:") # user types a response, e.g. 5
>>> print x + 2
7
```

You can illustrate the use of input by a simple series of statements to convert a temperature from Celsius to Fahrenheit:

```
>>> c = input("what is the temp in Sault Ste. Marie, Ontario?")
what is the temp in Sault Ste. Marie, Ontario?
17
>>> f = c * 9.0 / 5.0 + 32
>>> print 'across the river, in Sault Ste. Marie, Michigan, it is ', f
across the river, in Sault Ste. Marie, Michigan, it is 62.6
```

Indexing (Slicing)

We have been using *strings* so far for many of our examples. Strings are the way that Python manipulates textual information. A string, like a word in English, is a compound value that is formed by a succession of smaller values termed *characters*. The string 'Python' for example is formed by the characters *P y t h o n*. Individual characters in a Python string can be accessed by providing their *position* within the string. The position, or index, can be thought of as representing the number of characters from the start of the string. The first character is therefore found at position 0, as there are zero characters between the start of the string and this value. The second character is found at position 1, and so on.

P	y	t	h	o	n

The operator used to access a character is termed an *indexing* operator, which is written using a pair of square brackets:

```
>>> 'Python'[0]
'P'
>>> 'abc'[1]
'b'
```

Notice that a character is actually just a string that has only one position. Looking at it another way, indexing is returning a portion, or a *substring*, of the original value. This idea can be generalized to a concept termed a *slice*. A slice is formed when two integers are written, separated by a colon. The second value is an ending position. A portion of the string starting at the given position up to but not including the ending position is produced.

```
>>> 'realtor'[2:6]
'alto'
```

You should at this point stop reading and experiment with the slicing operator with various different strings and argument values until you are comfortable with the notation.

If a colon is used but the last number is omitted, the result is the remainder of the string starting from the given position:

```
>>> 'recurrent'[2:]
'current'
```

Finally, if no number is used before the colon, the result is the initial string up to but not including the given position:

```
>>> 'halter'[:4]
'halt'
```

String are *immutable*, meaning they cannot be changed once they are assigned. If you try to assign to an indexing expression you will receive an error message. (Try it!) If you want to manipulate a string, say to move characters around, you must create a new string.

```
>>> word = 'red'
>>> word[1] = 'a' # show word cannot be changed
Traceback (most recent call last):
File "<stdin>", line 1, in ?
TypeError: object doesn't support item assignment
>>> word = 'b' + word[:2] + 'a' + word[2:]
>>> word # change red to bread
'bread'
```

Slicing might seem like a complicated technique, but is an extremely powerful operation. You should experiment with different slicing possibilities until you are comfortable with the technique. And remember that whenever you are in doubt about the meaning of an expression, you can simply try some examples at the keyboard.

The concepts of indexing and slicing are also used with the list and dictionary data types, which are investigated in Chapters 4 and 5.

Modules and Dot Notation

Another common syntax is termed *dot* (or class) notation, in which a name can be qualified by the *class* or *module* in which it is defined. Classes will be discussed in Chapter 7. A *module* is a library of functions used to provide a service. Most Python programs will use one or more modules. An example is the math module, which defines a number of common mathematical functions. To tell the Python system you want to make use of the services provided by the module, you type an *import* statement, such as the following:

```
>>> import math
```

After the import statement, you can use the functions defined in the math module. Each value or function is preceded by the name of the module in which it is defined.

```
>>> math.pi # a value defined in the math module
3.1415926535897931
>>> math.sin(math.pi/2.0)
1.0
>>> math.sqrt(1000)
31.622776601683793
```

Many modules are defined in the standard Python distribution, and many more can be downloaded from public sources. The use of these modules greatly simplifies the creation of Python applications.

Let's use the math library to write statements that will solve a quadratic equation. A quadratic equation has the form $ax^2 + bx + c = 0$. Recall that such an equation has two solutions for the value of x, and these are given by the formula $x = -b \times \sqrt{(b^2 - 4ac)} / 2a$.

The input to our program consists of the three values a, b, and c. These can be read using the input function. The outputs are the two values provided by the formula.

```
>>> import math
>>> a = input('type the value for the coefficient a')
>>> b = input('type the value for the coefficient b')
>>> c = input('type the value for the coefficient c')
>>> d = b * b−4 * a * c
>>> d = math.sqrt(d)
>>> print 'first root is ', (-b + d) / (2 * a)
>>> print 'second root is ', (-b − d) / (2 * a)
```

What happens if the argument given to the square root function is negative? Try it and see for yourself!

AN ATTITUDE OF EXPLORATION

So far in this chapter, you have learned many new concepts and expressions. You might feel overwhelmed by the amount of information you have to remember. Don't worry. With experience and practice all these ideas become second nature. As noted in the discussion on slicing, an important part of gaining experience is experimentation. The interactive nature of the Python system makes experimentation extremely easy. Even experienced Python programmers will frequently start an interactive session just to type small statements and expressions to remind themselves how a particular operator or function works. You should develop this attitude of exploration, and whenever you are in doubt about a feature, try it out!

BITWISE OPERATORS*[1]

If you have explored the meaning of the various operators provided by the Python system, you might have been confused by the operators <<, >>, &, |, ^, and ~. These operations make sense if you understand that computers process information in a different form than we humans do.

Humans work with numerals in a base-10 system. When we see a value, such as 4,372, we read this as representing 4 times 1,000 (that is, 10^3), plus 3 times 100 (10^2), plus 7 times 10 (10^1), plus 2. Internally, computers work in a much simpler system. They work with only two values, *0* and *1*, termed *bits*, and a number system based on 2.

Any number can be written in base 2. Consider, for example, the number *42*. In base-2 numerals this is written like so: 101010. To convert back and forth, read the numeral from the right side, rather than the left: 101010 is 0 times 1 plus 1 times 2 plus 0 times 4 (2^2) plus 1 times 8 (2^3) plus 0 times 16 (2^4) plus 1 times 32 (2^5). 2 + 8 + 32 = 42.

The operators <<, >>, &, and | are best understood if you convert their arguments into this internal binary representation. Take, for example, the left shift operator, <<. This operation returns the value in which the left argument represented in base 2 has been shifted by an amount given by the right argument. For instance, consider the expression *5 << 3*. The value *5* is *0101* in binary. Shift this left by three places, and you have *0101000*. Convert this back to base 10, and you have the value *40*.

```
>>> 5 << 3
40
```

The >> operator returns the value in which the argument has been shifted to the right. See if you can figure out the binary representation for the value *15*. Then, using that representation, explain the following behavior:

---

[1] Sections marked with an asterisk indicate advanced and/or optional material and can (probably should) be omitted on your first reading. Once you have grasped the remainder of the chapter, come back and examine the more advanced sections.

```
>>> 15 >> 2
3
```

The operators & and | perform a bit-by-bit *and* and *or*, respectively. This is called a *bitwise* operation. A 1 bit can be thought of as corresponding to the logical value true, and a 0 as the logical value false. An *and* of two bits equals 1 if both bits are 1, and an *or* is 1 if either bit is 1. This is just like a logical *and* is true if both arguments are true, and a logical *or* is true if either argument is true. So the bitwise & of 5 and 12 (0101 and 1100, respectively) is 4 (0100), while the bitwise | is 13 (1101).

```
>>> 5 & 12
4
>>> 5 | 12
13
```

The ^ operator is known as an *exclusive-or*. The exclusive-or of two bits is 1 if either is 1, but not both. So 5^12 is 9 (1001).

```
>>> 5 ^ 12
9
```

The unary operator ~ performs a *bitwise inverse*. In the result, every bit that was 0 becomes 1 and every bit that was 1 becomes 0. Because of the way that negative numbers are stored in the computer, a positive value becomes negative, and a negative value will become positive.

```
>>> ~4
-5
>>> ~ -7
6
```

A version of the int function that takes a string and a base can be used to convert base-2 numbers (or any other base, for that matter) into base-10 integers:

```
>>> int("0101," 2)
5
```

Bitwise operations are useful in certain situations, but are infrequent in practice.

ENCODINGS*

The underlying hardware for a computer works with simple 0s and 1s. These are called *bits*. All values manipulated by a computer must ultimately be represented by bits. How the bits are interpreted gives meaning to the values.

You started to explore this in the preceding section, where you experimented with the encoding for integer values. An integer value such as 42 is encoded as a string of bits, such as 101010. For efficiency reasons, computers normally work with a fixed block of bits. Some of the more common blocks are the *byte* (8 bits) and the *word* (on most machines, 32 bits). Integers, for example, are commonly stored as a 32-bit word. This means that the value 42 is really 00000000000000000000000000 101010 in binary.

A good part of what we mean by *type* is really a shorthand for *encoding*. To say that a value is an integer means that we will interpret the bits as described. (This is not to say that this is all that *type* means. For instance, another aspect of type is the set of operations that can be applied to values. You can divide integer typed values, for example, but not strings).

A single character is normally stored as a byte, that is, an 8-bit quantity. You can find the integer value of a character, as an integer, using the function named ord (short for *ordinal*):

```
>>> ord('a')
97
```

This tells you that internally the character *a* is stored as the integer value *97*. The mapping of characters to integer values is provided by a standard, called the American Standard Code for Information Interchange (ASCII). So the ASCII code representation of the character *a* is *97*.

An 8-bit byte allows 256 different values. This is fine for Roman-based languages with a small number of letters (for example, 26 letters in the English alphabet) but is insufficient for scripts such as Chinese or Korean. Characters in these languages are encoded in a 16-bit form, termed *Unicode*. You can search the Web to find the Unicode values for characters in various languages.

A string is represented internally by a series of 8-bit bytes. For example, the word *Python* is represented internally like this:

80	121	116	104	111	110

You can see this by combining indexing and the ord function:

```
>>> ord('Python'[2])
116
```

The numbers are the ASCII code representation for the six characters. A block like this is sometimes called an *array*. You'll learn much more about arrays in Chapter 4. An integer that is larger than 32 bits is similarly represented by an array of integers.

By the way, the function chr (short for character) is the opposite of ord. It takes an integer value and returns the corresponding character:

```
>>> print chr(97)
'a'
```

The letters in the ASCII code are in order. This means you can manipulate string values by converting them to numbers, manipulating the number values, and converting them back into strings:

```
>>> chr(ord('a') + 7)
'h'
```

```
>>> ord('f')—ord('a')
5
>>> chr(ord('A') + (ord('f')—ord('a')))
'F'
```

A floating-point number is typically represented using two integers, similar to the idea of scientific notation. In scientific notation, a value of *24.35* can be represented as $2435 * 10^{-2}$. The base can be omitted, and only the two integers *2435* and *-2* need to be represented.

-2	2435

Computers, as noted earlier, work in base 2 rather than base 10, but the underlying idea is the same.

Larger data types require a more complicated encoding. Ultimately, however, everything must be reduced to bits. Consider a digital image, for example. You might know that images are made up of little dots called *pixels*. Each of these dots is a distinct color. You might also know that in a computer, a color is often encoded as 3 bytes that represent the amount of red, green, or blue. This is termed the *RGB encoding*. Each pixel in this system requires 24 bits (that is, three colors times 8 bits for each color).

A simple way to represent a picture would be an array of pixels. In a 640×480 pixel picture (a common size for digital images) this would require 921,600 bytes (that's 640 × 480 × 3). Because large images are relatively common, various, more sophisticated techniques can be used to represent pictures that use less memory than the array of pixel format, but the ideas are similar.

Sounds, movies, and in fact all data values manipulated by a computer must ultimately be encoded as a series of bits.

EXERCISES

1. Examine each of the following expressions. Predict what the result should be, and then evaluate the expression using the Python interpreter to check your predictions. Explain the type for each expression. If an expression is illegal, explain why.
   a. 10 / 5
   b. 5 / 10 (or 5 // 10 in newer Python systems)
   c. 5.0 / 10
   d. 10 % 4 + 8 / 4
   e. 3 ** 10 / 3

2. Translate each of the following mathematical expressions into an equivalent Python representation.
   a. (3 + 4)(7)
   b. n (n − 1) / 2
   c. sqrt(a * a + b * b)

3. Explain the difference between 42 + 2 and "42" + "2." What is the + operator doing in each case?

4. What is wrong with this version of the quadratic formula?
   rl = (-b + d) / 2 * a

5. Write a series of Python statements that will first ask the user to type today's exchange rate between US dollars and euros. Next, ask the user to type a value in dollars. Finally, print the equivalent value in euros.

6. Write a Python statement that reads a numeric value from the user, placing it into a variable named x. Then write a print statement that will print the values x, x^2, x^3, and x^4. Use tab characters to separate the four resulting values. Write a second print statement, but use newline characters instead of tab stops.

7. Write three Python statements. The first should read a number from the user that represents a temperature in Fahrenheit, placing the value into a variable named f. The second statement should convert the value into Celsius, placing the result into a variable named c. The third statement should print the values of f and c with a descriptive notation.

8. Write a series of Python statements that will read a number from the user that represents the radius of a circle. Then use a print statement to show the circle's diameter, circumference, and area. You can import the math module and use the constant `math.pi` to represent the constant π (pi).

9. Write a series of Python statements that will import the math module, read a number from the user that represents an angle given in radians, and then prints the sine and cosine for the given angle.

10. The interactive Python system provides a special variable written as a single underscore character. Execute the following sequence of statements, and explain what this variable holds. Try some other statements to test your hypothesis.

    ```
    >>> 3 + 7
    >>> print _
    >>> 'abc'
    >>> print _
    >>> 3 * 'abc'
    >>> print _
    ```

11. Try writing a print statement that uses the escape character \b. What do you think this is doing? Try placing several characters before and after the \b. Try typing several in a row after a series of characters.

12. Try writing a print statement that uses the escape character \a. What do you think this is doing? Can you think of a use for this feature?

13. Python supports 18 different binary operators. Experiment with each of these, using arguments that are both integer, both floating point, and both string. Not all operators work with each argument type. Fill in the following table. For each operator, provide either a short description and indicate the type of the result or the words *NOT LEGAL*.

Operator	Integer	Floating point	String
+			
-			
*			
**			
/			

Continued

Operator	Integer	Floating point	String
%			
<<			
>>			
&			
|			
^			
<			
>			
<=			
>=			
==			
!=			
<>			

14. Assume the variable named *n* holds a positive integer value. How do you determine the last digit of *n*? (Hint: what does the % operator do?)

15. You have probably discovered that the % operator performs the remainder operation when used with two positive integer arguments. But what does it do when one or both arguments are negative?

```
>>> 11 % 3
2
>>> 11 % -3
-1
>>> -11 % 3
1
>>> -11 % -3
-2
```

Try to come up with an explanation of this behavior. To do so, make a chart of the values from –15 to 15, and for each compute the result when used with the mod operator and the value *3*. Then do the same chart with *–3*. Can you see a pattern? From this pattern can you explain the behavior of the mod operator?

16. Your explorations of the chart in exercise 13 might not have led you to explore what happens if the arguments are different types. Try each of the 18 operators using the value *'abc'* as the left argument and the value *2* as the right argument. Which of the 18 operators are legal? Can you explain what the result represents? Reverse the arguments, using *2* as the left argument and *'abc'* as the right. Which are still legal?

17. Can you select values for *x* and *y* in the expression $-x + y$ that will help you determine the precedence of the unary – operation in comparison to the binary + operator?

18. Python allows relational operators to be *chained*. If *x* is a number, what do you think the expression $3 < x < 5$ means? Can you design an experiment to test your guess? What about $5 > x > 2$. Does an expression such as $2 < x > 4$ make any sense? If so, what does it mean?

19. You might have noticed that integers come in two flavors: normal integers and long integers. You can see this using the exponential operator. A value 2^8 is a normal integer, while 2^{100} is long.

```
>>> 2**8
256
>>> 2**100
1267650600228229401496703205376L
```

The L at the end of the number indicates the value is long. (If your system does not supply the L, the same information can be found using the function named type). Find experimentally the smallest integer I for which 2 ** I is long.

20. Each row in the following table consists of a starting word and an ending word. Assign the starting word to the name *w*. Then using only indexing and slicing commands, convert the starting word into the ending word. The first is done for you as an example.

Starting word	Ending word	Command
w = 'kyoto'	'tokyo'	w[3:] + w[:3]
'bread'	'bead'	
'kartasura'	'surakarta'	
'listen'	'silent'	

21. What happens when you try to index a string value with a number that is out of range? Such as `'abcdef'[9]`? What happens when you use a negative number, such as `'abcdef'[-2]`? How about `'abcdef'[-9]`? Provide a rule to explain the results.

22. Assume that the name *w* is assigned the value *'abcdef'*. Explain the meaning of each of the following: w[2], w[2:], w[:2], w[2:4], w[:].

23. Try typing the following expressions: `'abc'[0]`, `'abc'[0][0]`, `'abc'[0][0][0]`, and `'abc'[0][0][0][0]`. What is going on here?

24. What happens if you try to divide an integer value by zero?

25. What happens if you press control-D (ctrl-Z on Windows machines) when the Python system is waiting for input from a call on `raw_input`?

26. Assume that a year contains 365 days (that is, ignore leap years). Let *y* be the name holding a value that represents an age in years (for example, 23). Write an expression that represents the number of seconds in that period (for example, the number of seconds in 23 years).

27. Using the fact that the unary ~ inverts each bit in an integer and the knowledge of the binary representation for positive numbers, experimentally discover the representation of negative numbers. For example, you know the representation of *5* is *0101*. The following tells you that the internal representation of *–6* is the inverse—that is *1010*. Experiment with other values. Can you develop a general rule that explains the representation of a negative number as the inverse of a positive number?

```
>>> ~ -6
5
```

28. The functions `max` and `min` can also be used with string arguments. What is the value of `max('abc')`? Of `min('abc')`? Can you explain the meaning of the result? Using `max` and `min`, can you tell which is larger, the lowercase letter *a* or the uppercase letter *A*? What about *a* and *0*?

29. Include the module named *random*, and then print the value of the expression `random.random()`. Do it several times. What do you think the expression represents? Try typing `random.randint(a, b)` with various different integer values for *a* and *b*. What does it return? What happens if you use noninteger arguments with `randint`?

30. What happens if you take the square root of a negative number? Try importing the *cmath* module and using `cmath.sqrt()` instead. Now what happens?

31. Most of the assignment operations can be combined with a binary operator to form what is known as an *assignment operator*. For example, what do you suppose is the value of the variable *a* after the following two commands? Write down the statements you might use to verify your guess. Give examples to demonstrate what various other assignment operators do. What would happen if the following example used strings instead of integers?

```
>>> a = 7
>>> a += 5
```

32. The function `int` can be used to convert a float into an integer, as in `int(2.9)`. It can also be used to convert a string containing an integer into an `int`, as in `int("2")`. You might then be tempted to think that it could convert a string containing a float into an `int`, as in `int("2.9")`. Does this work?

33. What is the value of `int("0101", 3)`? Explain how this value is derived. Then do the same for `int("0101", x)` for values of *x* between 4 and 10.

34. How many different possibilities can be represented using two binary digits (or bits)? How many with three? With eight?

35. The section on encodings provided hints about how floating-point numbers could be encoded as a pair of integers. Do a web search using the terms "floating point encoding" and find a more detailed description of the actual encoding used by most computers.

2 CHAPTER

Creating Python Programs

Having to create and re-create the same commands to perform the same tasks can become tiresome. Fortunately, Python provides an easy and powerful alternative to such repetition. You can store Python command statements in a file and then direct the Python system to read and execute commands from that file, rather than from the console. Such a file is termed a Python *program*.

```
# a simple python program
5 + 2
print 5 + 2
name = raw _ input("what is your name?")
print 'hello' , name
```

COMMANDS

Commands that are typed at the console and those read from a file are treated a bit differently in Python. To see these differences, try typing the lines shown above directly into the Python system. Then enter the lines into a text file using a text editor, such as Notepad, SimpleText, or Emacs. (If you use a word processor, such as MS Word, make sure you save the document as a text file first.) Traditionally, Python programs are stored in a file with the extension *.py*. Name your new file *hello.py*. Now start the Python system and type the file name on the command line, as follows:

```
python hello.py
```

Can you see any differences in execution? Notice that simple expressions, such as the line *5+2*, are displayed when Python is running an *interactive* session, but they do not appear when the input comes from a file. The only output you see will come from the print statements.

Now experiment by making changes in the file hello.py and executing the resulting file. If you have not already done so, try introducing an error, such as misspelling a name or leaving out a value for the addition operator. What happens? How is the error message from executing the file different from the error message you get in the interactive session?

A Temperature Conversion Program

Here's an example from Chapter 1 that you can rewrite as a program. Type the following statements into a file named tempConv.py:

```
# tempConv.py
# A Celsius to Fahrenheit conversion program
# written by Robin Smith, July 2009

print "This program will convert a temperature in Celsius"
print "to the equivalent temperature in Fahrenheit"
c = input("What is the temperature in Celsius you wish to convert?")
f = c * 9.0 / 5.0 + 32
print "The equivalent temperature in Fahrenheit is", f
```

Notice some of the features of this file that are characteristic of Python programs. First, the program begins with some informative comments. These should always include the purpose of the file, as well as the name of the author and date of creation. Often, as shown here, the first line will include the name of the file in which the program is stored; however, this convention is not always followed.

The body of the program contains the statements that will be executed when the program is run using the Python interpreter. A common feature is for these statements to begin with some helpful print statements that remind the user what the program is doing and what the inputs represent.

After saving the file tempConv.py, you should try executing the file several times using different numbers for the input value. Can you discover the temperature at which the Celsius and Fahrenheit values are the same?

No program should ever be considered finished without having been tested first. What values should you use to test your program? For a program such as this, you can start with values for which you know the correct answer. The following two well-known values are correct:

```
$ python tempConv.py
This program will convert a temperature in Celsius
to the equivalent temperature in Fahrenheit
What is the temperature in Celsius you wish to convert? 0
The equivalent temperature in Fahrenheit is 32.0

$ python tempConv.py
This program will convert a temperature in Celsius
to the equivalent temperature in Fahrenheit
What is the temperature in Celsius you wish to convert? 100
The equivalent temperature in Fahrenheit is 212.0
```

After a few more test values, you can be assured that this simple program is working properly. (This is not to say that testing is always this easy, because it's not. You'll learn more about testing programs after you've been introduced a bit more to Python syntax.)

Now try rewriting the quadratic equation solver from Chapter 1 as a program. What values might you use to test your program? As you are testing, can you find any deficiencies in the program?

STATEMENTS

A Python program consists of a sequence of *statements*. The term *code* is often used to describe statements that have been organized into a program. In Chapter 1 you encountered three forms of statement: the assignment statement, the print statement, and the import statement. Two of these are used in the temperature conversion program. Here you will learn about several more forms of statements.

Writing a Python program has many advantages over immediately executing a statement. First, it allows you to execute the same series of statements over and over. For example, you might want to perform the same calculation using different input values. Second, it allows for the possibility that one person (the *programmer*) might create a Python program that will then be executed by somebody else (the *user*). The user might not know the Python programming language, or how to program, or even know that the program they are using was written in Python. Third, you have undoubtedly noticed that it is difficult to write more than a few statements in Python without making mistakes. Common mistakes include using an incorrect name or an improper operator, leaving out punctuation, and so on.

When Python statements are collected into a program, you can correct any errors by editing the file. The revised program can then be easily executed, without the need to retype any statements. The process of removing the errors is termed *debugging* ("bugs" is another word for errors in computer lingo). Fourth, a Python program is an *artifact*, an object that can be shared with others. Good programmers learn by reading each others' code, as much as from reading books such as this. As your programming skills mature, you should practice reading code as a form of literature, noticing what makes a program easy to read and what features make programs difficult to read.

Assignments

In Chapter 1, you were introduced to the assignment statement. The assignment is used to associate a name with the result of evaluating an expression. Here's an example:

```
f = c * 9.0 / 5.0 + 32
```

This form is actually a special case of the assignment. The assignment statement can be generalized in two ways. First, several variables can be assigned at once, as long as they are all being assigned the same value:

```
a = b = c = 3.0
```

Second, Python permits any number of variables to appear on the left side of the equal sign, separated by commas. The same number of expressions must then appear on the right side, again separated by commas, like so:

```
sum, diff, prod = x + y, x-y, x * y
```

The expressions are evaluated, and each is assigned to the corresponding variable. In this case, the effect is the same in all three statements:

```
sum = x + y
diff = x - y
prod = x * y
```

This example is sometimes termed a *simultaneous assignment statement*. One use for simultaneous assignment is to read more than one value from the user in a single statement. For example, you could read all three coefficients in the quadratic solver from Chapter 1 with the following statement:

```
a,b,c = input("type the coefficients a, b, and c, separated by commas")
```

This form of assignment can occasionally be useful. Here is a more subtle example. The statement:

```
x, y = y, x
```

will exchange the values of the variables *x* and *y*. Try typing the statements in an interactive session to convince yourself that it has this effect. Now try the simple rewriting used above and see what happens:

```
x = y
y = x
```

Why doesn't this sequence of statements have the effect you want? An exchange of values in two variables is a common requirement in many programs, and Python provides a powerful yet simple solution to this difficulty.

Conditionals

Another common task is to choose between two or more alternative possibilities depending upon the outcome of a test. Each alternative is termed a *conditional*. To see a conditional being used in practice, consider the program shown at right. The program prompts the user to enter a value, performs a simple calculation, and prints the result. In this case, it converts a test score (a number between 0 and 40) into a percentage. As a final step, however, the program tests the value stored in the variable named percent. If this value is larger than 90, an encouraging statement will be printed. If the value is not greater than 90, no statement will be printed.

```
print 'The exam had 40 points'
score = input("What was your score?")
percent = 100 * score / 40.0
print 'Your percentage was',percent
if percent >= 90.0:
    print "Congratulations, you got an A"
```

You should experiment by executing this program with various values and noticing the way it works. You can also try typing the same statements in an interactive session. An important feature to note is the use of spaces and tab stops. Up to now, all our statements have started in the first column. In this program, the pattern changes. The statement following the *if* statement is indented by striking the tab character once.

At this point, if you have embraced the experimental approach advocated in Chapter 1, a number of questions should be entering your thoughts. What happens if I forget to type the tab character? What happens if I use spaces instead of tabs? What happens if I type two tabs instead of one? Rather than telling you the answer, I'll tell you to try these alternatives immediately and see the results for yourself.

More than one statement can be controlled by a conditional. To see this, simply type each statement using the same indentation—that is, the same number of tab stops. When the indentation returns to the previous level, the statements are no longer being controlled by the if. You can see this behavior by replacing the *if* statement with something similar to the statements shown below.

```
if percent >= 90.0:
    print "congratulations, you got an A"
    print "you are doing well in this class"
print "see you in class next week"
```

An *if* statement produces one of two outcomes: Either the condition is true, in which case the indented statements are executed, or it is not true, in which case control moves to the next statement at the original level of indentation. Sometimes you'll want to perform an action in the latter case, one that will not be executed if the condition is true. This can be accomplished by an *else* statement, as shown below. Experiment with the *else* statement and notice how Python executes statements depending on the result of the condition test.

```
if percent >= 90.0:
    print "congratulations, you got an A"
    print "you are doing well in this class"
else:
    print "you did not get an A"
print "see you in class next week"
```

If statements can be nested inside each other. To do this, simply indent the new statement, inserting one new tab for the new level of control. But you need to be careful, because an *else* statement is matched to a preceding *if* by the indentation level. Compare the following two examples. Predict what the outcome of each will be, and then execute the programs to test your prediction.

```
if percent >= 90.0:
    if percent >= 95.0:
        print 'you get an A+!'
    else:
        print 'you get an A'
```

```
if percent >= 90.0:
    if percent >= 95.0:
        print 'you get an A+!'
else:
    print 'you get an A'
```

Nested if *Statements and* elif

Often a series of tests can have a number of outcomes. One way to write this would be to use nested *if* statements. Here's an example:

```
if percent >= 90.0
    print 'congratulations, you got an A"
else:
    if percent >= 80.0:
        print 'you got a B'
    else:
        if percent >= 70.0:
            print 'you got a C'
        else:
            print 'your grade is less than a C'
```

This situation is common, and the nested statement solution is less than ideal since it tends to creep across the page, and lining up the correct number of tabs can be a problem. To solve this, Python uses the *elif* statement, which is a combination of *else* and *if*. The preceding statement can be written as follows:

```
if percent >= 90.0:
    print 'congratulations, you got an A'
elif percent >= 80.0:
    print 'you got a B'
elif percent >= 70.0:
    print 'you got a C'
else:
    print 'your grade is less than a C'
```

Flow Charts

It is sometimes easier to understand a sequence of nested conditional statements if they are written in a two-dimensional graphlike representation, which is called a *flow chart*. By moving your pencil along a path through the graph, you can trace the movement of control through the program.

To form a flow chart, you draw each conditional represented by a diamond-shaped box, with two possible outcomes. The question being asked by the conditional is written inside the box, and the outcomes are labeled with the values "yes" or "no" to indicate which direction to move depending on the outcome of the conditional.

Statements are indicated by a square box, with the actions to be performed.

A series of statements is represented by combining these two forms. Which of the two earlier examples of indentation does the following flow chart represent? Can you draw a flow chart that represents the other?

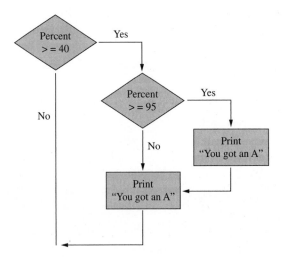

Single Statements

Frequently, the statement under control of an *if* or *else* (called the *body* of the condition) is only a single statement. If the statement is short, it can appear on the same line as the *if* or *else*, following the colon:

```
if percent >= 90.0: print 'Congratulations, you got an A'
elif percent >= 80.0: print 'You got a B'
elif percent >= 70.0: print 'You got a C'
else: print 'Your grade is less than a C'
```

This format can make programs considerably shorter, although slightly more dense and hence possibly difficult to read.

Testing Conditional Statements

When you are testing a program that contains conditional statements, you should strive to follow these principles:

- For each conditional statement, make sure you examine at least one test case in which the conditional is true and one in which the conditional is false.
- Make sure you execute every statement in the program.
- When a conditional includes relational comparison statements (less than, less than or equal, and so on), try to come as "close as possible" with a comparison that is true and one that is false. If possible, include a value in which the comparison is equal, so that you can catch errors where a less than or equal (<=) is written that should have been a simple less than (<).

Let's use these principles to test our program, which we will assume has been stored in a file named examEval.py:

```
$ python examEval.py
The exam had 40 points
What was your score? 40
Your percentage was 100.0
Congratulations, you got an A

$ python examEval.py
The exam had 40 points
What was your score? 37
Your percentage was 92.5
Congratulations, you got an A

$ python examEval.py
The exam had 40 points
What was your score? 36
Your percentage was 90.0
Congratulations, you got an A

$ python examEval.py
The exam had 40 points
What was your score? 35
Your percentage was 87.5
You got a B

$ python examEval.py
The exam had 40 points
What was your score? 32
Your percentage was 80.0
You got a B

$ python examEval.py
The exam had 40 points
What was your score? 31
Your percentage was 77.5
You got a C
```

```
$ python examEval.py
The exam had 40 points
What was your score? 25
Your percentage was 62.5
Your grade is less than a C
```

If the comparison operations had used the wrong operations (< instead of <=), the values *36* and *32* would have produced the wrong results. It is only after you have tested your program on a number of different inputs and understand how those inputs are forcing the flow of control through your program that you can have some degree of confidence that it is producing the correct result.

While Loops

You might need to execute a statement repeatedly; this is called a *loop*. The simplest type of loop is a *while* loop. To illustrate a *while* loop consider the calculation of compound interest. If *d* dollars is being compounded at *p* percent interest, the interest earned at the end of one year is *d * p / 100.0*. Assuming you compound the interest, the new balance will be the old balance plus the interest. To calculate the result for one year, you could write a program such as the following:

```
d = input("what is your initial balance?")
p = input("what is the interest rate (as a number)?")
d = d + d * p / 100.0
print "your new balance after one year is", d
```

If you want to determine how much money you will have after five years, it can be computed as follows:

```
d = input("what is your initial balance?")
p = input("what is the interest rate (as a number)?")
year = 1
while year <= 5:
    d = d + d * p / 100.0
    print 'your new balance after year', year, 'is', d
    year = year + 1
print 'your final balance is', d
```

Study the program carefully. Notice which statements are indented and which statements are not. Again, try experimenting with variations. What will happen if (by mistake) you forget to indent the statement year = year + 1? What changes do you want to make if instead of five years you want to calculate the balance after seven years? What if you want to read the number of years from the user? Imagine that you do the latter, and the user enters the value *0* for the number of years. What will your program do then?

The condition being tested by a *while* loop can be any true/false value. Here is another simple program that will read a series of values from the user, count the number of items, and print their average. The user indicates the end of the input by typing the special value, *–1*.

```
sum = 0.0
count = 0
num = input("enter your number:")
while num != -1:
    sum = sum + num
    count = count + 1
    num = input("enter your number:")
print "average is", sum / count
```

What will happen if the user enters *–1* the very first time, without entering any numbers? Predict the outcome in this case, and then try the program and see if it matches your prediction. Is the result very helpful? Can you think of a way, using *if* statements, to produce a more helpful result in this case and still produce the same result in the normal case?

Flow Charts for While Loops

Flow charts for *while* loops are formed using the same components you have seen already, except an arrow can be used to return to a previously defined connector:

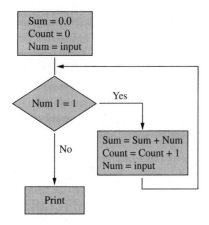

Testing While Loops

Just as guidelines exist for testing conditional statements, good guidelines are available for testing loops, such as the following:

- If a loop can execute an indefinite number of times, try to come up with an input that will force the loop not to execute at all—that is, will force it to execute zero iterations. This is probably the most easily overlooked error.
- Try to find an input that forces the loop to execute only once.
- Find an input that forces the program to execute more than once.

- If an upper bound has been set on the number of iterations of the loop, try to find values that barely meet the upper bound, meet the upper bound, and exceed the upper bound.

Using these guidelines, you could easily uncover an error in this program:

```
$ python ave.py
enter your number: 12
enter your number: -1
average is 12.0

$ python ave.py
enter your number: 12
enter your number: 9
enter your number: 18
enter your number: -1
average is 13.0

$ python ave.py
enter your number: -1
average is
Traceback (most recent call last):
File "ave.py", line 8, in ?
print 'average is', sum / count
ZeroDivisionError: float division
```

Break, Continue, and Pass Statements*[1]

It is not uncommon to want to end a loop in the middle of execution. The *break* statement allows you to do this. It "breaks" out of the current loop. For example, rather than writing two different calls in the input function, the average computing loop could be written as follows:

```
sum = 0.0
count = 0
while True:
    num = input("enter your number:")
    if num == -1:
        break
    sum = sum + num
    count = count + 1
print "average is", sum / count
```

---

[1] Sections marked with an asterisk indicate advanced or optional material that can be skipped on first reading.

Compare carefully this version of the loop with the version provided earlier in the "*While* Loops" section. Can you see any advantages to this approach? Can you identify any drawbacks?

The *continue* statement is similar to a break, except it immediately returns to the condition test of the loop ("continuing" execution of the loop).

Finally, a *pass* statement does nothing at all. This is useful in two common situations: It's sometimes easier to express a positive condition than a negative one. This can then be written as a conditional statement that does nothing, followed by an *else* that does real work:

```
if a<b and x<3:
   pass # do nothing here
else:
   doRealWork(x, y)
```

Pass statements are also sometimes used in the body of a function. Examples of this are provided in Chapter 3.

For *loops*

Loops that run through an arithmetic progression, such as 1, 2, 3, 4, 5, tend to be the most common. The loop provided earlier in the chapter that counted years from 1 to 5 was a typical example. For this particular case, a simpler type of statement, a *for* statement, can be used and could be written as follows:

```
for year in range(1, 6):
   d = d + d * p / 100.0
   print 'your new balance after year', year, 'is', d
```

There is actually more going on here than meets the eye. The function `range` is behind the scenes constructing a list containing the elements 1, 2, 3, 4, and 5 (that is, values up to but not including the second argument). The *for* statement then iterates over elements of the list. However, lists aren't discussed until Chapter 4. And, in truth, most Python programmers think of this construct as an *idiom* without even recognizing that `range` is a function or that it is producing a list. Instead, this is simply a convenient way to write a loop that runs through a simple sequence.

A *for* statement is, in the strictest sense, never necessary. That is, anything that can be done using a *for* can be done using a *while*. For example, the preceding statement could be written as follows:

```
year = 1
while year < 6:
   d = d + d * p / 100.0
   print 'your new balance after year', year, 'is', d
   year = year + 1
```

The *for* statement has advantages over the *while*, however. Notice that the *while* loop requires a separate statement to perform both the initialization of the variable year as well as the increment. If either of these statements is omitted, the program will fail to work properly. Furthermore, the *for* statement makes it clear that the type of loop being produced is an arithmetic progression, something that is discovered only after careful analysis of the *while* loop version. For these reasons, the *for* statement should be used when it is appropriate.

The range function can take one, two, or three arguments. Try executing the following, substituting the expressions range(5) (as shown), range(2, 8), and range(2, 8, 3). Then write a short description of what the range function does when presented with one, two, or three arguments.

```
for i in range(5):
  print i
```

The *for* statement can also be used to loop over the letters in a string. Try executing the following:

```
for ch in 'abacadabra':
  if ch in 'aeiou':
      print 'letter', ch, 'is a vowel'
  else:
      print 'letter', ch, 'is not a vowel'
```

This is another example of a *for* loop used with a string. Based on your exploration of the ord and chr functions in Chapter 1, can you predict what the loop will print?

```
for ch in 'A Very Good Thing':
  if 'a' <= ch <= 'z':
      print chr(ord(ch)-ord('a') + ord('A'))
  elif 'A' <= ch <= 'Z':
      print chr(ord(ch)-ord('A') + ord(a'))
  else:
      print ch
```

The exercises at the end of the chapter will help you hone your skills using conditionals and loops in Python programs.

LEVELS OF ABSTRACTION

Abstraction is the process of purposefully hiding some details so that you can more easily see others. It is the principle means by which we handle complex systems. If you look at a map of the world, for example, you will see very large structures, such as mountain ranges or oceans, but you will not see individual streets as you would if you looked at a map of a city or town. In the first map, the small details have been *abstracted away*, so that the larger details can be more easily understood.

Abstraction is used in computer programming as well. As noted, the creation of a program opens the possibility that one person, the *programmer*, might create a Python program that will then be executed by somebody else, the *user*. Each of these individuals views the program at different levels of abstraction. The user simply needs to understand the purpose of the program and its input and output behavior. For example, users feed the program a number that represents a temperature in Celsius, and the program returns a number that represents the equivalent temperature in Fahrenheit. The programmer, on the other hand, understands the program at an entirely different level of abstraction. The programmer must understand the *process* by which the program produces the correct result for a given input.

As you progress through your exploration of Python, you will see this idea repeated several times in different forms. That is, you will encounter mechanisms (such as functions, the topic of Chapter 3), that allow the user to experience two or more levels of abstraction. As with programs, these can usually be described as the "what" level of abstraction that help you understand what is being done, and the "how" level of abstraction that help you understand how the task is being accomplished.

Curiously, because details can become so numerous, it is what you can safely *forget* that is often much more important than what you must *remember*. For instance, most users need to know only that the function named `sqrt` in the Math module produces square roots of numeric arguments. They don't generally want to, and certainly don't need to, know exactly how this result is produced.

THE SOFTWARE DEVELOPMENT PROCESS

Although the programs you are developing at this point are exceedingly simple, it is not too early to begin thinking about the process that occurs when any new computer application is created. In general, this process is divided into a number of stages or steps outlined here.

Following is an idealized view of the software development process, but the realities are often somewhat different. As you progress through your studies of computer science, you will encounter several other approaches. One popular current approach is termed *extreme programming (Xp)*. Using Xp, the client works side-by-side with the developer, programs are written rapidly (*rapid prototyping*), and they are frequently tossed out and rewritten (*refactored*). However, it is still useful to know the various stages in the ideal design process, if for no other reason than to help you decide what to do next.

Step 1: Analyze the Problem

If you are creating the program for somebody else (a client), try to determine exactly what the client needs and understand the problem that needs to be solved. Create a few test cases that can be used to see if you are on the right track, and find agreement with the client on what the correct input and output values should be for these test cases.

Step 2: Create Initial Specifications

Describe in as formal fashion as you can what your program will do. Create a *scenario* (or use-case), a simple story that shows what it will "look like" to use the

program. This can be accompanied by pictures or mock-ups. Have the client examine
the scenario to make sure it is in agreement with the original vision. It is important
here to describe the essential "look and feel" of the application, as well as *what* it will
do, and not *how* it will produce the desired result.

Steps 3 and 4: Create and Implement the Design

Using the specifications and the scenarios, create a design for the overall structure of
the program. This is where you start to worry about how each task is to be performed.
It is not uncommon during this part of the process to uncover unanticipated details,
exceptional conditions, or possibilities for generalizing your program to a wider
range of values. When this happens, you can create new scenarios and again work
with the client to see if these scenarios satisfy the original vision.

Then translate your design into a working Python program. Remove all the
syntactic errors in the program, until it appears to be working for a reasonable set of
values.

Step 5: Test and Debug the Program

Once you think your program is working, test it in a systematic fashion. Begin with
the test cases you created during your analysis of the program. If any of these produce the wrong results, it might be necessary to go back and change your design or
your implementation. Once you have the program working on these inputs, consider
the guidelines presented earlier for testing conditional statements or loops. Do the
test cases you have written already satisfy these guidelines? If not, create new test
cases for these situations. Once you have the program working correctly with these
new test cases, make sure you show them to the client to verify that the correct result
is being produced.

Step 6: Maintain the Program

Few programs remain untouched once they are released for others to use: perhaps
new bugs are discovered, or users decide they want new abilities that were not en-
visioned in the original design. Changes that are made after an initial release are
termed, somewhat euphemistically, *maintenance*. Many program evolve quite dra-
matically over years of use.

EXERCISES

1. Write a series of Python statements that will read three numeric values from the user, and
   then print the largest of the three.

2. Write a series of Python statements that will read three strings from the user, and then
   print them in dictionary order. (Note: you can compare two strings using the relational
   operators.)

3. Three numbers, *a, b,* and *c,* are called a *Pythagorean triple if* $a^2 + b^2 = c^2$. An example is the triple *3, 4,* and *5,* since *9 + 16 = 25*. Pythagorean triples can represent, for example, the length of sides in a right triangle. Write a series of Python statements that will read three numbers into variables named *a, b,* and *c* and then print a message saying whether or not they are a Pythagorean triple.

4. Using a *for* loop, print of table of Celsius/Fahrenheit equivalences. Let *c* be the Celsius temperatures, ranging from 0 to 100. For each value of *c,* print the corresponding Fahrenheit temperature.

5. Using a *for* loop, print a table of powers of *x,* where *x* ranges from 1 to 10. For each value *x,* print the quantity *x,* x^2, and x^3. Use tab characters in your print statement to make the values line up nicely.

6. Using a *while* loop, produce a simple table of sines, cosines, and tangents. Make the variable *x* range from 0 to 3 in steps of 0.1. For each value of *x,* print the value of *math.sin(x),* *math.cos(x),* and *math.tan(x).*

7. Using a series of nested *for* loops, find all Pythagorean triples consisting of positive integers less than or equal to 20.

8. Remember the formula for the roots of a quadratic equation. For the equation $ax^2 + bx + c = 0$, the roots are $b \pm \sqrt{(b^2 - 4ac)} / 2a$. If the discriminant (the quantity under the square root) is positive, there are two real roots; if 0, there is one double root; and if negative, there are two complex roots. Write a program to read the values *a, b,* and *c* and produce a message saying how many roots the equation has and their forms.

9. Write a program that will accept as input a series of names and salaries. Use the name *End* to mark the end of the sequence of values. After the values have been entered, print the average salary and the names and salaries of those individuals with the highest and lowest salaries.

10. Hourly workers typically earn overtime when they work more then 40 hours per week. For example, overtime pay might be 150 percent of the regular salary for the additional hours. Write a Python program that will ask the user for her hourly wage and then for the hours she has worked in the past week. With these two values, print the wages earned for the week.

11. A driver computes his miles per gallon by recording his odometer reading each time he fills the gas tank. Subtracting the previous odometer reading yields the miles traveled, and dividing by the gallons entered yields the miles per gallon. Write a program that reads values from the user until he enters the value *–1* for the odometer reading. After the second set of figures, print the miles per gallon for each fill-up.

12. What is the effect of a print statement that ends with a comma? Try writing two such statements in succession in a program. Can you think of a use for this behavior?

13. Perhaps surprisingly, a number can be used as the conditional portion of an *if* or a *while* statement. Experiment with this idea. Under what conditions is a number considered to be true? Can you think of a situation for which you might want to use a *while* loop with an integer condition?

14. Perhaps even more surprising, a string can also be used as the conditional in an *if* or a *while* statement. Explore this use. Under what conditions is a string considered to be true?

15. Having answered the preceding question, what would you think would be the result of the expression 0 or expression 3? Try it. What does it actually produce? Try various other expressions using integers and the operators *and* and *or*. Can you come up with a rule to predict the outcome? Does your rule explain expressions such as 3 and 4 and 5?

16. Having solved the previous exercise, predict the output of the following statements, and then test your answer. What was your prediction? Was it correct?

```
x = 'able'
while x:
        print x
        x = x[1:]
```

17. A year is a leap year if it is divisible by 4, unless it is divisible by 100 and not by 400. Write a program that reads an integer value, and prints "leap year" or "not leap year."

18. Write a program that reads an integer value *n* from the user and then produces *n* lines of output. The first line contains one star, the second two stars, and so on until the last line, which should have *n* stars. Can you write this using only a single loop? Hint: Remember what the expression '+'*5 does.

```
Enter a size: 5
+
++
+++
++++
+++++
```

19. Write a program that reads two integer values *n* and *m* from the user and then produces a box that is *n* wide and *m* deep, such as the following:

```
Enter a width: 5
Enter a height: 4
@@@@@
@   @
@   @
@@@@@
```

20. What does the range loop do if it is given negative numbers? Experiment with negative values in the first, second, or third location and try to come up with a general rule.

21. Write a program that reads a word and prints the number of letters in the word, the number of vowels in the word, and the percentage of vowels.

```
Enter a word: sequoia
Letters: 7
Vowels: 5
Percentage of vowels: 71.42
```

22. Python has a feature that is somewhat unusual for programming languages. The *for* and *while* loops can also take an *else* clause, just like an *if* statement. The following is an example:

```
year = 0
i = 0
while year < 5:
        i = i+ year
```

```
        year = year + 1
    else:
            print 'year is', year
```

Experiment with various loops and the *else* statement, and see if you can discover the rule that tells you under what circumstances the *else* statement is executed. Try using a loop with a *break* statement. Describe the experiments you performed, their results, and your conclusions.

23. Import the module named `sys`, and try executing the function `sys.exit` (*"message"*) with some string value. What is the result? Try putting this statement in the middle of a loop. What does it do?

24. The function `random.randint` from the random module can be used to produce an integer from a range of values. For example, `random.randint(1,6)` produces the values 1 to 6 with equal probability. Such a value can be used, for example, to simulate the roll of a die. Using this technique, write a program that will play several rounds of the popular dice game known as craps. The rules of craps are as follows: A player rolls a pair of dice. If the sum of dice is either 7 or 11 on the first throw, the player wins. If the sum is 2, 3, or 12 on the first throw, the player loses. Any other sum becomes the player's "point." To win, the player must continue rolling the dice until a roll matches the point. This is termed "making the point." If the player rolls a 7 before making the point, the player loses.

25. Use a random number generator to create a program to play "guess my number." The computer selects a random number and prompts the user for a guess. At each step, the computer responds either "you are right," "too low," or "too high." The loop continues until the user guesses the correct number.

26. Random numbers can also be used to create a simple tutoring program. For example, suppose you are teaching multiplication. A program might randomly select two numbers between 1 and 9 and then ask a question such as the following: How much is 6 times 8? The student types the answer, and the computer checks that it is either correct or not, issuing an appropriate message. Write a program that will loop 10 times producing questions of this form and checking the answers.

3 CHAPTER

Defining Functions

In the previous chapter you learned how to create a Python *program* by placing a series of Python statements into a file. Programs make it easy to execute the same pattern of statements more than once. They also allow a user (either the original programmer or another person) to execute a group of Python statements without having detailed knowledge of how it all works.

After reading Chapter 2, you know that *abstraction* is the process of purposefully hiding some details so that you can more easily see others. The use of a program allows us to separate the "*what* is the task to be done" from the "*how* is the task done"—that is, we separate the description of the task to be accomplished from the details of how the task is performed. Through abstraction, the user of the temperature conversion program, for example, could think merely of the task being performed and not about the details of how this task was accomplished.

The same issues frequently arise *within* a program during the course of execution—that is, the same operations can be required several times in different parts of a program, and the programmer might wish to collect a series of statements together so that she can think about them as a unit. The easiest way to do this is to create a *function*.

A function is a way of packaging a group of statements for later execution. The function is given a name that becomes a shorthand, or handle, to describe the process. Once the function is defined, the user can think of the task by its name and not by the steps involved to accomplish the task. Once again, this concept separates the "what" from the "how."

You have actually been using functions since Chapter 1. In this chapter, you will learn how to define your own functions.

A function is created using a *def* statement (short for *definition*). As you have seen, most functions require some initial information in order to perform particular tasks. This information is passed by *parameters*. When you call functions, you place parameter values inside a parenthesized list. Inside a function definition is another list of parameter names that are matched to particular arguments. The values passed to the function are attached (that is, assigned) to the names when the function is executed. The following is an example function definition:

```
def areaOfRect (w, h):
    # compute the area of a rectangle with width w and height h
    return w * h
```

Notice that the *syntax* for the function definition follows a pattern similar to the *if* and *while* statements you learned about in Chapter 2. The colon (:) indicates the beginning of a group of statements. The statements being collected (which can be one or more) are distinguished by being indented one tab stop. These are termed the *body* of the function. New features include the keyword (def) and the *parameter list*—the list of names enclosed in parentheses following the function name. A new type of statement, the *return* statement, indicates the value that will be used as the value of the expression in the caller's program after the function finishes execution. It is common (although not required) that a *comment* be placed inside the function to describe its purpose.

You have already seen the syntax used to invoke a function. The name of the function to be executed is given, followed by a list of *arguments*, or values that will be matched to the names given in the parameter list. Following the function call, the statements in the body of the function will be executed. When the function returns, the resulting value will be used as the value of the expression.

> Sometimes functions do not return a value. You will see an example in the next section. If the end of the function body is encountered without finding a *return* statement, control is passed back to the point of execution.

```
print 'the area of rectangle 2 by 3 is', areaOfRect(2, 3)
print 'the area of rectangle 2.5 by 3.2 is', areaOfRect(2.5, 3.2)
print 'the area of rectangle 2 by 7.2 is ', areaOfRect(2, 7.2)
print 'silly values produce silly results', areaOfRect('abc', 3)
```

You can create function definitions in interactive mode as well, although it is not common to do so. Simply insert a tab before each line that will be part of the body of the function, and press the return key after all the statements have been entered.

You should at this point stop reading and try creating several functions, both in interactive mode and in a program, until you are comfortable with the syntax for both function creation and function invocation. For example, try creating a function that converts a temperature in Celsius to the equivalent temperature in Fahrenheit. Another function could return the *cube* of the argument (that is, the argument multiplied by itself three times). Write a function that takes the radius of a circle and returns its area. Write a function that returns the minimum of three argument values. Using the functions ord and chr, write a function that takes a character as input, and if it is lowercase, returns the uppercase equivalent.

Functions are useful for several reasons—two of the most important being that it *raises the level of abstraction* and is a form of *software reuse*. *Raising the level of abstraction* means that the programmer can now think of the function as a "black box." Raising the level of abstraction allows the programmer to concentrate on *what* needs to be done, rather than *how* it is performed. For example, when you invoke the function math.sqrt, you can simply think of it as the square-root function. You do not need to know that a complicated series of actions is required to calculate the square root of a value.

Functions also serve as a form of *software reuse*. Programs are much easier to create when they are constructed out of high-level building blocks rather than low-level statements. You may have noticed this already in the use of modules, such as the math module. You can reuse the facilities provided by the math module without needing to rewrite them in every program that uses a trig function or a square root.

Eventually you will learn how to create your own modules and share your own functions with other Python programmers.

Functions can use information from their surrounding program. For example, suppose you want to write a program to compute the volume of a sphere given its radius. The formula, you may remember, is $v = 4\pi r^3/3$. The value π (pi) is given by a symbolic constant in the math module. You can import this module into the program, and then use the value in a function definition:

```
import math
. . .
def volumeOfRadius ( r ):
  # compute volume of sphere given radius
  return 4 * math.pi r * r * r / 3
```

Using this function, you could, for example, determine how many planet Earths could fit into the planet Jupiter:

```
>>> ve = volumeOfRadius (6378000) # earth radius in meters
>>> vj = volumeOfRadius (71492000) # Jupiter radius
>>> print 'volume of earth', ve
>>> print 'volume of jupiter', vj
>>> print 'ratio of volumes', vj / ve
```

Parameters can often be used to generalize one problem, making it applicable to a wider range of cases. We can illustrate this with a function to print the Roman numeral equivalent of an integer. Recall that the Roman number system has the following digits: I = 1, V = 5, X = 10, L = 50, C = 100, D = 500, and M = 1000. The first nine numbers seem to follow no easy pattern, so we write it simply as a long sequence of *if/elif* statements:

```
def romanNumber(n):
  # return equivalent of n written in roman numerals
  if n == 0: return '' # romans had no zero
  elif n == 1: return 'I'
  elif n == 2: return 'II'
  elif n == 3: return 'III'
  elif n == 4: return 'IV'
  elif n == 5: return 'V'
  elif n == 6: return 'VI'
  elif n == 7: return 'VII'
  elif n == 8: return 'VIII'
  elif n == 9: return 'IX'
  else print 'number is out of range', n
```

This example illustrates a useful Python shorthand: If the body of an *if* or *elif* is only a single statement, it can be written on the same line as the conditional test. When we consider numbers larger than 10, we discover an interesting pattern. Values larger than 10 are treated in exactly the same way, except that X, L, and C are used instead of I, V, and X. That is, a number such as 70 is written LXX. The ones place is

simply appended to the end, so that a number such as 74 is written as LXXIV, which
is LXX and IV appended. If we generalized the Roman digit function with the characters to print for I, V, and X, then we could use one function for both purposes:

```
def romanDigit(n, onechar, fivechar, tenchar):
    # return equivalent of n written in roman numerals
    # using given chars for one, five and ten
    if n == 0: return '' # romans had no zero
    elif n == 1: return onechar
    elif n == 2: return onechar + onechar
    elif n == 3: return onechar + onechar + onechar
    elif n == 4: return onechar + fivechar
    elif n == 5: return fivechar
    elif n == 6: return fivechar + onechar
    elif n == 7: return fivechar + onechar + onechar
    elif n == 8: return fivechar + onechar + onechar + onechar
    elif n == 9: return onechar + tenchar
    else print 'number is out of range', n


def romanNumber (n):
    # print equivalent of n written in roman numbers
    return romanDigit(n/10,"X","L","C")+romanDigit(n%10,"I","V","X")
```

The function shown will work for values up to 99; the generalization to 1000s
simply requires adding another call with "C" for the ones digit, "D" for the 500, and
"M" for the 1000.

If you are reading this as text, you most likely skimmed over the code written
above and thought to yourself, "Well, OK, if you say so." If this is the case, you should
stop reading immediately and explore the program using the Python system. Try it out.
Give it some values. See if you can understand why a division is needed in the first
part of the expression above and a modular division is required in the second. What
numbers do these two expressions produce? Now can you expand this function to work
for numbers larger than 100? Some experimentation is probably necessary to find the
proper combination of division and mod operators to isolate the desired digits.

```
>>> print 2847 % 10 # use mod to get last digit
7
>>> print 2847 /10 # use division to remove last digit
284
>>> print (2847 / 10) % 10 # combine to get tens digit
4
>>> print (2847/100) % 10 # generalize to hundreds digit
8
```

Python programmers frequently start an interactive session to experiment with
expressions and remind themselves of the use of operators during the course of
developing a program. Having seen the general pattern, we can then create the
Roman number function:

```
def romanNumber (n):
  # print equivalent of n written in roman numbers
  return (romanDigit((n/100) % 10, "C", "D", "M") +
      romanDigit((n/10) % 10, "X", "L", "C") +
      romanDigit(n%10, "I", "V", "X"))
```

Note the use of parentheses to allow the expression to span multiple lines. The key idea here is that we have generalized the basic function by adding parameters. This then allowed us to use the generalized function as part of another function, calling on the first function with a variety of different parameters.

```
>>> print romanNumber(47)
XLVII
>>> print romanNumber(847)
DCCCXLVII
>>> print romanNumber(2007)
MMVII
```

Let's examine another example. In Chapter 2, you used the formula to compute the money earned on a given balance assuming a fixed interest rate. You could encapsulate this in a function as follows:

```
def interestEarned (balance, rate):
  # amount earned by balance invested at given rate
  return balance * rate / 100.0
```

Rate is written as a number, such as 4.5; the division by 100 is used to convert the number into a percentage (and, by the way, to convert any integer values into floating point). Now suppose you wanted to determine how many years it would take for $1000 invested at 4.5 percent interest to grow to $1200. This could be computed by the following loop:

```
bal = 1000
year = 0
while bal <= 1200:
  bal = bal + interestEarned(bal, 4.5)
  year = year + 1
print 'it will take', year, 'years'
```

Typically, a program will contain many functions, and it is common for one function to invoke another. For example, suppose you wanted to create a separate function to record the action of compounding—that is, adding the interest back into the balance. You could write this as follows:

```
def compound (balance, rate):
  # return the updated balance if interest is compounded
  return balance + interestEarned (balance, rate)
```

Now if you wanted to find out how much $1700 would grow in 10 years assuming a 5 percent return rate, you can write the following statements:

```
bal = 1700
for i in range(0, 10):
  bal = compound(bal, 5)
print 'after 10 years the balance is', bal
```

Suppose you wanted to take this one step further and encapsulate the loop for the year iteration inside a function. You could write this as follows:

```
def compoundYear (balance, rate, numYears):
  # return balance assuming compounding for n years
  for year in range(0, numYears):
      balance = compound(balance, rate)
  return balance
```

Now you can easily answer questions such as, How much will $1350 become after five years with a 7 percent rate of return? Just use this line:

```
print '$1350 at 7% after 5 years is', compoundYear(1350, 7, 5)
```

FUNCTIONS AS BUILDING BLOCKS

The Roman number example illustrated the idea of treating a function as a building block, using one function in the development of another. Here is one more example. Many style guidelines suggest putting all program code inside function definitions. The principle function is often termed main. (The use of the name main is merely convention in Python; however, in many other programming languages, such as Java or C, the principle function is required to use this name).

For example, here is how we could have rewritten the temperature program from the previous chapter:

```
def main():
  # A Celsius to Fahrenheit conversion program
  # written by Robin Smith, July 2007

  print "This program will convert a temperature in Celsius"
  print "to the equivalent temperature in Fahrenheit"
  c = input("What temp in Celsius do you wish to convert? ")
  f = c * 9.0 / 5.0 + 32
  print "The equivalent temperature in Fahrenheit is", f

main()
```

The only statement, outside of function definitions, is the one invocation of the function `main` (which, by the way, is also an example of a function with no return statement). However, this function suffers from a common programming design flaw, which is to combine too many actions into one unit. In particular, a good design will almost always separate interaction (that is, input and output statements) from computation. What if in the next program you needed a similar Celsius to Fahrenheit conversion, but these were embedded in a larger task, or the messages you wanted printed were different?

The solution is to abstract away the conversion calculation, putting it into its own function:

```
def convCelsiusToFahrenheit ( c ):
  # convert a temp in Celsius to equivalent Fahrenheit
  return c * 9.0 / 5.0 + 32

def main():
  # A Celsius to Fahrenheit conversion program
  # written by Robin Smith, July 2009

  print "This program will convert a temperature in Celsius"
  print "to the equivalent temperature in Fahrenheit"
  c = input("What temperature in Celsius do you wish to
convert? ")
  f = convCelsiusToFahrenheit ( c )
  print "The equivalent temperature in Fahrenheit is", f
```

You should think of functions as building blocks. By separating the calculation from the output, we have created a more general-purpose building block that can now be more easily used in different projects. You should practice the art of identifying "chunks" of computations that can be abstracted into useful building blocks.

TESTING FUNCTIONS

In earlier chapters, we discussed guidelines for testing statements, such as conditionals and loops. Testing a function simply involves finding parameter values that will test the statements in the body of the function. For example, can you find parameter values that will force every conditional to be both true and false? Can you find parameter values that will force a loop to execute zero times?

To illustrate this process, the following example program purposely includes an error; you can see how systematic testing can uncover the error. Along the way we will introduce another useful debugging technique, the *code walkthrough*.

Imagine you need to write a function that will take three sides of a triangle and characterize them as either equilateral (all sides equal), isosceles (two sides the same), or scalene (all sides different). You might write a function similar to this:

```
def triType (a, b, c):
    # characterize triangle: equilateral, isosceles, or scalene
    if a == b:
        if b == c:
            return 'equilateral'
        else:
            return 'isosceles'
    elif b == c:
      return 'isosceles'
    else:
      return 'scalene'
```

On the surface, this function looks reasonable. So the first step is to define a few test cases from the specification itself. Certainly you need a set of values that are all equal (such as 2, 2, 2) and a set that is all different (such as 2, 3, 4). Then you need values in which two sides are equal. How many ways can this occur? There appear to be three possibilities, represented by (2, 2, 3), (2, 3, 2), and (3, 2, 2). Notice that these initial test cases were produced simply by thinking about the specifications of the problem itself, and not considering anything at all about the design of the program.

If we test the program using these five values, we get a surprising result:

```
>>> print triType(2,2,2)
equilateral
>>> print triType(2,2,3)
isosceles
>>> print triType(2,3,2)
scalene
>>> print triType(3,2,2)
isosceles
>>> print triType(2,3,4)
scalene
```

Oops! Why does the value (2, 3, 2) produce a wrong result? To find out, you can perform a *code walkthrough*. Sit down with paper and pencil and simulate the action of the computer on the given input. Like the computer, you will need to remember the values of the various variables. So you write down the current values, as shown at right.

a = 2

b = 3

c = 2

Then pretend you are the computer, executing statements in turn. You can use something like a tick mark, or you can cross out a statement after you have simulated it, to remember where you are:

```
def triType (a, b, c):
    # characterize triangle: equilateral, isosceles, or scalene
    if a == b:
        if b == c:
            return 'equilateral'
        else:
```

```
            return 'isosceles'
    elif b == c:
        return 'isosceles'
    else:
        return 'scalene'
```

In this fashion, you arrive quickly at the last return statement, about to return the result scalene, even though two of the three input values are the same. This shows you that you need to perform one more test before the end:

```
elif a == c:
    return 'isosceles'
else:
    return 'scalene'
```

You should practice the art of testing functions, and remember to test all functions in your program before you decide that everything is working properly.

NAME SCOPES

In an earlier chapter you learned how to attach a name to a value using an assignment statement. A function provides another way to create names and give them values. When the function is invoked, the arguments are evaluated, and then the resulting quantities are assigned to the parameter names. Once the parameters are initialized, the statements in the body of the function are executed.

If you simply use a name from the surrounding (that is, global) scope, the values are as you would probably expect:

```
>>> x = 4
>>> def scopeTest (a):
...         return x + a

>>> print scopeTest(3)
7
>>> print 'x is', x
x is 4
```

However, if you define (or redefine) a global variable name, the results may seem surprising:

```
>>> x = 4
>>> def scopeTest (a):
...         x = 7 # reassign value of x?
...         return x + a

>>> print scopeTest(3)
10
```

```
>>> print 'x is', x
x is 4
```

Why didn't the value of *x* change? The answer is that a new variable named *x* was created. Parameter names, and any variable that is assigned inside the function, are *local* to the function in which they are defined. This means that the name can be used only inside the body of a function. We call the body of the function the *scope* of the parameter names. The function is said to create a *local scope*, whereas names defined outside the function have a *global scope*. A local name that is the same as a global name is sometimes said to create a value that *shadows* the global, since you cannot (easily) see the global value. Once a function returns, the name and values of parameters are no longer meaningful. Changing the local values inside the function has no effect on the global scope.

You can think about scopes as a collection of nested boxes. Names defined at the top level are in the outermost box. Each function creates a new box, representing the new scope. Names assigned within the function live in this box. When the Python system searches for the meaning to attach to a name, it starts from the innermost box and looks outward until it finds a matching name.

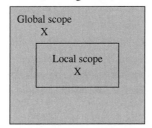

You should at this point stop and experiment with function definitions and assignment statements in order to get a better feel for Python's scope rules.

As with the naming of global variables, you should carefully consider the naming of parameters. Names should be chosen that make the meaning of the program clear—they should be evocative and easy to understand. Short names are often easier to read, but do not make them too short. Using "balance" to hold a bank balance is often a better choice of names than either "b" or "checkingAccountBalance."

Why do programming languages have name scopes? Without scopes, all names would have to be unique. An analogy will help illustrate the concept. City names are in some sense similar to variable names. The normal resolution rule in the United States is that no two cities can have the same name if they are both in the same state. You cannot have two cities named Springfield in the state of Illinois, for example. But nothing prevents two cities from having the same name if they are in different states. Cities in both Oregon and Illinois, as well as many other states, use the name Springfield. The scope of the name is the state, and while within the scope the name is unique, across two or more scopes there can be multiple values with the same name.

The scope rule allows programmers to use simple variable names, such as n or p, without worrying that a different function in another part of the program will end up modifying the value held by a variable. This permits several programmers to work on the same job, and it allows a programmer to use the work of another programmer (such as with an *import* statement) without having to worry about what names the module might alter in the current scope.

WRITING A FUNCTION THAT CALLS ITSELF

Suppose you want to write a function that will convert an integer into its text name. The value 347, for example, should produce "three hundred forty seven." Such a function might be useful in a program to print a check. If the number is less than 20, the structure of the program is tedious, but not complex:

```
def numToString (num):
  if num == 0: return ''
  elif num == 1: return 'one'
  elif num == 2: return 'two'
  . . .
  elif num == 19: return 'nineteen'
```

Complete this function definition and verify that it produces the correct result for values between 0 and 19. (You can argue with producing an empty string for 0, but assume that is the desired output for now.)

What about a number such as 27? It would be tedious to go through all 10 values between 20 and 29, particularly when they have such a simple structure. The "twenty" part is easy. To get the "seven" part, we can notice that this is a problem that we have *already solved*. That is, we know how to convert the value 7 into "seven"— we simply call the function numToString. With that insight, we can add the clauses that return the result for these values as follows:

```
elif num <= 29: return 'twenty' + numToString(num%10)
```

Study carefully what is happening in the previous line. The value num%10 is returning the remainder after the value num is divided by 10. That is, for a value such as 27, it will return 7. Invoking numToString on this value will produce the string "seven." The addition operator is concatenating this to the string "twenty." Type in this new part of the program and verify that it works for values between 20 and 29. Using this as a pattern, finish the definitions for values in the range 30 to 99.

What about 347? This should produce "three hundred forty seven." But notice again that portions of this result are simply values we already know how to produce. For example, if we compute num//100 it will yield 3, which we can then transform into "three."[1] Examine the following lines:

```
elif num <= 999:
  return (numToString(num//100) + ' hundred ' +
  numToString(num%100))
```

The expression in the *return* statement has been placed in parentheses simply to make it easier to break over multiple lines (recall that Python continues reading mul-

---

[1] Prior to Python version 3 this could have been written num / 100. After version 3, the division operator will return a float value. To return integer division the // form must be used.

tiple lines until it finds matches for all parentheses). Study these lines carefully until you understand what they are doing. Then add this to the function `numToString`, and verify that it produces the correct result for values in the range 100 to 999. Then do the same for thousands. A number such as 347982 should produce "three hundred forty seven thousand nine hundred eighty two." Finally, add the rule for millions.

A function that calls itself is said to be *recursive*. The creation of recursive functions is an extremely powerful technique. Any recursive function can be divided into two parts: First one or more *base cases* must exist; these are values that are handled without the benefit of recursion. In our example, the base cases are the integers 0 to 19. Next, there are *recursive cases*, values that are handled by "reducing" the problem to a "simpler" problem of the same form. The words "reducing" and "simpler" are placed in quotation marks because the meaning will be different in each new situation. In this case, *reducing* means using division, and a *simpler* problem means a number that is smaller than the original. The function is then invoked on the simpler problem, and the result is used to construct the solution to the original problem.

The exercises at the end of the chapter will give you the opportunity to explore recursive functions in more detail.

A Cautionary Tale Regarding Recursive Functions*[2]

Recursive functions can, in the right circumstances, be extremely powerful, as the example of converting a number into the text equivalent shows. However, they can involve dangers that the programmer should avoid. A classic cautionary tale involves the computation of *Fibonacci numbers*. Fibonacci numbers are defined using a recursive formula as follows: $fib(0) = 0$, $fib(1) = 1$, $fib(n) = fib(n - 1) + fib(n - 2)$. They were introduced in 1202 by a mathematician named Fibonacci in the following simple story:

> A certain man put a pair of rabbits in a place surrounded on all sides by a wall. How many pairs of rabbits can be produced from that pair in a year if it is supposed that every month each pair begets a new pair which from the second month on becomes productive?

The first few Fibonacci numbers are 0, 1, 1, 2, 3, 5, 8, 13. This series turns up in a surprising number of places. For example, the ratio of successive Fibonacci numbers converges to a constant value approximately 1.618. This has been termed the *golden ratio*. The golden ratio appears in many places in nature, as well as in architecture in the size of windows and rooms.

Computation of the *i*th Fibonacci number can be performed with a relatively straightforward function:

```
def ifib(n):
    a, b = 0, 1
    for i in range(0, n):
        a, b = b, a+b
    return a
```

---

[2] Sections with a trailing * indicate optional or more complicated material that can be omitted on first reading.

You should try this function out on a few examples to verify that it works. For example, what is the 35th Fibonacci number? Because the definition is recursive, it is temping to write a recursive version of the function, as follows:

```
def rfib(n):
   if n == 0: return 0
   if n == 1: return 1
   return rfib(n-2) + rfib(n-1)
```

You should verify that this function also works and produces the correct result. If you try to calculate the 35th Fibonacci number, what happens? Why is the recursive version so much slower than the program that used the loop? The answer is that for each value of n, the recursive program is making two calls on itself. For a large number, each of these would require two calls. Each of these in turn also requires two calls. So to compute the nth Fibonacci number requires approximately $2 * 2 * 2 * \ldots * 2$ recursive calls, or 2^n. This is termed *exponential complexity* and can bring even the fastest computers to their knees.

You should be careful not to draw the wrong lesson from this story. It is not telling you that recursion is dangerous or bad; it merely means that you must understand what you are doing. Problems in which at each step you either handle a base case or make a single recursive call are generally just as fast in either a recursive or nonrecursive form. It is only when one step makes two or more recursive calls that you need to think carefully. In later courses, you will learn techniques termed *complexity analysis* that can be used to estimate the running time of various algorithms.

USING GLOBAL NAMES INSIDE OF FUNCTIONS*

At times you will want a function to modify a variable from the global name scope. To accomplish this, you must first tell the Python system that you intend to use the global name. This is accomplished using the *global* statement. Compare the execution of the following example program with the earlier example, and note carefully the differences:

```
def scopeTest (a):
   global b
   b = 8
   print 'inside the function a is ', a
   print 'inside the function b is ', b

a = 1
b = 2
scopeTest(7)
print 'after the function, a is', a
print 'after the function, b is', b
```

A function that does anything other than returning a value is said to be producing a *side effect*. Typical side effects are printing some output or changing a value. The function shown here does both.

Can you do anything useful with this feature? Here is an example function that counts the number of times it has been called:

```
def callCount ():
  global counter
  counter = counter + 1
  print 'function has been called ', counter, 'times'
counter = 0
```

```
>>> callCount()
function has been called 1 times
>>> callCount()
function has been called 2 times
```

You should think carefully about using the global statement—or in general using any side effects at all. Notice, for example, that nothing in the name of the function indicates it will, as a side effect, alter the value of the variable *b*. If you need only to *access* a variable, you do not need the global statement; it is necessary only if you want to change a global variable. Use a global statement only when you find no other alternative way to accomplish the same task.

RAISING EXCEPTIONS

What will happen in the `compoundYears` function if the interest rate is negative? Or if the number of years is less than zero? Even if the arithmetic does not produce an error, such a situation is much more likely to be the result of an error in logic than an expected outcome. What should the function do in situations like the following?

```
def compoundYear (balance, rate, numYears):
  # return bal assuming interest compounded n years
  for year in range(0, numYears):
      balance = compound(balance, rate)
  return balance
```

One possibility is to do nothing and let the execution continue. The most common consequence of this choice is for an error to be compounded by further errors, until a result that is totally meaningless is produced. Another possibility is to print a message but then proceed anyway. This was the technique we used in the Roman number conversion program. A far better alternative is to check your values for validity, and if they are not valid, immediately halt execution and tell the user. This is known as *defensive programming*.

How should you tell the user that something is wrong? The proper way to do this in Python is to use a *raise* statement. This is known as *raising an exception*. The following rewriting of the function `compoundYear` shows how this is done:

```
def compoundYear (balance, rate, numYears):
  # return bal assuming interest compounded n years
  if rate < 0:
      raise RuntimeError, 'Negative interest rate'
```

```
    if numYears < 0:
        raise RuntimeError, 'Negative number of years'
    for year in range(0, numYears):
        balance = compound(balance, rate)
    return balance
```

Now if the user tries to invoke the function with an improper value, an error message will be produced, just like those generated for bad arguments to the built-in operations:

```
>>> print 'after 10 years', compoundYear(1000, -5, 3)
Traceback (most recent call last):
  File "compound.py", line 21, in ?
        print 'after 10 years', compoundYear(1000, -5, 3)
  File "compound.py", line 12, in compoundYear
        raise RuntimeError, 'Negative interest rate'
RuntimeError: Negative interest rate
```

Whenever possible, you should check the validity of arguments inside a function, and raise a `RuntimeError` if they are incorrect. In a later chapter, you will learn the flip-side of exceptions, how to catch and handle an exception that has been raised by a function.

At this point, go back and add error checking to some of the earlier functions we developed in this chapter. What condition needs to be tested in the function that returned the volume of a sphere? Add a statement to check this condition and raise an exception if it is not satisfied. The Roman number conversion program simply printed a message when the input was invalid. Replace this with a statement that raises an exception.

FUNCTIONS ARE VALUES*

A function is really just another type of value, and the *def* statement is really just a special sort of assignment statement:

```
def newfun(a):
  print 'the argument is', a


>>> print newfun
<function newfun at 0x64bb0>
```

Just like any other value, you can assign a function value to a different variable. You can then use that variable as if it were a function:

```
>>> x = newfun
>>> x(3)
the argument is 3
```

As with all variables, function names can be reassigned, either with an assignment or another *def* statement:

```
>>> newfun = 7.5
>>> print newfun
7.5
```

Function definitions are in fact executable statements, just like an assignment or a *print* statement. It is legal to place a function definition inside a conditional, for example:

```
if a < b:
   def minvalue():
        return a
else:
   def minvalue():
        return b
```

The uses of this feature are, perhaps not surprisingly, rare.

A FEW WORDS ABOUT NOTHING*

Suppose you write a function that finishes without returning a value, but you nevertheless save the result in a variable. What is the value of that variable? To find out, try writing the following function and discovering the outcome of the indicated statements:

```
def nothing():
   print "sorry, nothing here"

>>> a = nothing()
>>> print a # fill in with the result you discover

>>> print type(a)
```

The value None is the sole instance of the class NoneType. It is used in a variety of situations for which a placeholder value is necessary but no other obvious candidates present themselves. You can access this value using the name None. For example, you might want to use this to initialize a variable when you don't know what value it will eventually hold.

EXERCISES

1. The program to convert integers into their string equivalents does not correctly handle either negative numbers or zero. This is most easily fixed by creating a second function that recognizes these as special cases, and then invokes the recursive function in the general case. Write this second function. Why can't the recursive function return "zero" when it is given the value 0?
2. Many programs loop until the user indicates they want to stop. Write a function named cont () that takes no arguments. The function should print the message "continue?" and wait for the user to respond. If the user types Yes, y, or Y, then return true; otherwise return false.

3. An exercise in the previous chapter described how to use the function `random.randint` to simulate the roll of a die. Embed this technique in a function named `diceroll` that takes no arguments but returns a value from 1 to 6, marking the number of dots on a dice roll. Use this function to rewrite your craps program from the earlier chapter.

4. A year is a leap year if it is divisible by 4, unless it is divisible by 100 and not by 400. Write a function that takes an integer value representing a year and returns a Boolean result indicating whether or not the year is a leap year.

5. Using your leap year function, and your knowledge of the number of days in each month, write a function that takes a year and a day number and returns a string representing the month and date. For example, the input 2006 237 would return Friday, August 25, 2006.

6. Write a function that takes a positive integer n, and then produces n lines of output. The first line contains one star, the second two stars, and so on until the last line, which should have n stars. Can you write this using only a single loop? Hint: remember what the expression `'+'*5` does.
   Enter a size: 5

   ```
   +
   ++
   +++
   ++++
   +++++
   ```

7. Numbers in base 16 are termed *hexadecimal*. The letters A through F are generally used to represent the digits *10* through *15*. If a number x is larger than 16, the quantity $x\%16$ yields the smallest digit, while the quantity $x/16$ yields the value to the left of the smallest digit. Using these observations, write a function that takes an integer value and returns the hexadecimal equivalent expressed as a string.

8. The number of combinations of n things taken m at a time is written $\binom{n}{m}^3$. This can be defined recursively by the following formulas. $(n\ 0) = 1$, $(n\ n) = 1$, $(n\ m) = (n - 1\ m) + (n - 1\ m - 1)$. Write a recursive function named `comb(n, m)` to compute this value.

9. If a is a number and n is a positive integer, the quantity a^n can obviously be computed by multiplying a, n times. A much faster algorithm uses the following observations. If n is 0, a^n is 1. If n is even, a^n is the same as $(a * a)^n/2$. If n is odd, a^n is the same as $a * a^{n-1}$. Using these observations, write a recursive function for computing a^n.

10. If a function finishes without a *return* statement, what is the value returned? To find out, try writing a function without a *return* statement, and then print the value returned by an invocation. What information can you discover when you use the `type()` function on this value?

11. What happens when you use a function name, without arguments, in a *print* statement? What value is produced when you use the `type()` function on a function name?

12. A very simple recursive function is *factorial*. The definition of *factorial* (written *n!*) says that 0! is 1, and in general *n!* is $n * (n - 1)!$. For example, 5! is 120, which is $5 * 4 * 3 * 2 * 1$. What is the base case? What is the induction case? What should you do if the argument is less than zero? Write the factorial function using your ideas.

13. Using your factorial function, write a function that estimates the value of the mathematical constant e using this formula:

$$e = 1 + 1/1! + 1/2! + 1/3! + 1/4! + \ldots$$

Stop after 10 terms. Print both your computed value and the value stored in the math module as *math.e*.

14. Is the value *None* considered to be true or false? That is, if you use this value in an *if* statement, is the attached statement executed or not?

15. Try executing the following program. Can you explain what is going on?

```
def outer(x):
    def inner(y):
        return x + y
    return inner

x = outer(3)
print x(4)
```

16. What happens if a global statement refers to a variable that has not been assigned in the global scope? Make a prediction as to what you think should happen, and then write a program to test your hypothesis.

17. A *palindrome* is a word that reads the same both forward and backward—for example the word *rotor* or the sentence *rats live on no evil star*. Testing for the palindrome property is easy if you think recursively. If a string has zero or one character, it is a palindrome. If it has two or more characters, test to see if the first character matches the final character. If not, then the word is not a palindrome. Otherwise, strip off the first and final characters, and recursively perform the palindrome test. Write a recursive function using this approach.

18. Normally, palindromes are allowed to have capital letters, embedded spaces, and punctuation, all of which is ignored in the palindrome test. Examples of this form are *A man, a plan, a canal, Panama!* or *Madam, I'm Adam*. The palindrome test you wrote in question 17 can be easily extended to allow this form. If the first letter is uppercase, convert it to lowercase and test the resulting word. If the first letter is a space or punctuation, remove it and test the remainder. Otherwise, do the same with the final letter. Rewrite the palindrome test function using this approach.

19. Another classic problem that illustrates the power of recursive definitions is the "towers of Hanoi." In this problem, three poles are labeled A, B, and C. Initially, a number of disks of decreasing size are all on pole A. The goal of the puzzle is to move all disks from pole A to pole B without ever moving a disk onto another disk with a smaller size. The third pole can be used as a temporary holding place during this process.

    If you try to solve this problem in a conventional fashion, you will quickly find yourself frustrated trying to determine the first move. Should you move the littlest disk from A to B, or from A to C? But a recursive version is very simple. Rewrite the problem as a call on `Hanoi(n, x, y, z)` where n is the size of the stack, and x, y, and z are strings representing the starting pole (initially 'A'), the target pole (initially 'B') and the temporary pole (initially 'C'). The task can be thought of recursively as follows. If n is 1, then move one disk from pole x to pole y. Otherwise, recursively call Hanoi to move $n-1$ disks from x to z, using y as the temporary. Then move one disk from x to y, which leaves pole x empty. Finally move $n-1$ disks from z to y, using x as the temporary. Write the towers of Hanoi as a recursive function, printing out a message each time a disk is moved from one pole to another. Would using zero as a base case work even better? What action is required to move zero disks from one pole to the next?

CHAPTER

Strings, Lists, Tuples, and Sets

In Chapter 1, you encountered the *string* data type. This chapter will explore strings in more detail, and you'll be introduced to two other related data types in the Python programming language: *list* and *tuple* data types.

LISTS

A list is created inside square brackets. At its simplest, a list is a collection of values, separated by commas:

```
>>> lst = [1, 4, 7, 9, 12] # create a list with five elements
>>> lst
[1, 4, 7, 9, 12]
```

A list need not contain elements of the same type. The following example creates a list consisting of an integer, a real, a float, and another list:

```
>>> lsttwo = [1, 2.4, 'abc', lst]
>>> lsttwo
[1, 2.4, 'abc', [1, 4, 7, 9, 12]]
```

Just as an open parenthesis makes the Python system continue reading until it is closed, an open bracket starts a list that can extend over multiple lines:

```
>>> lstthree = [1, 2
...     3, 4,
...     5]
>>> lstthree
[1, 2, 3, 4, 5]
```

A list is similar to a string, and many of the operations you explored in Chapter 1 can be applied to either type. These include indexing, slicing, the *in* test, using the plus operator (+) for concatenation, using the multiplication operator (*) for repetition, the `len` function, and the `max` and `min` functions. The function list can be used to convert a string into a list of characters. Examples of these are shown below.

```
>>> lst[2]
7
>>> lst[1:3]
[4, 7]
>>> lst[2:]
[7, 9, 12]
>>> lst[:2]
[1, 4]
>>> 4 in lst
True
>>> 5 in lst
False
>>> lst + [3, 4]
[1, 4, 7, 9, 12, 3, 4]
>>> len(lst)
5
>>> [2, 3] * 4
[2, 3, 2, 3, 2, 3, 2, 3]
>>> max(lst)
12
>>> min(lst)
1
>>> list('abc')
['a', 'b', 'c']
```

Unlike a string, a list is *mutable*, which means that the elements in a list can be changed after the list is created. This can occur in a number of ways—for example, as a result of using an index as target of an assignment:

```
>>> lst = [1, 4, 7, 9, 12]
>>> lst[1] = 5
>>> lst
[1, 5, 7, 9, 12]
```

A slice can also be the target of an assignment. The value on the right side of the equation must also be a list, but it is not necessary that this list have the same number of elements as the slice. The list can be enlarged or reduced in size as necessary.

```
>>> lst[1:3] = [9, 8, 7, 6]
>>> lst
[1, 9, 8, 7, 6, 9, 12]
```

The *del* statement can be used to delete an element from a list. This is effectively the same as assigning a one-element slice with an empty list:

```
>>> del lst[3]
>>> lst
[1, 9, 8, 6, 9, 12]
```

Lists also provide a number of operations that can be written using *dot notation*, in which the list being modified is followed by a dot, and then the name of the operation and an argument list appear.

The following table summarizes the operations that use this form:

Operation	Description
s.append(x)	Appends element x to s
s.extend(ls)	Appends (extends) list s with list ls
s.count(x)	Counts number of occurrences of x in s
s.index(x)	Returns the index of the first occurrence of x
s.pop()	Returns and removes the last element from s
s.pop(i)	Returns and removes element i from s
s.remove(x)	Searches for x and removes it from s
s.reverse()	Reverses elements of s in place
s.sort()	Sorts elements of s into ascending order
s.insert(i, x)	Inserts x at location i

The value to the left of the dot is the list being manipulated. The following illustrates the use of some of these operations:

```
>>> lst = [1, 7, 3, 9, 2]
>>> lst.append(4)
>>> lst
[1, 7, 3, 9, 2, 4]
>>> lst.extend([8, 5])
>>> lst
[1, 7, 3, 9, 2, 4, 8, 5]
>>> lst.count(5)
1
>>> lst.index(5)
4
>>> lst.pop()
5
>>> lst
[1, 7, 3, 9, 2, 4, 8]
>>> lst.sort()
>>> lst
[1, 2, 3, 4, 7, 8, 9]
```

Often lists are grown, using the append operation, starting from an empty list. A simple pair of square brackets is used to create the initial empty list:

```
>>> lst = [ ]
>>> lst.append(3)
>>> lst
```

```
[3]
>>> lst.append(7)
>>> lst
[3, 7]
```

Example: Finding Average and Standard Deviation

In Chapter 2 you saw a program that would compute the average for a list of numbers. The end of the list was indicated by the value -1:

```
sum = 0.0
count = 0
num = input("enter your number:")
while num != -1:
   sum = sum + num
   count = count + 1
   num = input("enter your number:")
print "average is ", sum / count
```

Suppose now you want to compute some other statistics. A common statistic is the *standard deviation*. The standard deviation tells you how the values are scattered—a small value means they are clustered together, and a large value indicates they are widely separated. To compute the standard deviation, you must first compute the average. Let's call this value *ave*. Next, you compute the difference of each value from the average. This tells you how far the value is from the average. The difference is squared so as to remove the positive/negative distinction, and all the differences are summed. The sum is divided by the size of the collection, so it will be independent of the number of elements. Finally, the standard deviation is the square root of the resulting sum. Here's the equation:

$$\text{Standard Deviation} = \sqrt{\left(\sum (x_i - \text{ave})^2 / n\right)}$$

Let's rewrite the program from Chapter 2 so that it first places all the elements into a list, and then uses functions to compute the different statistics. First, the main program:

```
def main (): # use the main program convention from last
chapter
   # compute average, standard dev of list of numbers
   print "enter values to be analyzed, use -1 to end list"
   data = [ ] # our list of values
   num = input("enter your number:")
   while num != -1:
       data.append(num) # add value to data list
       num = input("enter our number:")
   ave = average(data)
   print 'average of data values is ', ave
```

```
std = std(data, ave)
print 'standard deviation is ', std
```

The main function copies values into a list. The `average` function must examine each element in this list. You have seen already how this can be done, but you may not have recognized it. The `range` function constructed a list, and the *for* statement was used to iterate over the elements of the list:

```
for year in range(0, 10):
```

But, in fact, the *for* statement can be used to cycle over any list of values, and not simply those produced by a `range`. So the function `average` can be written as follows:

```
def average (data):
   # compute average of a list of numbers
   sum = 0.0 # make sum into a floating point number
   for x in data:
       sum = sum + x
   if len(data) == 0: return 0
   else: return sum / len(data)
```

Since lists can be indexed, an alternative way to write the loop is to loop over the set of index values, as follows:

```
for i in range(0, len(data)):
   sum = sum + data[i]
```

Or you could even use a *while* loop:

```
i = 0
while (i < len(data)):
   sum = sum + data[i]
   i = i + 1
```

Which of these alternatives do you find easier to read and understand?

What does the function `average` return if no elements appear in the data list? Does this seem like a reasonable value? Do you think it would have been better to raise an exception in this situation?

The function to compute the standard deviation uses `sqrt` from the math module. You need to remember to import this module in the program sometime before the function is defined.

```
import math
```

```
def std (data, ave):
   # compute standard deviation of values from average
   diffs = 0.0
   for x in data:
       xdiff = x-ave # compute difference from average
       diffs = diffs + xdiff * xdiff # squared
```

```
if len(data) == 0: return 0
else: return math.sqrt(diffs/len(data))
```

You will find that lists of numbers can be extremely useful in all sorts of applications.

Example: Case Conversion

You learned back in Chapter 1 that although strings can be indexed, they are *immutable*—they cannot be changed. Lists, on the other hand, can be both indexed and modified; they are *mutable*. Many operations that work on strings are therefore developed by converting a string to a list, manipulating the list, and converting the list back into a string. Converting a string into a list is simple:

```
>>> list('abc')
['a', 'b', 'c']
```

Converting a list back into a string is slightly more complicated. The simplest technique is to use the join operation. This operation combines the values of a list, placing a string value between each list element. Using an empty string as the separator provides the result you want. (The join function and other string functions are described in a more systematic fashion in the section String Functions..)

```
>>> ' 'join(['x', 'y', 'z'])
'xyz'
```

You can combine these ideas in the following function. The function takes as argument a string. It first converts the string into a list. Using the chr and ord functions you explored in earlier chapters, all lowercase letters are converted to uppercase, and all uppercase letters are converted to lowercase. Having modified the values in the list, the list is then converted back into a string:

```
def convertCase (st):
    stChars = list(st)
    for i in range(0, len(stChars)):
        if 'a' <= stChars[i] <= 'z':
            stChars[i]=chr(ord(stChars[i])-ord('a')+ord('A'))
        elif 'A' <= stChars[i] <= 'Z':
            stChars[i]=chr(ord(stChars[i])-ord('A')+ord('a'))
    return ''.join(stChars)
```

This example shows the function in operation:

```
>>> print convertCase('Rats Live on No Evil Star')
rATS lIVE ON nO eVIL sTAR
```

Example: Silly Sentences

In Chapter 1 you learned about the *random* module. One of the functions in that library takes a list as an argument and returns a value selected at random from the list. You can use this function to write a program that prints silly sentences. All your sentences will have the form *subject verb object*. All you need to do is select a subject at random from a list of possibilities, and similarly a verb and an object.

```
import random
subjects = ['fred', 'jane', 'fido']
verbs = ['likes', 'eats', 'hits', 'ignores']
objects = ['an apple', 'a cat', 'me']

for i in range(0, 3):
  print random.choice(subjects),random.choice(verbs),random.
choice(objects)
```

Example sentences could include the following:

jane likes a cat
fred hits an apple
fido ignores me
jane eats an apple

Fixed Size Lists and Arrays

Sometimes you'll want to create a fixed size list, but you won't know until later what values will be stored in the list. This type of object is similar to an *array* in other programming languages. The typical Python solution is to use the repetition operator and a list containing the value *None*:

```
>>> a = [None]*5
>>> a
[None, None, None, None, None]
```

The variable is now a list with five elements, but the positions do not yet have any useful values stored in them. In some applications the array will hold numeric data, and zero (0) is a more appropriate initial value:

```
>>> data = [0]*5
```

An exercise at the end of the chapter will illustrate one use for an array of numbers.

A *two-dimensional array* is usually represented in Python by a "list of lists." However, the initialization of such a value is not as easy as the initialization of a one-dimensional list. Here is an example that illustrates the most common technique for creating a two-dimensional array:

```
>>> data = [None] * 5
>>> for i in range(0,5):
... data[i] = [0] * 5
...
>>> data
[[0, 0, 0, 0, 0], [0, 0, 0, 0, 0], [0, 0, 0, 0, 0], [0, 0, 0, 0, 0],
[0, 0, 0, 0, 0]]
>>> data[2][2] = 7
>>> data
```

Append Works by Side Effect

Note carefully that append and extend work by *side effect*, altering the list to the left of the dot. The value these functions return is the constant *None*.

```
>>> lst = [1, 2, 3]
>>> print lst.append(4)
None
```

A common beginner's mistake is to reassign the value returned by this function to the list variable. The results can be surprising.

```
>>> lst = [1, 2, 3]
>>> lst = lst.append(4)
>>> print lst
None
```

```
[[0, 0, 0, 0, 0], [0, 0, 0, 0, 0], [0, 0, 0, 0, 0], [0, 0, 0, 0, 0],
 [0, 0, 0, 0, 0]]
```

Lists and Loops

In Chapter 2, you learned how the *for* statement can be used to loop over the characters in a string, and how the range function can be used with the *for* statement to loop over an arithmetic progression. In fact, range is simply a function that produces a list of values:

```
>>> range(1, 6)
[1, 2, 3, 4, 5]
```

The *for* statement can be used with any list. Elements are examined one by one, assigned to the loop variable, and the body of the loop is executed:

```
>>> lst = [3, 5, 7]
>>> for x in lst: print x
3
5
7
```

An interesting function named zip takes two lists and produces a list of *tuples* representing their pairs:

```
>>> zip([1, 2, 3],[5, 6, 7])
[(1, 5), (2, 6), (3, 7)]
```

When combined with the multiple assignment you learned about in Chapter 2, this produces an easy and elegant way to loop over two lists in parallel:

```
>>> one = [1, 2, 3]
>>> two = [5, 6, 7]
>>> for x, y in zip(one, two):
```

```
...            print 'x', x,'and y',y
x 1 and y 5
x 2 and y 6
x 3 and y 7
```

What happens if the lists are different lengths? You can try a sample program and discover this for yourself.

Assignment and References

Now that you have created a mutable data type, you can move on to a subtle but nevertheless very important concept. This is the idea of *references*—and, in particular, the fact that an assignment copies *references*, not *values*.

Imagine that you create a list and assign it to a variable named *a*. Next you assign the variable *a* to variable *b*. Finally you make a change to part of *b*. What do you think will be the value held in *a*?

```
>>> a = [1, 2, 3]
>>> b = a
>>> b[1] = 7
>>> a
[1, 7, 3]
```

Are you surprised at the answer? After all, it was variable *b* that was changed, not variable *a*. What is going on here? The answer is that assignment makes the name on the left *refer* to the same object as the value on the right. Or, you could say that the variable name *b* is an *alias* for the value stored in variable *a*. In technical terms, we say that Python uses *reference assignment*. This can be visualized as follows:

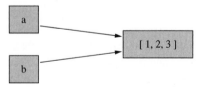

It is important that you understand the semantics of assignment for lists, because this can frequently be the source of subtle programming errors. Any time you are changing the value in a list, you need to think carefully about whether any other variable refers to the same list. (By the way, not all programming languages use reference semantics for assignment. Some use the alternative, termed *copy semantics*. As you proceed through your career as a programmer, you will undoubtedly learn many programming languages. Each time you learn a new language, you should carefully examine aspects such as the meaning of term *assignment*.)

Sometimes you'll want to avoid the trap of reference assignment by making a *true copy*. The easiest way to do this in Python is to use a *slice*, as in the following:

```
>>> a = [1, 2, 3]
>>> b = a[:] # use a slice instead of a simple name
>>> b[1] = 7
>>> a
```

```
[1,  2,  3]
>>> b
[1,  2,  3]
```

The slice makes a copy of the value, so that a change to one will not alter the other. (There is a deeper subtlety concerning what sort of copy you make. This will be explored in the exercises at the end of this chapter.)

Function parameters act like a form of assignment, and arguments also pass references, so the same alias situations can arise. Consider the following sneaky function:

```
def sneaky (n):
    n[1] = 'a'
```

The function changes one of the locations in the argument value. You can see this by passing a list and looking at the result after the function call:

```
>>> a = [1, 2, 3]
>>> sneaky(a)
>>> a
[1, 'a', 3]
```

Sometimes you want to be able to change a list that is passed through a parameter. But just as often you will not want this to occur. Bottom line, be aware of the semantic rules for assignment and parameter passing, and make sure you write the statement that will provide the effects you intended.

Identity and Equality

The concept of a mutable type leads us to introduce another import concept, the difference between *identity* and *equality*. A joke will help illustrate the difference. A man walks into a pizza parlor. He sits down, and the waiter approaches him and asks what he would like to order. He looks around, points to a nearby patron and says, "I'll have what she is eating." The waiter immediately goes to the woman, picks up the pizza in front of her, and places it in front of the man.

This story is funny because in normal discourse, we use the concept of *equality* in two very different ways. Sometimes we use *equality* to mean two things are exactly the same (for example, we say that the planet Venus is the evening star). Sometimes we use *equality* to mean that two things are functionally similar in all important aspects, even if they're not exactly the same thing (one pepperoni pizza is about the same as another).

When values are immutable, such as with numbers or strings, the distinction is largely unimportant. You can't change the values, so you don't notice that two variables are holding exactly the same thing. But the difference becomes relevant when we have mutable types, such as lists (and, later, dictionaries and classes). For this reason two separate operators are involved. The operator you have seen, ==, is for testing equality. The identity testing operator is called `is`. Two lists are equal if they are the same length and their corresponding elements are equal. Two lists are identical if they are exactly the same object. You can see the difference with a simple test, such as the following:

```
>>> if [1, 2, 3] == [1, 2, 3]: print 'equal'
equal
>>> if [1, 2, 3] is [1, 2, 3]: print 'identical'
>>>
```

The two lists are equal, but not identical. On the other hand, if you assign a value stored in one variable to another variable, then the values held by the two variables are both identical and equal:

```
>>> a = [1, 2, 3]
>>> b = a
>>> if a is b: print 'identical'
identical
```

Use the identity testing operator `is` if you need to determine whether two variables hold exactly the same object. Use the equality operator `==` if you need to know whether they have the same value, even if they are not the same object.

Sorted Lists

A *sorted list* is a list in which the elements appear in order. A sorted list is often needed when output is produced—for example, if string values are printed in alphabetical order. You can produce a sorted list in two major ways. The built-in function named `sorted` will produce a sorted version of a list:

```
>>> sorted([4, 2, 6, 3, 1])
[1, 2, 3, 4, 6]
```

Alternatively, the member function `sort` will reorder the values in a list so that they appear in order:

```
>>> lst = [4, 2, 6, 3, 1]
>>> lst.sort()
>>> lst
[1, 2, 3, 4, 6]
```

The `sort` function can alternatively take a comparison function as argument. The comparison function takes two arguments and returns a negative value if the first is smaller than the second, zero if they are equal, and a positive value if the first is larger. Such a function is needed if the list contains values that do not recognize the standard comparison operators or if the sense of the ordering is not strictly increasing.

```
def smallerThan(x, y):
   if x < y: return 1
   if x == y: return 0
   return -1

>>> lst.sort(smallerThan)
```

```
>>> lst
[6, 4, 3, 2, 1]
```

Sorted lists are important because they can be searched much more quickly than unsorted lists. To understand why, think about how you locate a telephone number in a telephone book. It's easy to do, because the telephone book lists names in alphabetical order. Now think about trying to find the name attached to a given number. This is much more difficult, because you would need to compare the number to each entry in the book.

Searching a sorted list is similar to the "guess my number" game. You begin by comparing the test value to the middle of the list. If it is smaller, you next search the first half of the list. If it is larger, you search the last half. You break the section of the list you are searching in half and look for the element in the smaller section. In this fashion, you are first searching the entire list, then half the list, then a quarter, then an eighth, and so on. This process is termed *binary search*. As the telephone book example illustrates, binary search is extremely fast. A list of 1 billion elements can be searched with as few as 20 comparisons.

While writing a binary search algorithm is an interesting exercise (see the examples at the end of the chapter), you'll usually want to use the version that is provided as part of the standard Python distribution. The function is found in the module named *bisect*. The function `bisect.insort(lst, item)` places the item into a sorted list. The function `bisect.bisect(lst, item)` returns the index of the point in the list where an item could be inserted in order to maintain the sorted property. It is an easy matter (again, see the exercises at the end of the chapter) to use this to test a value to determine whether it is in the collection or to remove a value from the collection.

EXAMPLE: SORTED LIST OF NAMES AND AGES

This example illustrates a number of the features that have been discussed so far by creating a simple program that reads a list of names and ages, and then prints the list sorted by ages. Your first decision to make is the representation for the name-age combination. An easy solution is to use a two-element list, so that the final data will be stored as a lists of lists something like the following:

```
[['fred smith', 42], ['robin jones', 38], ['alice johnson', 29]]
```

The program will read the name and age information in separate lines, using raw_input for the first, since we want a string, and input for the other, so that it will be converted into a number:

```
data = []
name = ''
while name != 'done':
    name = raw_input("enter name, or 'done' to finish: ")
    if name != 'done':
        age = input("enter age for " + name + ": ")
        data.append([name, age])
```

Once the loop completes, all the information will be contained in the list named `data`. If you try to sort this list you will get an error, because list elements cannot be compared to each other. Instead, you need to define a comparison function. As you saw in the previous section, this function must take two arguments and return an integer value. In this case, the two arguments are lists, and you can compare the `age` field:

```
def compareIndexOne (x, y):
  # compare two lists based on index value 1
  if x[1] < y[1]: return -1
  if x[1] == y[1]: return 0
  return 1
```

Using this function, you can then complete the program by sorting the `data` list, and then you can print each element:

```
data.sort(compareIndexOne)
for element in data:
  print 'name: ', element[0], ' age: ', element[1]
```

TUPLES

A *tuple* is similar to a list, but it is formed using parentheses instead of square brackets. Like strings, tuples are immutable, meaning they cannot be changed once they are created. In all other respects, they are identical to lists. This means that any of the list operations that do not change the value of the tuple are valid. A list can be changed into a tuple, and vice versa.

```
>>> tup = (1, 2, 3, 2, 1)
>>> 2 in tup
True
>>> list(tup)
[1, 2, 3, 2, 1]
>>> tuple(['a', 'b', 'c'])
('a', 'b', 'c')
>>> tuple('abc')
('a', 'b', 'c')
```

A common use for tuples is to return two or more values from a function. The following function, for example, takes a string or list as argument and returns both the largest and the smallest element as a tuple:

```
def minAndMax (info):
  # return both largest and smallest
  return (min(info), max(info))

>>> minAndMax('abcd')
('a', 'd')
```

```
>>> minAndMax([1, 2, 5, 7])
(1, 7)
```

In Chapter 2, you encountered a *multiple assignment*. What we did not tell you at that point was that a multiple assignment works by creating a tuple of expressions from the right side of the argument and a tuple of targets from the left, and it then matches each expression to a target. Because a multiple assignment uses tuples to work, it is often called a *tuple assignment*. The number of names must match the number of elements in the tuple. In the following example, `minAndMax` is returning a two element tuple. These values are assigned to the variables *x* and *y*.

```
>>> x, y = minAndMax('abcd')
>>> x
'a'
>>> y
'd'
```

The comma operator implicitly creates a tuple. This is used in the following common programming idiom. Try executing the instructions as shown and examining the resulting values. Can you explain what is happening using the idea of tuple assignment?

```
>>> x = 'apples'
>>> y = 'oranges'
>>> x, y = y, x
```

A tuple assignment also works inside lists. The following assigns the values of variables *x* and *y* to 3 and 4, respectively:

```
>>> [x, y] = [3, 4]
```

Upon first hearing about tuples, students frequently ask why they are necessary. They seem to be less useful than lists, since their entire behavior is a subset of the things you can do with a list. The answer is that tuples are immutable. Once created, you are guaranteed they can never be changed. Sometimes, such guarantees are important. You will see one such place in Chapter 5, where only immutable values can be used as an index into a dictionary. But many more examples exist.

Tuples and String Formatting*[1]

Tuples are sometimes used to encapsulate an indefinite (or variable) number of arguments, so that a function or operator can deal with a single entity. An example is the *string formatting operator*, written as %. If you followed the advice in Chapter 1 to experiment with this operator, you might have been confused by an odd error message:

```
>>> "abc" % 'def'
Traceback (most recent call last):
    File "<stdin>", line 1, in ?
```

---

[1] Section headings marked with an asterisk indicate optional or more complicated material that can be skipped on first reading.

```
TypeError: not all arguments converted during string
formatting
```

Here is a more proper example of the use of this operator:

```
>>> 'int %d float %g and string %s' % (17, 3.14, "abc")
'int 17 float 3.14 and string abc'
```

Notice how the argument for the % operator at right is a tuple that wraps several values. The left argument is a *formatting string* that can contain a number of special markers that indicate where values from the tuple are to be inserted and what type they should be. Some of the markers are %d for integers (decimal), %g for floats, %s for strings, and %% for a literal percent sign. The result is a string with the values inserted in the specified locations. This somewhat cryptic technique is based on a function found in the C standard library. A more complete explanation of the string formatting operator can be found in Appendix A.

STRING FUNCTIONS

A number of useful operations can be performed with strings. Among them are the following:

Operation	Description
s.capitalize()	Capitalizes the first character of s
s.capwords()	Capitalizes the first letter of each word in s
s.count(sub)	Counts the number of occurrences of sub in s
s.find(sub)	Finds the first index of sub in s, or -1 if not found
s.index(sub)	Finds the first index of sub in s, or raises a ValueError if not found
s.rfind(sub)	Finds last index of sub in s, or -1 if not found
s.rindex(sub)	Finds the last index of sub in s, or raises a ValueError if not found
s.lower()	Converts s to lowercase
s.split()	Returns a list of words in s
s.join(lst)	Joins a list of words into a single string with s as separator
s.strip()	Strips leading/trailing white space from s
s.upper()	Converts s to upper case
s.replace(old, new)	Replaces all instances of *old* with *new* in string

One of the most useful of these functions is split. This function takes a string (typically a line of input from the user) and splits it into individual words. A *word* is defined as a sequence of characters not including spaces or tabs. Another useful function is lower, which converts text into lowercase. The following illustrates the use of these functions:

```
>>> line = raw _ input("What is your name?")
What is your name? Timothy Alan Budd
```

```
>>> lowname = line.lower()
>>> print lowname.split()
['timothy', 'alan', 'budd']
```

Other useful functions will search a string for a given text value or strip leading or trailing white space from a string.

An alternative version of `split` takes as argument the separator string. The string is broken into a list using the separator as a division. This can be useful, for example, for breaking a file path name into parts:

```
>>> pathname = '/usr/local/bin/ls'
>>> pathname.split('/')
['usr', 'local', 'bin', 'ls']
```

The inverse of `split` is the function `join`. You have seen `join` in an example presented earlier in this chapter. The argument to join is a list of strings. The value to the left of the dot is the separator that will be placed between each element. Often this is simply an empty string. The values in the list are laminated along with the separator to produce the result string.

```
>>> lst = ['abc','pdq','xyz']
>>> print '::'.join(lst)
abc::pdq::xyz
```

Note: In earlier versions of Python, the functionality described here was provided by a module. Users needed to import the string module. In addition, the prefix for operations was the name `string`, and the string itself was passed as the first argument:

```
import string
. . .
>>> print string.split(string.lower(line))
```

This style is found in many Python programs, and users should be familiar with both techniques. However, the string module is now deprecated, and it is likely that these functions will be dropped from a future version of the language.

SETS: UNORDERED COLLECTIONS

The most recent data type added to the Python programming language is the *set*. A set differs from a list in three important ways. First, the elements of a set are unique. If you try to add a value to a set and the value is already in the collection, nothing happens. Second, sets are unordered. While you can iterate over the elements in a set, you cannot assume that they will be produced in any particular sequence. Finally, the set data type supports a number of set operations. The most significant of these are set intersection and set union.

The majority of functions that can be used with lists can also be used with sets. No special syntax is used for the set data type. Instead, the function `set(x)` constructs a new set out of an existing sequence, generally a list. However, sets can also be constructed using a tuple, although the syntax (with two adjacent parentheses) can seem confusing.

```
>>> print set([1, 2, 3])
set([1, 2, 3])
>>> print set([7, 8, 3, 8, 9])
set([8, 9, 3, 7])
>>> print set((7, 8, 3, 8, 9))
set([8, 9, 3, 7])
>>> s = set([1, 2, 3])
>>> s.add(5)
>>> s.add(3)
>>> print 2 in s
True
>>> print 4 in s
False
>>> s.remove(3)
>>> print 3 in s
False
>>> rs = set([1, 7, 5])
>>> print s.intersection(rs)
set([1, 5])
>>> print s.union(rs)
set([1, 2, 5, 7])
```

Because sets are a relatively new addition to the Python language, many programmers still use lists for tasks involving set operations.

Example: Palindrome Testing

You were introduced to palindromes in Chapter 3's "Exercises" section. Writing a function to test for the palindrome property is both a good exercise in string functions and a good example of a recursive function. Strings with a length of zero or one are obviously palindromes. For a longer string, strip off the first and last characters, and if they are different, the input is not a palindrome. However, if they are the same, recursively call the testing function with the string that results when the first and final characters are removed:

```
def palTest (s):
    if len(s) <= 1: return True
    elif s[0] != s[-1] : return False
    else: return palTest(s[1:len(s)-1])

>>> print palTest("rotor")
True
>>> print palTest("refried")
False
>>> print palTest("rats live on no evil star")
True
```

More complicated palindromes allow both uppercase and lowercase letters, as well as punctuation. To handle these, you can simply add new cases to your palTest function. If the first character is not a letter, it is stripped away. Similarly if the last character is not a letter it is stripped away. Only when you know that both values are letters do you compare their lowercase value:

```
def isLetter ( c ):
  # return true if c is a letter
  return ('a' <= c <= 'z') or ('A' <= c <= 'Z')

def palTest (s):
  if len(s) <= 1: return True
  elif not isLetter(s[0]): return palTest(s[1:])
  elif not isLetter(s[-1]): return palTest(s[:-1])
  elif s[0].lower() != s[-1].lower(): return False
  else: return palTest(s[1:len(s)-1])

>>> print palTest("A man, a plan, a canal, Panama!")
True
```

Example: Date Conversion

The `split` function is one of the most useful string functions, and you will find it in many different applications. For example, suppose you want to write a function that converts a date of the form *4/1/2007* into the form *Apr 1, 2007*. You can simply split the original using a slash (*/*) as a separator, and then use month (which is an integer) to index into a list of month names. Remember that index values go from zero to the list size, whereas we normally use 1 to represent the first month. To handle this, subtract 1 from the month value:

```
def longDate (date):
  monthNames = ['Jan', 'Feb', 'Mar', 'Apr', 'May', 'Jun',
       'Jul', 'Aug', 'Sep', 'Oct', 'Nov', 'Dec']
  month, day, year = date.split('/')
  return monthNames[eval(month)-1] + ' ' + day + ', ' + year

>>> print longDate('4/1/2007')
Apr 1, 2007
```

Note that the split returned a collection of strings, so that the month would be represented by the string value *4*. It was necessary to use the `eval` function to convert this into an integer to index into the list of month names.

Example: Encryption

Suppose you want to pass a message to a friend, but you don't want other people to be able to read it. To do this, you must disguise the text in some fashion. This process is known as *encryption*. The reverse process, taking the encrypted message and retrieving the original, is known as *decryption*.

Many encryption algorithms work by treating a character value as a number. You might remember that in Chapter 1 you encountered the function `ord` that did just that:

```
>>> print ord('a')
97
```

A simple encryption function would take a string, translate each character into a number, convert each number into a string, and concatenate these together to obtain the hidden message:

```
def encrypt (text):
   result = ''
   for c in text:
       result = result + ' ' + str(ord(c))
   return result


>>> hidden = encrypt("Mike loves mary")
>>> print hidden
77 105 107 101 32 108 111 118 101 115 32 109 97 114 121
```

To decrypt the hidden message, break the input into the text of individual numbers, convert each text number into an integer, and then convert each integer into a character:

```
def decrypt (text):
   result = ''
   for num in text.split():
       result = result + chr(eval(num))
   return result
```

Decryption now undoes the work of encryption:

```
>>> print decrypt (hidden)
Mike loves mary
```

This encryption scheme is not entirely satisfactory. In particular, the encoded string is much longer than the original. A common alternative that avoids this problem is called *rot13*, a variation on the Caesar cipher. In rot13, letters are "rotated" 13 positions forward in the alphabet, so that *a* becomes *n*, *b* becomes *o*, and so on. One nice property of rot13 is that the same function both encodes and decodes a message.

To define the rot13 function, we first need to figure out how to translate a single character. Let's assume that we are working only with lowercase letters. We could use the function `ord`. But there's another possibility. If we define a variable holding the alphabet, we can use the string function named `index` to convert a letter into a number between 0 and 25. To find the rot13 equivalent, we add 13 to this value, and then take the remainder when divided by 26. This once more gives us a value between 0 and 25. This is a value we can use as a subscript in our alphabet to yield a new character. Putting all this together looks like this:

```
def rot13char (c):
  alphabet = 'abcdefghijklmnopqrstuvwxyz'
  idx = alphabet.find( c )
  idx = (idx + 13) % 26
  return alphabet[idx]
```

The `rot13char` algorithm should be called only with lowercase character values. To do this, we can easily convert a string into all lowercase, and then test to see if a character is in the given range. If so, we convert it. If not, it stays unchanged:

```
def rot13 (s):
  result = ''
  for c in s.lower():
      if 'a' <= c <= 'z':
          result = result + rot13char(c)
      else: result = result + c
  return result
```

The encoded string is now no longer than the original:

```
>>> print rot13("I'm happy to see this!")
v'a unddm hc grr huvg!
```

Even more important, two encodings return the original string (albeit with all lowercase letters):

```
>>> print rot13(rot13("Rats live on no evil star"))
rats live on no evil star
```

Example: Eliza

We can illustrate the use of string and list functions with a simple but amusing program. This is a rewriting of a classic and well-known computer game, originally called Eliza. The program simulates a *Gestalt* psychotherapist and conducts a sort of question-and-answer session with the user. An example session might look like this:

```
Hello. Welcome to therapy. What is your name? Tim
Well Tim. What can we do for you today? I am writing a book
on Python
Tell me more. Do you know Python?
Why do you want to know? Even my mother is learning how to
program in Python
Tell me more about your mother.
. . .
```

Although it seems intelligent, the Eliza program has no innate understanding of the words. Instead, the program simply looks for simple patterns in the reply and responds with one of many canned phrases. For example, the program looks at the first two words. If they are *I feel* or *I think*, the program will ask the user why he feels that way. If the user mentions a relative, such as his mother, the program asks for more information. If the user simply presses return without a reply, the program tells the user to talk. If no other pattern matches, a simple open-ended reply is given. These are only a small sample of the rules that can be written—all to simulate intelligence where there is none.

```
# Eliza—a gestalt therapy program written by Tim Budd

import string

def getReply (line, words):
  # find a reply based on the words
  if len(words) == 0: return "You have to talk to me. "
  if line[-1] == '?': return "Why do you want to know? "
  if "mother" in words: return "Tell me more about your mother. "
  if "father" in words: return "Tell me more about your father. "
  if "uncle" in words: return "Tell me about your uncle. "
  if "sister" in words: return "Tell me about your sister. "
  if "brother" in words: return "Tell me about your brother. "
  if words[0] == "i" and words[1] == "feel":
      return "Why do you feel that way? "
  if words[0] == "i" and words[1] == "think":
      return "Do you really think so? "
return "Tell me more. "

name = raw _ input("Hello. Welcome to Therapy. What is your name? ")
print "Type quit any time you want to finish."
line = raw _ input("Well " + name + ". What can we do for you today? ")

while line != "quit":
  line = line.lower()
  reply = getReply(line, line.split())
  line = raw _ input(reply)
```

Notice how the function `string.lower` is used to convert characters to lowercase, and the function `string.split` is used to break the input line into individual words. Once broken, the patterns (and many others) are easy to describe.

TRIPLE QUOTED STRING, RAW STRINGS, AND ESCAPE CHARACTERS*

In addition to single and double quotes, triple quotes can be used to define strings. These are written using three single (`'''`) or double (`"""`) quotation marks. Triple-quoted strings can both span multiple lines and include single or double quotation marks:

```
>>> line = '''Robin said:
"don't shoot!" just as the
rifle went off'''
>>> print line
Robin said:
"don't shoot" just as the
rifle went off
```

String literals can also include *escape characters*. These characters are preceded by a backslash (\). The backslash indicates that the following character is to be given a special meaning. Examples include \t for the tab character, \n for a newline character, \' and \" for single and double quotation marks, and \\ for a backslash character itself. These can be used, for example, to create a string that includes both single and double quotation marks:

```
>>> line = "she replied: \"I didn't mean to do it!\" "
>>> line
she replied: " I didn't mean to do it!"
```

The newline character produces a move to a new line when it is printed:

```
>>> print "red\nbeans\nand\nrice"
red
beans
and
rice
```

Finally, *raw strings* turn off the processing of escape sequences. This is useful when you want to create a string that contains many backslash characters. A raw string is preceded by the character r:

```
>>> print r'red\nbeans\nand\nrice'
red\nbeans\nand\nrice
```

EXERCISES

1. Perhaps surprisingly, a list can be used where a condition is expected, such as in the test part of an *if* or *while* statement. Experimentally investigate this use. Under what situations is a list considered to be true? Under what situations is it false? Provide examples to illustrate your answers.
2. The list function can be used to convert a string into a list, as in list('abc'). Explain how to convert the resulting list back into a string.
3. The *del* statement deletes a single element from a list. It is claimed that this is effectively the same as assigning an empty list to a one-element slice. Demonstrate this by providing the equivalent assignment statement to the following example of del:

```
>>> lst = [1, 9, 8, 7, 5]
```

```
>>> del lst[3]
```

4. Can slices be used with the *del* statement? Provide an example to show what will happen.

5. Why is it necessary to have both the functions append and extend? What is the result of the following expression that uses append and which probably intended to use extend?

```
>>> lst = [1, 2, 3]
>>> lst.append([4, 5, 6])
```

6. Can you use the addition assignment operator, +=, with two lists? What is the result?

7. Show how to use the is operator to demonstrate that assignment creates a duplicate reference, and not a true copy. Then use the same operator to demonstrate that a slice assignment does create a copy.

8. What happens if you pass a three-element tuple to the function sneaky? What error message is produced? What happens if you pass a three-element string?

9. Show how to get the effect of the lst.append operation with a combination of lst.insert and len.

10. Suppose you use the lst.remove operation to remove an element that is repeated in a list—for example, removing the value *3* from the list [1, 2, 3, 4, 3, 5, 3]. Which value is removed? What is the effect of lst.remove if the element is not found in the list?

11. What does lst.index do if you search for an element that is not found in the list?

12. What does the lst.insert function do if you pass it a negative offset?

13. What does lst.pop do if you pass it a negative offset? What does it do if you pass it an offset that is larger than the number of elements in the list?

14. Comparison of two strings is based on the ASCII ordering. This means that uppercase letters (all of them) come before lowercase letters. Many applications require a sort that is case-independent, such as you find in a dictionary. Show how to achieve this effect by writing a comparison function for the sort operation. Hint: Convert both arguments to lowercase using the function lower(), and then compare the resulting values.

15. The function randint from the *random* module can be used to produce random numbers. A call on random.randint(1, 6), for example, will produce the values 1 to 6 with equal probability. Write a program that loops 1000 times. On each iteration, it makes two calls on randint to simulate rolling a pair of dice. Compute the sum of the two dice, and record the number of times each value appears. After the loop, print the array of sums. You can initialize the array using the idiom shown earlier in this chapter:

```
times = [0] * 12 # make an array of 12 elements, initially zero
```

16. A classic problem that can be solved using an array is the random walk. Imagine a drunken man standing on the center square of a sidewalk consisting of 11 squares. At each step, the drunk can elect to go either right or left. How long will it be until he reaches the end of the sidewalk, and how many times will he have stood on each square? To solve the problem, represent the number of times the drunk has stood on a square as an array. This can be created and initialized to zero with the following statement:

```
times = [0] * 11
```

Use the function `random.randint` from the random module to compute random numbers. The function `random.randint(0,1)` will produce the values 0 and 1 with equal probability. Maintain a value that indicates the current location of the drunk, and at each step of the simulation move either right or left. Display the value of the array after each step.

17. The two-dimensional variation on the random walk starts in the middle of a grid, such as an 11-by-11 array. At each step, the drunk has four choices: up, down, left, and right. Earlier in the chapter you learned how to create a two-dimensional array of numbers. Using this data type, write a simulation of the two-dimensional random walk.

18. One list is equal (==) to another if they have the same length and the corresponding elements are equal. It is perhaps surprising that lists can also be compared with relational operators, such as <. Experiment with this operator and see if you can develop a general rule to explain when one list is less than another.

```
>>> [1, 2] < [1, 2, 3]
True
>>> [4, 5] < [1, 2, 3]
False
>>>
```

19. When you use the + operator to concatenate two lists, does it make a copy or a reference of the arguments? Show an example to demonstrate your answer.

20. What does the following statement do? Can you think of a good use for this type of statement?

```
a, b, c, d = range(4)
```

21. While the slice trick is a common idiom for making a copy, it works only if the elements in the list are themselves simple values. To see the problem, examine the following. What do you predict will be printed as the value of c? Try executing the statements. Did the result match your prediction? Explain the outcome using the concept of references.

```
>>> a = [1, 2]
>>> b = [a, 3]
>>> c = b[:]
>>> a[0] = 7
>>> b[1] = 8
>>> c
```

The slice assignment trick is returning what is termed a *shallow copy*. A true and complete copy of a multi-level value is termed a *deep copy*. To make a deep copy you can include the module named *copy* and invoke the function `copy.deepcopy(x)`. Show that if this function is used in the example above, the result is different from the shallow copy outcome.

22. Examine the result, and explain the difference between the following two expressions:

```
>>> lst = [1, 2, 3]
>>> lst * 3
. . .
>>> [ lst ] * 3
. . .
```

23. Take the second expression in exercise 22, and subsequently change the value `lst`; what happens to the result? Explain this behavior using the ideas of deep and shallow copies from earlier questions.

```
>>> lst = [1, 2, 3]
>>> arr = [ lst ] * 3
>>> lst[1] = 7
>>> print arr # what will you see?
```

24. What if you tried to avoid the problem above using the slice copy idiom? What happens if you change an element in the array? Explain the result using the ideas of deep and shallow copy and references.

```
>>> lst = [1, 2, 3]
>>> arr = [ lst[:] ] * 3
>>> arr[1][1] = 7
>>> print arr # what will you see?
```

25. What does the `string.count` function do if the pattern overlaps with itself? For example, suppose you want to count the number of times that the string "sis" occurs in the word "frisisisisip." Two values are possible—the overlapping count and the non-overlapping count. Which is produced by the function? Describe a way to find the other value.

26. What does the `string.replace` function do if the pattern value overlaps with itself? For example, suppose you want to replace all the occurrences of "sis" in "frisisisisip" with "xix"?

27. What does the `string.replace` function do if the replacement introduces new instances of the pattern? For example, what if you replace the string "sis" with "xsis" in "frisisis"?

28. A variation on the `split` function uses an argument. What does the following produce? Try various other expressions, and explain what value is returned by this version of `split`.

```
>>> line = '12:43:13:24:43"
>>> print line.split(":")
```

29. The module random provides a number of functions that produce random numbers. The most useful are the functions `random.random()`, which returns a floating point value in the range (0.0, 1.0), and the function `random.randint(a, b)`, which produces a random integer N, distributed a <= N <= b. Using the latter, write a function that takes a list and returns a randomly selected element.

30. Many more rules can be added to the response generator for the Eliza program. Examples include responding to "I want" or "I think" with a question that asks why the client wants or thinks that way (perhaps even including the text of the material that follows the first two words), a randomly generated generic response taken from a list of different possibilities if nothing else is appropriate, searching for a key word such as "computer" and responding with something like "computers can be so annoying, can't they?" Think of some more question and answer patterns and implement them in your own version of Eliza.

31. In Chapter 2, you learned that the `range` function, normally used in a for statement, actually produces a list. With the benefit of your knowledge of lists, explain what the function `range(x, y, z)` produces.

32. A polygon can be represented by a list of (x, y) pairs, where each pair is a tuple: $[(x_1, y_1),$ $(x_2, y_2), (x_3, y_3), \ldots (x_n, y_n)]$. Write a recursive function to compute the area of a polygon. This can be accomplished by "cutting off" a triangle, using the fact that a triangle with corners $(x_1, y_1), (x_2, y_2), (x_3, y_3)$ has area $(x_1y_1 + x_2y_2 + x_3y_2 - y_1x_2 - y_2x_3 - y_3x_1) / 2$.

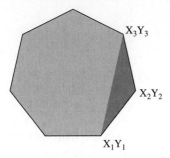

X_3Y_3

X_2Y_2

X_1Y_1

33. As noted in this chapter, the function `bisect` in the module of the same name takes as argument a sorted list and an element. It returns the index where the element could be inserted, if desired, so as not to violate the sorted characteristic of the list. Show how to use this function to create a simple collection abstraction. Your collection should implement the following functions:

    `add(lst, ele)` to add the element into the collection
    `test(lst, ele)` to return true if the element is in the collection; false otherwise
    `remove(lst, ele)` to return the element from the collection if it is there; otherwise do nothing

34. Write the function `bisect` that matches the definition given in the previous question. That is, `bisect(lst, ele)` should return the position in `lst` where the element could be inserted so as not to violate ordering. Do this using the binary search idea. That is, first compare the element to the value stored in the middle of the list. Then search either the first half or the second half of the list. Do this repeatedly until you have found the proper position. Hint: Maintain variables low and high that are indices of the lowest possible and largest possible position, and loop as long as low is different from high.

5 CHAPTER

Dictionaries

The next built-in Python type we will examine is the *dictionary*. A dictionary is an indexed data structure that uses the same square bracket syntax used for indexing in a list. However, in a dictionary the indices are not positions, but values. Any immutable type can be used as an index. Strings are most common, but numbers and tuples work as well. An example will help illustrate the idea. An empty pair of curly braces creates a new dictionary, just like an empty pair of square brackets are used to create an empty list. New elements are placed into the dictionary simply by using an index in an assignment.

```
>>> dct = { } # create a new dictionary
>>> dct['name'] = 'chris smith'
>>> dct['age'] = 27
>>> dct['eyes'] = 'blue'
```

The index expression is called a *key*, while the element stored in association with the key is called a *value*. Dictionaries are also sometimes called *maps*, *hashes*, or *associative arrays*. Just as individual elements in a list can be accessed by indexing, values are returned from a dictionary using the indexing operation. An equivalent function is get. Both will produce an error if the index has not yet been assigned; however, a useful two-argument version of get will return the second argument if the index is not valid. The value stored with a key can be changed simply by assignment.

```
>>> print dct['name']
chris smith
>>> print dct.get('age')
27
>>> print dct['weight']
Traceback (most recent call last):
  File "<stdin>", line 1, in ?
KeyError: 'weight'
>>> print dct.get('weight', 0) # use 0 as default value
0
>>> dct['age'] = 28 # change the value
>>> dct['age']
28
```

As with a list, the function `len` can be used to determine the number of elements (the length) of the dictionary. In addition, the `del` function can be used to delete an element from a dictionary:

```
>>> del dct['age']
>>> print dct['age']
Traceback (most recent call last):
  File "<stdin>", line 1, in ?
KeyError: 'age'
```

Just as a list can be created with an initial set of values, a dictionary can be initialized at the time it is created. Each key/value pair is written using a colon (`'name':'robin jones',`), and the list of these pairs are separated by commas:

```
>>> info = {'name':'robin jones', 'age':53, 'weight':203}
>>> print info['name']
robin jones
```

As with parenthesized expressions and lists, an open curly brace for a dictionary literal makes the Python system keep reading until the closing curly brace is reached:

```
>>> info = {'name' : 'robin jones',
...     'age' : 53,
...     'weight' : 203}
```

The most common operations for a dictionary are shown in the table below. At this point, you should try creating a few dictionaries and examining the results of various expressions.

`len(d)`	Number of elements in d
`d[k]`	Item in d with key k
`d[k] = v`	Set item in d with key k to v
`del d[k]`	Delete item k from dictionary d
`d.clear()`	Remove all items from dictionary d
`d.copy()`	Make a shallow copy of d
`d.has _ key(k)`	Return 1 if d has key k, 0 otherwise
`d.items()`	Return a list of (key, value) pairs
`d.keys()`	Return a list of keys in d
`d.values()`	Return a list of values in d
`d.get(k)`	Same as d[k]
`d.get(k, v)`	Return d[k] if k is valid, otherwise return v

The function `has_key` can be used to test whether a given value is a legitimate key. This can be used to avoid the error message that will be produced if an illegal key is used:

```
if info.has _ key('age'):
  ageinfo = key['age']
else:
    ageinfo = 21 # use 21 as a default value
```

However, notice that this common idiom can be replaced using the alternative form of the function `get`:

```
ageinfo = info.get('age', 21)
```

Despite the relatively small set of operations available for dictionaries, they are one of the most powerful and commonly used data types in Python programs. Dictionaries indexed by strings are often used to store records of information. (Taking the place of data types such as `struct` in C or `record` in Pascal). Dictionaries whose elements are themselves lists or other dictionaries are used to store hierarchical values. You will see an example in the concordance program at the end of this chapter.

Dictionaries indexed by integers can be used like lists. You might wonder why you would ever want to do this. Consider sparse vectors, for example: Imagine you have a list of integers, but most of the elements have a value of zero. There are non-zero entries at positions 2, 17, and 523. Using a list, you would need to have at least 524 positions. Using a vector, you need only store the elements that are nonzero:

```
data = {2:27, 17:329, 523:42}
```

Using the second form of the *get* statement to access elements, the default value is returned on all but the nonzero elements:

```
>>> data.get(523, 0)
42
>>> data.get(525, 0)
0
```

Example: Counting Elements

The `get` function that allows for a default value can greatly simplify many problems. For example, the following simple function takes a list and returns a dictionary representing a count of the number of times each value appears:

```
def frequency (lst):
  counts = { }
  for ele in lst:
      counts[ele] = counts.get(ele, 0) + 1
  return counts
>>> frequency(['abc', 'def', 'abc', 'pdq', 'abc'])
```

```
{'abc': 3, 'pdq': 1, 'def': 1}
>>> frequency('the best of the best'.split())
{'of': 1, 'the': 2, 'best': 2}
```

Let's use this idea to write a program that reads lines of text from the input until a line with the single word *quit* is entered. After each line is read, it is split into individual words, and a frequency count is kept of each word. Once the terminating line is found, the frequency of each word is reported.

```
def main ():
   freq = { }
   line = raw _ input()
   while line != 'quit':
        words = line.split()
        for word in words:
             freq[word] = freq.get(word, 0) + 1
        line = raw _ input()
   # now all words have been read
   for word in freq:
        print word + ' occurs ' + freq[word] + ' times'
```

If the input is this:

```
it was the best of times
it was the worst of times
quit
```

Output will be this:

```
of occurs 2 times
it occurs 2 times
times occurs 2 times
worst occurs 1 times
the occurs 2 times
was occurs 2 times
best occurs 1 times
```

Example: Tabulating Club Dues

Let's continue working with the preceding example with a simple variation. Imagine a club with several members who pay monthly dues. The dues each member has paid are recorded as follows:

```
chris:2.34
robin:1.50
fred:3.23
robin:3.75
chris:4.35
```

Breaking a Loop in the Middle

Notice how the call to `raw_input` is repeated twice, since this action is required before we can test for the quitting value. An alternative approach would be to place the call on `raw_input` at the top of the loop, and use the *break* statement to quit. This is called *breaking out of the middle of a loop*. Which form do you think is easier to read?

```
while true:
   line = raw _ input()
   if line == 'quit': break
   . . .
```

Notice that members may have contributed more than once (say, over several meetings). We need a program that will read inputs in this form, be terminated,[1] by a line containing the word *quit*, and then print a list of the amounts each member has contributed. The program will be structured similar to the example provided earlier. The major difference is that input will be split using the colon as spacer, and the second value will be converted into a number using the function `eval`:

```
def main ():
   dues = { }
   line = raw _ input()
   while line != 'quit':
       words = line.split(':')
       dues[words[0]] = dues.get(words[0], 0.0)+eval(words[1])
       line = raw _ input()
   # now all lines have been read
   for name in dues:
       print name,' has paid ',dues[name],' in dues'
```

COMBINING TWO DICTIONARIES WITH UPDATE

Two lists can be combined using concatenation, or an *append*. This concept does not make sense for dictionaries; however, a somewhat similar operation is provided by the `update` method. This method takes as its argument another dictionary. The values from the argument dictionary are copied into the receiver, possibly overwriting an existing entry. Here's an example:

```
>>> dictone = {'abc':3, 'def':7, 'xyz': 9}
>>> dicttwo = {'def':5, 'pdq': 4}
>>> dictone.update(dicttwo)
>>> print dictone
{'xyz': 9, 'abc': 3, 'pdq': 4, 'def': 5}
```

---

[1] At the moment, we are limited by the need to read input directly from the user. Soon enough, we will encounter file I/O, and when we do we can change our programs to read values from a file until end of file is reached.

MAKING COPIES

Remember that Python uses reference semantics from assignment. If you simply assign one dictionary to a new variable, they end up referring to the same collection. A change to one will end up modifying both:

```
>>> dictone = {'abc': 3, 'def': 7}
>>> dicttwo = dictone
>>> dicttwo['xyz'] = 12
>>> print dictone
{'xyz': 12, 'abc': 3, 'def': 7}
```

To make an independent copy of a dictionary, you can use the `copy` method:

```
>>> dictone = {'abc': 3, 'def': 7}
>>> dicttwo = dictone.copy()
>>> dicttwo['xyz'] = 12
>>> print dictone
{'abc': 3, 'def': 7}
```

When a dictionary is passed as an argument, the parameter is simply assigned the argument value. Hence both refer to the same value, and any change to the dictionary inside the function will remain after the function returns:

```
def sneaky (d):
   d['ha'] = 'ho'


>>> a = {'one':1, 'two': 2}
>>> sneaky(a)
>>> print a
{'one':1, 'two':2, 'ha':'ho'}
```

Sometimes, having the function fill in values in the dictionary is the behavior you want. Other times it is a sign of error. If you find a dictionary holding strange values, you can make copies of the dictionary before passing it into any function, in case the function is mistakenly filling in new values.

ZIP LIST INITIALIZATION*[2]

The `dict` function converts a list of two-element tuples into a dictionary, with the first element in each tuple representing the key and the second representing the value:

```
>>> x = dict([('name', 'fred'), ('age', 42), ('weight',175)])
>>> x
{'name':'fred', 'age':42, 'weight':175}
```

This might seem not particularly useful, since using the dictionary literal is so much easier. But remember the `zip` function? Many times you'll have a list of keys

---

[2] Sections marked with an asterisk indicate advanced or optional material and can be omitted on first reading.

and a separate list of values. The `zip` function makes it easy to convert this into a list of tuples, which can then be used to create a dictionary:

```
>>> keys = ['name','age','weight']
>>> values = ['fred',42,175]
>>> x= dict(zip(keys, values))
>>> x
{'name':'fred', 'age':42, 'weight':175}
```

LOOPS

Just as a *for* statement can be used to loop over the elements in a list, a `for` can also be used to cycle through the values in a dictionary. If you use the dictionary as the target of the *for* statement, the values returned are the keys for the collection:

```
>>> for e in info:
...     print e
'name'
'age'
'weight'
```

Sometimes (actually, rarely) you'll want to iterate over the set of values. This can be done using the `values()` function:

```
>>> for e in info.values():
...     print e
'fred'
42
175
```

The order in which the elements are stored in a dictionary is purposely undefined and may even change during the course of execution. Often you want to examine the elements in a particular sequence—for example, in ascending order of keys. This can be accomplished by sorting the list returned by the keys operation:

```
for e in sorted(info.keys()): # cycle through keys in sorted
order
```

Example: A Concordance

A *concordance* is an alphabetical listing of the words in a text string, along with the line numbers on which each word occurs. A dictionary is a natural data structure for representing a concordance. The words in the text will be used as a key, while the value will be the line numbers on which the words appear. Because a word can appear on more than one line, we use a list of line numbers. Our basic data structure is a dictionary, keyed by strings, holding a list of integers.

The concordance program breaks into two steps. In step 1, the input is read line-by-line from beginning to end. In this example, we will use a line with the single word *quit* to represent the end of input. (The chapter on files describes a better solution to this problem.) Once the input has been read, step 2 is to print the result.

Breaking the input into words is easy using the `split` function found in the *string* module. Here's a new feature: If you need only a single function from a module, you can use a *from* statement. The from statement `from module-name import function` imports a single function from a module. In addition, the function is placed into the *local scope*. This means the function can be used without the module qualification. In this case, it means the function is called `split` rather than `string.split`.

```
from string import split

def countWords (words, dct, lineNumber):
    # update dictionary for each word
    # with line number
    for word in words:
        lst = dct.get(word, [])
        lst.append(lineNumber)
        dct[word] = lst

# step 1, read lines until finished
line = raw _ input()
lineNumber = 0
dct = { }
while line != 'quit':
    lineNumber += 1
    countWords(split(line), dct, lineNumber)
    line = raw _ input()

# step 2, print results
for w in sorted(dict.keys()):
    print w, ':', dct[w]
```

The program is shown above. A function has been defined to perform the task of updating the counts on the words in a single line. An example execution might produce results such as the following:

```
$ python concordance.py
it was the best of times
it was the worst of times
quit
best : [1]
it : [1, 2]
of : [1, 2]
the : [1, 2]
times : [1, 2]
was : [1, 2]
worst : [2]
```

Several changes can be made to improve this program. For example, the same word might appear on one line more than once. So the line number should be appended to the list only if it is not already found in the list. Also, words with upper-case letters and lowercase letters should be combined. This can be accomplished easily by converting the line into all lowercase before it is split. Both of these changes should be relatively easy to make.

The following is somewhat more complicated: Punctuation should be removed, so that periods and commas are not counted as part of a word. One way to do this would be to translate each occurrence of a period or comma into a space. Can you figure out how to do this?

DYNAMIC PROGRAMMING*

Chapter 3 analyzed two different functions to compute the Fibonacci numbers. You learned that the recursive program ran much more slowly than the recursive version. However, you can make the recursive version run just as fast as the other. This technique, called *dynamic programming*, can be expressed as a pair of principles: Never compute anything until you need to, but having computed a result, remember it and don't compute it again.

You can use a dictionary to store values as they are computed. Because this dictionary must be shared across multiple calls to the Fibonacci function, it must be declared global. The revised function can be written as follows:

```
fibs = {0:0, 1:1} # base cases, fib(0) is 0, fib(1) is 1
def rfib(n):
   global fibs
   if not fibs.has_key(n):
       fibs[n] = rfib(n-2) + rfib(n-1)
   return fibs[n]
```

You can verify that the recursive version is now just as fast as the looping program presented in the earlier chapter.

PERSISTENT VARIABLES

A *persistent* variable can retain its value across multiple executions. Behind the scenes, such values are stored in a file, similar to those described in the next chapter. However, the user can make use of the persistence facilities without needing to use explicit file commands.

The easiest facility for providing object persistence is the *shelve* module. This can be imported using the statement import shelve. As its name suggests, a shelve can be thought of as a platform for storing values. Shelves are given names (behind the scenes, these are translated into file names). The user opens or creates a new shelve using the shelve.open function. This function returns the shelve, which can then be used as if it were a dictionary. Values stored into the dictionary are written to the shelve and are retained even after execution of the program is complete. Values are read from the shelve using the same indexing operations as the dictionary. The following is a simple example:

```
import shelve

data = shelve.open("information") # file is named information
data['name'] = 'fred smith' # put information into shelve
print data['name'] # get information out of shelve

data.close() # close the shelf before quitting
```

As with dictionaries, the `del` operation can be used to delete an item from a shelve, the function `has_key` can be used to see if a key is value, and the function keys can be used to produce a list of all legal key values.

Example: A Telephone Database

This example program will help illustrate the use of persistent variables. This program will maintain a telephone database. Commands to use the database are as follows:

- `whois phone-number` Find the information associated with a phone number.
- `add phone-number  information` Add phone number information to the database.
- `search keyword` Find all the entries that include *keyword*.
- `quit` Halt the application.

```
# telephone database application
# written by Tim Budd

import shelve

database = shelve.open("phoneinfo")
print "Commands are whois, add, search and quit"

line = raw _ input("command: ")
while line != 'quit':
  words = line.split()
  if words[0] == 'whois':
      print words[1],":",database[words[1]]
  elif words[0] == 'add':
      database[words[1]] = " ".join(words[2:])
  elif words[0] == 'search':
      for e in database.keys():
            if database[e].find(words[1]) != -1:
                print e,":",database[e]
  line = raw _ input("command: ")
database.close()
```

A shelve named `phoneinfo` is used to store the telephone database. A loop reads commands from the user. The `string.split` function is used to break the command into parts. The first word is used to determine which action to perform. Depending on the action selected, the database is consulted to find appropriate information. Before the application quits, the database is closed.

An example session with this program might go as follows:

```
Commands are whois, add, search and quit
command: add 2347531 fred smith
command: add 9842354 robin jones
command: quit
```

Later, another session could proceed as follows:

```
Commands are whois, add, search and quit
command: whois 2347531
2347531 : fred smith
command: search fred
2347531 : fred smith
command: search jones
9842354 : robin jones
command: quit
```

You should experiment with this program and verify that the information stored in the database is remembered between executions.

The program as given is simple but not very robust. You can easily make it better with a few simple additions. You should be able to make each of the following:

- If the user presses return without typing anything, the list stored in words will be empty. In this case, print a line reminding the user what commands are valid.
- If the telephone number provided by the `whois` command is not found, you should print a helpful message and not produce an indexing error (as will happen now).
- If the search for a pattern does not result in any value, you should tell the user.
- You should add a command named `delete` that will remove a given telephone number from the database.

Notice that the heart of the program is very small. However, making the program more robust in the face of errors will not only improve user satisfaction with the system but will also make the program considerably longer. Often, more than half of the length of a program is devoted to error handling and recovery. You need to remember this both when writing programs and when reading Python programs written by others. In examining the code for a new program, learn to identify the key ideas that are at the heart of the system.

INTERNAL DICTIONARIES*

Dictionaries and lists are used extensively throughout the Python system to store internal values. For example, the set of variable names that are valid at any point in time is stored in a dictionary. At the global level, you can access this dictionary using the `globals()` function. Within a function, you can access a separate dictionary used to store local variables using the `locals()` function. The following trivial program illustrates these values:

```
def test(a):
   b = 7
   print 'locals are:', locals()
   c = 12
   print 'locals are now:', locals()
test(5)
```

Executing this program produces the following:

```
locals are: {'a': 5, 'b': 7}
locals are now: {'a': 5, 'c': 12, 'b': 7}
```

Although these dictionaries are accessible and, in theory, can be modified by the user, doing so is tricky and can cause subtle errors.

EXERCISES

1. Using the function frequency, write a function that will produce a histogram from a list. A histogram shows, in a visual fashion, such as with stars, the number of times an item occurs in a list. For example, the histogram for the data used to illustrate the frequency function might appear as follows:

```
abc ***
pdq *
def *
```

2. Using lists, write the function `unique(lst)` that takes a list as argument and returns a list in which all duplicate values have been removed. For example, given the input `['abc,' 'def,' 'abc,' 'xyz,' 'def']` the function would return `['abc,' 'def,' 'xyz']`.

3. What is the result if you convert a dictionary into a list using the `list()` function?

4. What type of value is returned by has_key()? Explain why you can nevertheless use this value in a Boolean test, such as an *if* statement or a *while*.

5. What error message is produced if you index a dictionary with a mutable type, such as a list?

6. What is the effect of the following statements? Can you think of a use for such a construct?

```
num = raw_input("type a number less than 4")
print {1:"one",
   2:"two",
   3:"three",
   4:"four"}.get(num, "bad number")
```

7. Importing a function using a *from* statement has two benefits: It allows you to include a single function name, and it adds the function name to the local space. The latter actually produces faster execution, since it avoids a run-time lookup of the function. (That is, when you execute `string.split`, the Python system actually looks up the name `split` in the module string each time the function is executed.) To measure the improvements this can produce, try calling the function `split` on a fixed string in a loop that executes 10,000 times. Determine how fast this program will run when using an *import* statement and `string.split`, and when using a *from* statement. Is the difference significant?

6 CHAPTER

Files

You have already experienced creating files, such as the Python program file, using a word processor. After this experience, you should realize that a file is simply a sequence of characters stored on your computer or network. One of the things that makes a file different from a string or list of characters is that the file exists even after a program ends. This makes a file useful for maintaining information that must be remembered for a long period of time, such as the persistent values managed with the shelve module that you examined in Chapter 5.

Within a Python program, a file is represented by a value of type *file*. This value does not actually hold the contents of the file; instead, the value is a portal through which the user can access the contents of the file. A file stored on disk might easily contain more characters than can be held by a variable in memory. You can think of the file object as a window through which you can see the file itself. Like a window, the file variable allows you to view only a portion of the file at a time.

A file value is used in three distinct steps: First, the file is opened; this establishes the link between the file value in the Python program and the information stored on the disk. Next, values are read or written to the file; the process involves bringing characters in from the disk and storing them in a string in the Python program, or alternatively taking the contents of a string in your program and writing them out to the disk. When all values have been either read or written, the last step is to close the file. These operations are performed by the following commands:

`f = open("filename")`	Open a file, return file value
`f = open("filename", "w")`	Open a file for writing
`f.read()`	Return a single character value
`f.read(n)`	Return no more than n character values
`f.readline()`	Return the next line of input
`f.readlines()`	Return all the file as a list
`f.write(s)`	Write string s to file
`f.writelines(lst)`	Write list lst to file
`f.close()`	Close file

The most common way to obtain information from a file is through the command `readline`. This function returns the next line of text, including a newline character at the end. An empty line in the file will still contain the newline character.

The `readline` function returns an empty string when the end of the file is detected. The function `read` is used to obtain a fixed number of characters. It can return a smaller number of characters than requested if the end of file is reached before the requested number of characters have been found. The function `write` is used to copy a string into a file. The functions `readlines` or `writelines` can be used to read an entire file into a list or to copy an entire list into a file.

> Peas porridge Hot
> Peas porridge Cold
> Peas porridge in the Pot
> Nine Days Old!

To gain some experience with these functions, you can create a small test file. For example, create a file with the four lines shown at right, placing them into a file named peas.txt. Then try executing each of the programs shown next. Make a prediction of what the program will do before trying each one out. Are your predictions correct? Were you surprised at any output? Can you explain why programs 2 and 3 use the function `rstrip`? Why is this not needed in programs 4 and 5?

```
f = open("peas.txt")
line = f.readline()
while line:
    print line.swapcase()
    line = f.readline()
```

```
f = open("peas.txt")
line = f.readline()
while line:
    line = line.rstrip()
    print line.capwords()
    line = f.readline()
```

```
f = open("peas.txt")
line = f.readline()
while line:
    line = line.rstrip()
    lst = list(line)
    lst.reverse()
    print "".join(lst)
    line = f.readline()
```

```
f = open("peas.txt")
fout = open("peas2.txt", "w")
lst = f.readlines()
lst.reverse()
for x in lst:
    fout.write(x)
fout.close()
```

```
f = open("peas.txt")
fout = open("peas2.txt", "w")
lst = f.readlines()
lst.sort()
fout.writelines(lst)
fout.close()
```

Warning! Opening a File for Write Removes Old Values

Copy the four lines given above into a file named peas2.txt. Then try executing the following two lines:

```
>>> f = open("peas2.txt", "w")
>>> f.close()
```

Open the file with Notepad or a word processing program. What has happened? Remember that opening a file for writing causes the old values in the file to be deleted. This is true even if no new values are written into the file.

REWRITING THE WORD COUNT PROGRAM

Let's rewrite the word count program from Chapter 5 so that the input is now being read from a file, rather than directly from the user. Changes to the program include altering from where the input comes and the condition to test for end of file:

```
def freqCount (f): # f is a file of input
   freq = { }
   line = f.readline()
   while line:
        words = line.split()
        for word in words:
             freq[word] = freq.get(word, 0) + 1
        line = f.readline()
   return freq

def main ():
   f = open("text.txt")
   freq = freqCount(f)
   # now all words have been read
   for word in freq:
        print word,'occurs',freq[word],'times'
```

This example has employed some of the ideas of abstraction and encapsulation discussed in earlier chapters. This example separated the gathering of frequencies from printing the results and opened the file in the main program, passing the file value to the frequency counting function.

OPERATING SYSTEM COMMANDS

The operating system (such as Windows, Mac, or Unix) is normally in charge of file management. A number of useful operating system commands can be executed from within a Python program by including the os module. The two most useful commands are os.remove(name), which deletes (removes) the named file, and os.rename(oldname, newname), which renames a file.

```
>>> import os
>>> os.remove("gone.txt") # delete file named gone
>>> os.rename("fred.txt", "alice.txt") # fred becomes alice
```

You will see examples of both in the case study at the end of this chapter. Many other functions are available in the os module, but the use of these facilities is beyond the scope of this book. The most common and useful functions are described in Appendix A.

Files and For

A file value can be used in a *for* statement. The resulting loop reads from the file line by line and assigns the line to the for variable:

```
f = open("peas.txt")
for line in f:
  print line.reverse()
```

This can often make programs that manipulate files considerably shorter than the equivalent form using a *while* statement. For example, the frequency counting function is reduced to the following:

```
def freqCount (f): # f is a file of input
  freq = { }
  for line in f:
      words = line.split()
      for word in words:
          freq[word] = freq.get(word, 0) + 1
  return freq
```

RECOVERING FROM EXCEPTIONS

What happens if you try to open a file that does not exist? As you might expect, the Python system complains, and then responds by throwing an exception, an IOError. Normally the exception causes execution to halt with an error message. You have seen examples of this in earlier chapters and probably many more examples in your own programming.

Sometimes you might like to catch an exception and continue with execution, perhaps by performing some recovery action. This can be accomplished by using a *try* statement. Here's a classic example of a *try* statement with a file open:

```
try:
  f = open("input.txt")
except IOError, e:
  print 'unable to open the file input.txt'
else:
  ... # do something with file f
  f.close()
```

The open statement may or may not raise an IOError. If it does, the statements in the except part of the *try* statement are executed. If not, the statements in the else part are executed. The *try* statement is in this sense similar to a conditional, in which one of two alternatives is selected.

Any type of exception can be caught in a *try* statement. The variable name in the except part is attached to whatever text, if any, was used with the *raise* statement. You saw examples of the use of the *raise* statement in Chapter 3.

STANDARD I/O*[1]

The *print* statement, and the functions raw_input and input, are actually special uses of more general file commands. The *print* statement writes characters to a file that is normally attached to a display window, while the input functions read from a file that is attached to the user keyboard. These files can be accessed by importing the sys module. The standard input is available as the value of the variable sys.stdin, while the standard output is sys.stdout. Error messages are actually written to a different file, named sys.stderr, although normally this goes to the same place as sys.stdout.

One use for these variables is to take a program that is written as if it were reading from a file, but it is instead read from the console input. For example, we might invoke our frequency counting program developed earlier in the chapter as follows:

```
def main():
    # invoke frequency program, reading from console input
    freq = freqCount(sys.stdin)
    # now all words have been read
    for word in freq:
        print word,'occurs',freq[word],'times'
```

To mark the "end of file," the user presses control-D (or control-Z on Windows machines).

A more subtle use of the system module is to change these variables, thereby altering the effect of the standard functions. To see an example, execute the following program, and then examine the files output.txt and error.txt:

```
import sys
sys.stdout = open('output.txt', 'w')
sys.stderr = open('error.txt', 'w')
print "see where this goes"
print 5/4
print 7.0/0
sys.stdout.close()
sys.stderr.close()
```

---

[1] Sections marked with an asterisk contain optional or advanced material that can be omitted on first reading.

Several other functions and variables are defined in the `sys` module. The function `sys.exit("message")` can be used to terminate a running Python program. The function `sys.argv` is a list of the command line options passed to a program. On systems that support command line arguments, these are often used to pass information, such as file names, into a program. Assume that echo.py is the following simple program:

```
import sys
print sys.argv
```

The following might be an example execution:

```
$ python echo.py abc def
['echo.py', 'abc', 'def']
```

Notice that the name of the Python function is the first argument, while other command line arguments follow as string values.

Some of the other features of the sys module will be explored in the exercises at the end of the chapter.

PERSISTENCE AND PICKLE*

In Chapter 5, you learned about the shelve module. As you might expect, the implementation of the shelve module makes extensive use of file commands. Another module is also useful in saving and restoring the values of Python variables. This module is, humorously, known as *pickle*. (When you pickle a fruit or vegetable, you are saving it for long-term storage.) A more technical name for pickling is *serialization*.

The pickle module supplies two functions, `dump` and `load`. These can be used to save the contents of most Python variables to a file and later restore their values. The following is an example:

```
import pickle
. . .
object = . . . # create some Python value
f = open(filename, 'w')
pickle.dump(f, object)
```

Later, perhaps in a different program or at a different time, the contents of the variable can be retrieved from the file as follows:

```
import pickle
. . .
f = open(filename, 'w')
object = pickle.load(f)
```

Multiple objects can be saved and restored in the same file. However, the user is responsible for remembering the order in which values were saved. Most Python objects can be saved and restored using pickle and/or shelve. However, a few special objects, such as file values themselves, maintain an internal state that cannot be stored using these facilities.

Example—File Sort

It is easy to sort the lines of a file if your computer has sufficient memory to maintain the contents of the file in a list. Simply read the file into the list, sort the list, and then write the list out to a new file. But what if you have a very large file that is too big to fit into memory?

The algorithm used to solve this problem is known as *file sort*. This algorithm uses a number of temporary files as intermediate storage areas. The approach works in three steps. In step 1, the original file is read in small units, say 100 lines at a time. Each unit is sorted and written out to a temporary file. Once these units have been created, the second step begins. In this step, pairs of temporary files are merged into a new file. To merge two files requires only one line at a time from each, so memory size is not a problem. This merge process continues until just one file remains. This file will then have the desired outcome. In the final step, the single remaining temporary file is renamed to the desired result.

This application is considerably longer than any we have considered up to this point, so it can also be used as a vehicle to demonstrate an approach to designing large programs. This approach is known as *stepwise refinement*. It works by describing the initial program at a high level of abstraction using functions to represent major tasks, and then refining each of those functions in turn until the entire application has been developed.

Consider the program at the highest level of abstraction. Assume that the input is contained in the file input.txt, and the output should go into file output.txt. At a high level, the algorithm can be described as follows:

```python
import os
# step 1: make all the temporary files
try
    fin = open("input.txt")
except IOERROR:
    print 'unable to open input.txt'
else:
    tlist = makeTempFiles(fin)
# step 2: merge temp files
while len(tlist) > 1:
    mergeTwoIntoOne(tlist)
# step 3: rename the remaining temp file
tname = tlist.pop()
os.rename(tname, "output.txt")
```

Assuming that the yet-unwritten functions `makeTempFiles` and `mergeTwo IntoOne` do the right things, it is relatively easy to see that this program will work as we expect. The function `makeTempFiles` must read the file found in input.txt and break it into smaller units, storing each in a temporary file, and returning a list of the temporary file names. The function `mergeTwoIntoOne` should take this list of temporary files, remove two (we know there are at least two because of the *while* loop), merge the two into a new temporary file, and then place the new temporary back into the list. So we have reduced the problem of writing our original application to the simpler problem of writing these two functions. Let's take each one in turn.

The routine `makeTempFiles` is slightly tricky, because it is looping over two things at once. One loop reads lines from the input file, and another creates the temporary files and writes to each. The whole process ends when the `readline` from the original input file returns an empty string. A Boolean variable named `done` will help address this problem. This variable will be set to true once an end of file has been detected. With this insight, the structure of the function becomes clearer:

```
def makeTempFiles (fin)
    # read from fin and break into temp files
    tnames = [ ] # make empty list of temp files
    done = False
    while not done:
        tn = makeTempFileName()
        tnames.append(tn)
        fn = open(tn, "w")
        lines = [ ]
        I = 0
        while not done and I < 100:
            I = I + 1
            line = fin.readline()
            if line:
                lines.append(line)
            else:
                done = True
        lines.sort() # sort the last group of lines read
        fn.writelines(lines)
        fn.close()
    return tnames
```

A list of file names is created, which is initially empty. We don't know how many temporary files will be produced. The loop uses the Boolean variable `done` that will be set to `true` once an end of file is encountered. The routine `makeTempFileName` is used to make a new temporary file name. The temporary file is opened for writing and an inner loop reads no more than 100 lines. This loop can also terminate early if an end of input is encountered. Regardless of how the loop terminates, the lines are sorted and written to the temporary file.

We have used *stepwise refinement* in this design. During the process of writing the function, we have acted as if we already had written a function named `make-TempfileName`. Assuming that this function returns a new and unique temporary file name, we can examine the function `makeTempFiles` and convince ourselves that it is correct. So we have once more reduced the task to a simpler function.

The function `makeTempFileName` is one of those rare places where the *global* statement is useful. We want this function to create a stream of names such as t1.txt, t2.txt, t3.txt, and so on. We can easily do this using a *counter,* but the counter itself must exist at the global level and not have a scope local to the function. So we simply create the counter at the global level and use the *global* statement to indicate that within the function the name refers to the `global` variable.[2]

```
topTemp = 0
def makeTempFileName():
    global topTemp
    topTemp = topTemp + 1
    return "t" + str(topTemp) + ".txt"
```

Returning to the top level, we find we have not yet written the function `mergeTwoIntoOne`. This function takes the list of temporary file names, removes two files, creates a new temporary file, and merges the two files into one. We first abstract away the merge itself, so that we can concentrate on the steps required to manage the files:

```
def mergeTwoIntoOne (tlist):
    ta = tlist.pop(0) # first file name
    tb = tlist.pop(0) # second file name
    tn = makeTempFileName() # make output file name
    tlist.append(tn)
    fa = open(ta)
    fb = open(tb)
    fn = open(tn, "w")
    mergeFiles(fa, fb, fn)
    fa.close()
    fb.close()
    os.remove(ta) # remove temp files
    os.remove(tb)
    fn.close()
```

Notice that we have once again made use of the function `makeTempFileName` that we wrote earlier. Assuming that `mergeFiles` works as advertised, it is easy to see that this function is performing the correct task.

The remaining step is to write the routine `mergeFiles`. Once more, this is moderately tricky, because we are looping over two things at once—namely, reading lines from the first file and then from the second. One of these two will eventually reach an end of input, but we cannot predict which one it will be. So the algorithm divides into two sections. In the first step, lines are read from each file and the smallest line written to the output. This continues until one of the two files reaches the end. In the second step, any remaining lines from the remaining file are copied.

---

[2] In reality, we don't need to write the function `makeTempFileName`, since this service is provided by a function named `mktemp` in the tempfile module that is included as part of the standard library. (See Appendix A.) However, we couldn't pass up the opportunity to illustrate a legitimate use of the `global` command.

```
def mergeFiles (fa, fb, fn):
    # merge the contents of fa and fb into fn
    # step 1, merge as long as both files have lines
    linea = fa.readline()
    lineb = fb.readline()
    while linea and lineb:
        if linea < lineb:
            fn.write(linea)
            linea = fa.readline()
        else:
            fn.write(lineb)
            lineb = fb.readline()
    # step 2—write remaining lines
    # only one of the following will do anything
    while linea:
        fn.write(linea)
        linea = fa.readline()
    while lineb:
        fn.write(lineb)
        lineb = fb.readline()
```

That's it. We have started from a high-level description of the original problem, reduced each task to smaller problems, and then repeatedly addressed each of the smaller problems until everything is reduced to simple Python statements. All we have left is to put together the pieces and verify that it works as it should.

READING FROM A URL*

The `urllib` module provides a simple way to read the contents of a file stored at a specific URL. It returns an object that uses the same interface as a file:

```
import urllib

remotefile = urllib.urlopen("http://www.python.org")
line = remotefile.readline()
while line:
  print line
  line = remotefile.readline()
```

The `urllib` effectively hides all the details of network access, allowing the programmer to think just about what to do with all that data.

Let's use this feature to make a simple application. The National Oceanic and Atmospheric Administration (NOAA) provides current weather conditions at various airports throughout the United States on its Web site. If you open the web page at http://weather.noaa.gov/weather/current/KCVO.html, you can see a typical example. KCVO is the abbreviation for the Corvallis, Oregon, municipal airport. The contents of the Web page are represented in the HyperText Markup Language

(HTML) format. We won't discuss HTML here (it is discussed in more detail in Chapter 13), but if you use the View Source command on your web browser, you can see that the first occurrence of the word *Temperature* occurs in a pair of lines such as the following:

```
<TD ALIGN=RIGHT BGCOLOR="#FFFFFF"><B><FONT COLOR="#0000A0">
<FONT FACE="Arial,Helvetica"> Temperature
</FONT></FONT></B></TD>

<TD><FONT FACE="Arial,Helvetica"> 84 F (29 C)
```

This offers the insight we need to complete our program. We open the URL, read all the lines into one large string, then use the function find to locate the word *Temperature*. Once we have found this word, we creep forward one character at a time until we find a digit. This digit will be the start of the text we need. Once we have found a digit, we can once more use find to locate the next right parenthesis. The text between these two points is the information we want. Converting these ideas into Python gives us the following function:

```
def readTemperature (airportCode):
  urlName = 'http://weather.noaa.gov/weather/current/' +
airportCode + '.html'
  remoteFile = urllib.urlopen(urlName)
  fileContent = ''.join(remoteFile.readlines())
  start = fileContent.find('Temperature')
  while not ('0' <= fileContent[start] <= '9'): start = start + 1
  stop = fileContent[start:].find(')')
  return fileContent[start : start+stop+1]
```

The following shows the function being used to discover the current temperature in Corvallis:

```
>>> print readTemperature ('KCVO')
86 F (30 C)
```

EXERCISES

1. Write a program that will prompt the user for a file name and then print all lines from the file that contain the Python comment character #.

2. Write a program that will prompt the user for a file name, read all the lines from the file into a list, sort the list, and then print the lines in sorted order. (Alternatively, you can read the file name from the command line using sys.argv.)

3. Discover what exception is produced by each of the following points. Then, for each, write a small example program that illustrates catching the exception using a *try* statement and continuing with execution after the interrupt.

   • Division by zero
   • Opening a file that does not exist
   • Indexing a list with an illegal value

- Using an improper key with a dictionary
- Passing an improperly formatted expression to the function `expr()`

4. The sys module defines two string variables, `sys.ps1` and `sys.ps2`. In an interactive session, try printing the values of these variables. Try changing these to "+++" and "***" in an interactive session. Can you determine what they are used for?

5. Another variable defined in sys is `sys.maxint`. What is the value of this variable? What type of result do you get if you add 1 to this value? What if you take the arithmetic inverse of this value?

6. Write a program that asks the user for a file name, and then prints the number of characters, words, and lines in the file. (Alternatively, you can read the file names from the command line using `sys.argv`.)

7. Write a program that concatenates the contents of several files into one file. Prompt the user for the names of the source file and the destination file. (Alternatively, you can read the file names from the command line using `sys.argv`.)

8. Write a program that will prompt the user for a string and a file name, and then print all lines in the file that contain the string.

9. Most Unix systems have a list of correctly spelled words stored in the file /usr/dict/words. You can use this file to create a simple spell checker. Read the file into a data structure such as a list. Then read the text file, breaking it apart into individual words, and checking each word against the dictionary. Print any word you find that is not found in the dictionary.

CHAPTER

Classes

In Chapter 3, you learned about *encapsulation* as a technique for controlling complexity. In particular, the chapter introduced the concept of the *function* as a mechanism of encapsulation. Having written a function, the programmer can then think of the task the function is performing at a higher design level (for example, this function returns a new temporary file name) rather than at the low level of implementation details (for example, this function adds 1 to a global counter of file names, and then concatenates the resulting value with a string to produce a new name). We termed this process *abstraction*, as it allows the user to abstract away the "how" details and emphasize the "what."

CLASS BASICS

Many times, a collection of several functions and/or data values is unified in the sense of being linked to a common purpose—for example, the functions provide a *service* that can be used by other functions. It is useful to bundle these functions together into a *unit*. We want a mechanism that will encapsulate several functions and/or data values in much the same fashion that a function encapsulates a single action. This mechanism is called a *class*.

A class definition begins with the keyword `class`. The keyword is followed by the class name, a parenthesized list of parent classes, and a colon. We will have more to say about parent classes later in this chapter; for the moment, we'll simply use the standard parent class named `object`. Following the class heading, indented by a tab stop, is a series of function definitions. Functions defined within a class are known as *methods*. Here's an example:

```
class BankAccount(object):
    # define a class to simulate a bank account
    def __init__ (self):
        # initialize the bank account with zero balance
        self.balance = 0
    def deposit (self, amount):
        # deposit the given amount into the account
        self.balance = self.balance + amount
    def withdraw (self, amount):
```

```
        # withdraw the given amount from the account
        self.balance = self.balance—amount
    def getBalance (self):
        # return the balance in the account
        return self.balance
```

You should note that the class definition by itself does not create any instances of the class. (Instances are also known as *objects*.) Many different bank accounts can exist, just as many different integers are all instances of the same type. The class description defines the behavior common to all instances of the class. To create an instance of the class, the user invokes the class name as if it were a function. Several instances of the same class can exist.

```
>>> myAccount = BankAccount() # make instance of BankAccount
>>> secondAccount = BankAccount() # create another
```

The functions defined within the class description are invoked using the *dot notation* you are already familiar with from modules and the built-in types:

```
>>> myAccount.deposit(200)
>>> secondAccount.deposit(125)
>>> myAccount.withdraw(75)
>>> secondAccount.withdraw(50)
>>> print myAccount.getBalance()
125
>>> print secondAccount.getBalance()
75
```

If you have been reading carefully, you should already be asking yourself questions regarding several curious features of the class definition. First, if the function `deposit` as written used two argument values, why, when it was invoked, was there only one argument passed? (Similar questions exist for `withdraw` and `getBalance`.) The answer to this question is that the *receiver* for the command, that is, the value to the left of the dot, is *implicitly* passed to the function as the first argument. It is this feature that allows one to distinguish the two (or more) different instances of the class. By convention this first argument is named `self`, but in fact any legal name can be used.

An important responsibility of the class value is to store any data fields that the object requires. In this case, the one data field being maintained is the bank account balance. These data fields are written using the same dot notation that would be used if they were fields in the class value. Just as you created a new name by assigning a value to it, here a new data field is created the first time it is assigned a value. It is important to note that these data fields must always be qualified by the instance of the class in which they are found.

Notice once again the elements of abstraction and information hiding in the class mechanism. The programmer bundles together a series of related functions. The user of the class (who doesn't need to be the same as the original programmer) can once more characterize instances of this class by the services they are providing and need not have detailed knowledge of the ways in which these services are implemented.

CONSTRUCTORS

A curious feature of the class definition is the function named __init__. The Python system generally uses two underscore characters (__) before and after a name to designate functions or data values that are used implicitly, behind the scenes. You might have encountered a few of these, perhaps by accident, in your explorations of the Python system.

The init function is termed a *constructor*. It is used to initialize a newly created instance of the class. You never directly invoke the constructor. Instead, the constructor is called implicitly as part of the process of creating a new object.

In addition to the required class argument (that is, self), constructors can take other arguments. The value for these additional arguments must then be provided when the instance of the class is created. We might have wanted, for example, to allow an initial balance to be set when the object is first created. This would have been written as follows:

```
class BankAccount(object):
  # create a class to simulate a bank account
  def __init__ (self, initBalance):
      # create new account with given initial balance
      self.balance = initBalance
  . . .
```

The values for these additional arguments would be provided as part of the expression that created the new value:

```
>>> newAccount = BankAccount(500) # make bank account with $500
```

By the way, classes and objects maintain several internal data fields. Since these are normally not expected to be used by the programmer, they follow the double-underscore convention. A class, for example, maintains its name as a string:

```
>>> print BankAccount.__name__
BankAccount
```

Every instance of a class maintains a reference to the class that created it:

```
>>> print newAccount.__class__
__main__.BankAccount
```

Another internal value used by classes is the *instance dictionary*. This is stored in a field named __dict__. You can see this value by printing the field:

```
>>> print newAccount.__dict__
{'balance':500}
```

Internally, a statement such as

```
self.balance = self.balance + amount
```

is translated into

```
self.__dict__['balance'] = self.__dict__['balance'] + amount
```

It is even possible to make changes to the data fields by manipulating this field using dictionary commands, although this is not encouraged.

RESPECT CLASS BOUNDARIES

It is legal to access the data fields defined within an object directly, but this is generally considered poor form. For example, rather than using the method get Balance(), you could access the data field balance:

```
>>> # this is legal, but not encouraged
>>> print myAccount.balance
200
```

If accessing a data field is considered poor form, it is even worse to change the value of a data field from outside the object:

```
>>> # this is also legal, but really really not encouraged
>>> myAccount.balance = 500
>>> print myAccount.getBalance()
500
```

Readers with a background in Java or C++ will remember that those languages prevent this type of behavior using the visibility modifiers private, protected, and public. Python does not include this feature. In essence, everything in Python is public. But exploiting this ability by, for example, modifying the internal data values of an object from outside the class, is a guaranteed way to make your programs difficult to read, understand, and maintain. Always respect class boundaries and encapsulate all modification of class values within those boundaries. (See the section "Classes as Dynamic Records" later in this chapter for an exception to this rule.)

CALLING METHODS FROM INSIDE OTHER METHODS

It is possible for one method to invoke another in the same class. For example, suppose we wanted to add a transfer method to deal with banking. A transfer takes as arguments the amount to be moved and a second bank account into which the money should be placed. It then does a combination of withdraw and deposit. The transfer could be written as follows:

```
class BankAccount(object):
  . . .
  def transfer (self, amount, toAccount):
      # transfer the amount from one account to another
      self.withdraw(amount)
      toAccount.deposit(amount)
```

A transfer is invoked as follows:

```
>>> myAccount = BankAccount(500)
>>> newAccount = BankAccount(100)
>>> myAccount.transfer(200, newAccount)
>>> print myAccount.getBalance()
200
>>> print newAccount.getBalance()
300
```

Look carefully at the definition of the function `transfer`. Notice that to invoke the method `withdraw` you must explicitly name the object to which it refers (namely, our `self`), just as the `deposit` method names the account that it is changing. Again, users of languages such as Java or C++ are prone to forget this, as the value `self` (called `this` in those languages) can be omitted in this situation.

Exceptions within Methods

Good defensive programming requires you to verify that requests for action make sense before you attempt them. In this case, it would be better if our banking system checked that the balance was sufficient before performing a withdrawal. If insufficient funds are available, the program should raise an exception:

```
class BankAccount(object):

    . . .

        def withdraw (self, amount):
            if self.balance < amount:
                raise ValueError, "insufficient funds"
            self.balance = self.balance—amount
```

Normally, exceptions cause immediate termination and the display of an appropriate message:

```
>>> ba.withdraw(600)
Traceback (most recent call last):
  File "Chapter3.code", line 45, in ?
      ba.withdraw(600)
  File "Chapter3.code", line 30, in withdraw
      raise ValueError, "insufficient funds"
ValueError: insufficient funds
```

However, the programmer can catch exceptions using a mechanism called a *try statement*. If you place a call on a piece of code that might throw an exception within a *try* statement, the exception is caught by the *try* statement and a recovery is executed. Any statements within the *try* statement after the point the exceptions are raised are ignored.

```
>>> try:
        ba.withdraw(600)
        # notice the following will not be executed
        print "wow, free money!"
```

```
    except ValueError, e:
        print "no such luck"
        print "error message is ", e
```

```
no such luck
error message is insufficient funds
```

A try statement can be used to recover from an error and continue execution of the program in situations that otherwise would force the program to halt immediately.

OBJECTS ARE REFERENCES

Like lists, objects are internally stored as references. This is important for both assignment and parameter passing. Remember that when an assignment statement assigns an object to a new name, the new name and the old name reference the same value.

```
>>> bobsAccount = new BankAccount()
>>> bobsAccount.deposit(300)
>>> alicesAccount = bobsAccount
>>> alicesAccount.withdraw(250)
>>> print bobsAccount.getBalance()
50
```

The same result can occur when an object is passed as argument to a function. Consider the following function definition:

```
def winLottery (winner):
    winner.deposit(1000000)
```

```
>>> bobsAccount = BankAccount(50)
>>> winLottery(bobsAccount)
>>> print bobsAccount.getBalance()
1000050
```

When a program produces strange results and objects appear to be changing values inexplicably, carefully examine all the assignment statements for the objects and all the places that the value has been passed as an argument. An alias may be created for the object under a different name, and changes to the alias are being seen as changes to the original object.

PRINTING

What happens if you try printing a value of type `BankAccount` using a *print* statement?

```
>>> print bobsAccount
< __main__.BankAccount object at 0xd6db0>
```

As the programmer, you can control what information gets printed for a class. Try defining a method named __str__ (self). Remember that methods that begin with two underscores represent functions that are used internally and are not expected to be invoked directly by the user. In this case, the __str__ method is used to convert a value from type object to a string. You can produce whatever useful information you want with this string:

```
class BankAccount(object):
    . . .
  def __str__ (self):
        return 'Bank Account Object, balance = ' + self.balance
```

Now if you print the value of a bank account in a *print* statement, you will see a more informative message:

```
>>> print bobsAccount
Bank Account Object, balance = 1000050
```

INHERITANCE

Inheritance is used to build classes that are more specialized variations on an abstract concept. Imagine, for example, that you now need a representation for checking accounts. In addition to the behavior of standard bank accounts, a checking account has a method for recording checks. Checks are assigned a number and include a person or business to whom they are written as well as an amount. The information on checks that have been received is maintained in a dictionary. Another method allows you to query the information recorded for a particular check number:

```
class CheckingAccount (BankAccount):
  def __init__ (self, initBal):
        BankAccount.__init__(self, initBal)
        self.checkRecord = { }
  def processCheck (self, number, toWho, amount):
        self.withdraw(amount)
        self.checkRecord[number] = (toWho, amount)
  def checkInfo (self, number):
        if self.checkRecord.has_key(number):
            return self.checkRecord [ number ]
        else:
            return 'no such check'
```

The fact that BankAccount is listed in parentheses following the class name is the indication that inheritance is being used. This signals that a checking account is a more specialized type of bank account. The class BankAccount can be considered the *parent class*, and the new class CheckingAccount the *child class*. *Inheritance* means that the new class has access to all the functionality of the BankAccount class, as well as all the data fields. Note how the initialization method in the new class must explicitly invoke the initialization method in the parent class. When a class name is used to the left of the dot, the value self must be passed as an explicit argument, as shown here. When the value `self` is used to the left of the dot, it is omitted from the argument list.

The new class can define new data fields as well as new methods. Here we have added a data field that will hold a dictionary for recording the information on checks that have been processed. When a check is received, the information is stored in this dictionary. In addition, the amount written on the check is deducted from the account balance. Once more, notice the requirement that when invoking a method in the parent class, the receiver `self` must be explicitly written.

```
>>> # create a checking account with an initial balance of $300
>>> ca = CheckingAccount(300)
>>> ca.processCheck(100, "Gas Company", 72.50)
>>> ca.processCheck(101, "Electric Company", 53.12)
>>> print ca.checkInfo(100)
('Gas Company', 72.50)
```

Because the child class inherits methods from the parent class, you can invoke any of those functions as well:

```
>>> ca.deposit(50)
>>> print ca.getBalance()
224.38
```

Notice that the checking account performs the withdrawal of funds from the account before recording the check. If the withdrawal throws an exception, the control flows immediately to a surrounding *try* block. This means that the recording would *not* be performed.

```
>>> # following will throw exception
>>> ca.processCheck(102, "Cable Company", 800.12)
>>> print ca.getBalance()
224.38
>>> print ca.checkInfo(102)
no such check
```

When you develop code that uses exceptions, you should be aware of what statements could potentially cause an exception to occur and think about what you want to happen in that situation. For example, suppose you wanted to record checks even if insufficient funds are available to honor them. One possibility would be simply to place the code to update the dictionary before the call on `self.withdraw()`. Another possibility would be to catch the exception within the class `Checking Account`, handle the error (perhaps including other actions), and then, if you want, rethrow the exception so that it can be handled by any further *try* statements in the code that is using the check account.

```
class CheckingAccount (BankAccount):
  . . .
  def processCheck (self, number, toWho, amount):
      try:
          self.withDraw(amount)
```

```
except ValueError, e:
    print "check returned for insufficient funds"
self.checkRecord[number] = (toWho, amount)
raise ValueError, "insufficient funds " + amount
```

The is-a Test

Inheritance implies that one class is a more specialized form of another. This is often described as the *is-a relationship*, after a simple test you can use to determine whether inheritance is appropriate. To apply the is-a test, form an English sentence that links two concepts, such as "A checking account is a banking account." If the sentence "sounds right" in your mind, then inheritance is appropriate.

The is-a test relation can be compared to the *has-a* relation. For example, a bank account has a balance. Has-a implies containment: that is, the first type holds a data field of the second type. (A bank account holds a data field that maintains a balance.) Both types of relationships are important, and both use the services of an existing idea to build a new abstraction.

Because a class that uses inheritance automatically includes all the behavior and data fields defined in the parent class, an instance of a child class can be used where you might expect to find an instance of the parent class. This is termed *polymorphism*. Here's an example:

```
>>> # ba should be any type of BankAccount
>>> ba = CheckingAccount(100) # a checking account is-a BankAccount
>>> ba.deposit(50)
>>> ba.withdraw(40)
>>> print ba.getBalance()
110
```

Inheritance and Software Reuse

When inheritance is used to construct a new class, the code that is inherited from the parent class need not be rewritten. Often this can result in a significant savings in development time. This benefit is particularly useful when the same class is used as a parent class to multiple child classes. This savings in code development is known as *software reuse*.

The benefits of software reuse become even more pronounced when you can make use of a parent class developed by another Python programmer—perhaps a class distributed as part of an existing library. When this happens, you need to describe only what is new or different about the new class. Any methods or data values shared with the more general class are obtained for free as a benefit of inheritance.

Overriding

It is sometimes necessary for a child class to modify or replace the behavior inherited from the parent class. This is termed *overriding*. To override a method, the child class simply redefines the function using the same name and arguments. If the overriding function needs to invoke the original function in the parent class, the class name must be explicitly provided and the receiver moved to the first argument location. To illustrate, suppose the designer of the class CheckingAccount wants to print a message every time a withdrawal is made. This could be written as follows:

```
class CheckingAccount (BankAccount):
   . . .
   def withdraw (self, amount):
        print 'withdrawing ', amount
        BankAccount.withdraw(self, amount)
```

CLASSES, TYPES, AND TESTS

Each class definition creates a new type. This can be seen using the function type():

```
>>> print type(myAccount)
<type 'instance'>
>>> print type(BankAccount)
<type 'classobj'>
```

To test for membership in a class, use the built-in function isinstance(obj, cname). This function returns True if the object obj belongs to the class cname or any class derived from cname:

```
>>> print isinstance(myAccount, CheckingAccount)
True
>>> print isinstance(myAccount, BankAccount)
True
>>> print isinstance(secondAccount, CheckingAccount)
False
```

Similarly, the built-in function issubclass(A, B) returns True if the class A is a subclass of B:

```
>>> print issubclass(CheckingAccount, BankAccount)
True
```

By using various symbolic values found in the types module, the function isinstance can also be used to perform type checking for any of the built-in types. Here's an example:

```
>>> import types
>>> isinstance(3, types.IntType)
True
>>> isinstance(3, types.FloatType)
False
```

CLASS VARIABLES*[1]

It is possible for a class definition to include assignment statements made at the same level as method definitions:

---

[1] Sections marked with an asterisk describe advanced or optional material, and can (perhaps should) be omitted on first reading.

```
class BankAccount:
  accountType = "bank account"
  def __init__ (self, initialBalance):
  . . .
```

Such values are known as *class variables*. They can be printed using the same dot notation used to invoke methods:

```
>>> print newAccount.accountType
bank account
```

However, class variables are *shared* among all instances of the class. That is, only one value is stored for this variable, and the value is accessible using any instance of the class.

MULTIPLE INHERITANCE*

It is possible for a new class definition to specify inheritance from more than one parent class:

```
class A (object):
  def doA (self):
      print "I'm an a"

class B (object):
  def doB (self):
      print "I'm a b"

class C (A, B):
  def doC (self):
      print "I'm a c"
```

Instances of the new class can use methods from either parent:

```
>>> v = C()
>>> v.doC
I'm a C
>>> v.doA()
I'm an A
>>> v.doB()
I'm a B
```

This is termed *multiple inheritance*. While the idea seems appealing, several subtle issues are involved in the use of this technique. For example, what happens if the same method is inherited from both parents? In general, the use of multiple inheritance should be avoided whenever possible.

CLASSES AS DYNAMIC RECORDS*

Class data fields should never be used outside the class definition. However, an idiom that is common in the Python community directly violates this principle. Consider the following simple class definition:

```
class EmTee (object):
   pass
```

The class definition stores no variables and has a null class definition, which is required only because Python does not allow you to create totally empty class definitions. As you might expect, you can create an instance of this class.

```
>>> myData = EmTee()
```

What you might find surprising is that you can then assign new data fields to this object, as follows:

```
>>> myData.name = "Fred Smith"
>>> myData.age = 42
>>> print myData.name
Fred Smith
```

Python programmers often use this feature to create "one-off" records—that is, data structures that have only a single instance. This allows a number of values to be collected under one name—for example, to make them easy to pass to a function.

EXERCISES

1. Create a class `Rectangle`. The constructor for this class should take two numeric arguments, which are the `width` and `height`. Add methods to compute the area and perimeter of the rectangle, as well as methods that simply return the height and width. Add a method `isSquare` that returns a Boolean value if the rectangle is a square.

2. Define a class `Fraction` that represents a fractional value. The constructor for this class should take two integer values, which represent the numerator and the denominator for this class. Include methods to add, subtract, multiply, and divide two fractional values. What happens if you try to print a fractional value? Add a `__str__` method that converts a fractional value into a string.

3. One of the oldest known functions is Euclid's GCD function, which can be used to determine the *Greatest Common Divisor* of two positive integer values. The GCD function can be written as follows:

```
def gcd (n, m): # assume n, m > 0
   while n != m:
     if n > m: n = n—m
     else: m = m—n
   return n
```

Try the function with several different values to convince yourself that it is correct. Using the `gcd` function, rewrite the constructor for the fractional class to ensure that each fraction is placed in the lowest common denominator form. To do this, divide both the numerator and the denominator by their common divisor. Also make sure that the denominator is not a negative number. If the argument to the constructor has a negative denominator, invert the sign on both values. With these changes, a fraction such as `Fraction (2, -4)` would end up being the same as `Fraction(-1, 2)`.

4. What happens if you compare two fractional values? To fix this, you can implement the single method `__cmp__ (self, arg)`. All the relational operators use this one function. This function should take two fractional values and return a result that is negative if the first is less than the second, zero if they are equal, and positive if the first is larger than the second. After implementing this function, verify that each of the six relational operators now works as expected.

5. What happens if you use a fraction as a test in an *if* statement? Other numeric values are true if the value is nonzero, and false otherwise. To check this condition, the Python interpreter will try to execute a method named `__nonzero (self)`. Add this method to the class `Fraction` and verify that a fractional value can now be used in an *if* statement.

6. Suppose that Python did not have the complex data type. Write a class `Complex` for performing arithmetic with complex numbers. The constructor for this class should take two floating-point values. Add methods for adding, subtracting, and multiplying two complex numbers. Add a `__str__` method so that a complex number prints as the real and imaginary parts separated by a plus sign, with the letter `I` after the imaginary part.

7. What happens if you define a method and forget to use the first argument to hold the class instance? The following is an example. What message is produced if you create an instance of `TestError` (call it *a*) and invoke the `method a.value()`? What happens if you type the expression `TestError.value()`?

```
class TestError (object):
   def value(): # error, no self value
      return 4
```

8. Can you create a program that will illustrate the fact that class variables are shared among all instances of a class?

9. Class definitions, like function definitions, are actually a special type of assignment. What do you get if you print a class name? What happens if you reassign a class name (for example, use a class name in an assignment statement)? What happens if you assign a class name to another variable, and then use that variable as if it were the original class?

10. Another internal method that is occasionally useful to override is `__nonzero__`. This method is invoked implicitly when an object is used in a conditional, such as in an *if* or *while* statement. To see this, try creating a class such as the following:

```
class Box (object):
   def __init__ (self, ival):
      self.value = ival
```

What happens if you use an instance of the class Box in an *if* statement?

```
>>> aBox = Box(3)
>>> if aBox:
```

Now try defining the method __nonzero__(self) so that it returns True if the value held by the box is even, and False otherwise. Now what happens when you use the value in an *if* statement?

11. The definition of __nonzero__ in the preceding question can have a practical use. Many programmers familiar with Java or C miss the fact that assignment in those languages is an operator and can therefore be used in places such as a loop:

```
while (c = gets()) // will loop as long as c
    // returns a true, nonzero value
  . . .
```

This behavior can be simulated by a variation on our Box class. Define methods to get and set the value of the box. Then define the __nonzero__ method to return the current value. Show how these can then be used to perform an assignment as part of a larger Boolean expression:

```
data = Box()
while data.set(someexpression):
   print data.get()
```

12. The method __cmp__(self, other) is implicitly invoked by the relational operators such as <, <=, >=, >, ==, !=, and <>. Create the class Box as described in the preceding question. What error message is produced when you compare two instances of this class? Now define the method __cmp__ so that it returns -1 if the value held in the box is less than the value held in the box referenced by the parameter other, is 0 if they are equal, and 1 if the value is greater than the value of other. Test each of the relational operators to see that they now work.

13. The method __str__(self) is used to create a string representation of an object. What happens if you call str(aBox) on an instance of Box (described in the preceding question)? Override the method __str__ to produce the string "the value in the box is *x*", where *x* is the string representation of the value. Now what happens when you invoke the function str?

14. Each of the mathematical operations has a corresponding internal method name. For example, the + operation is internally performed by executing the method named __add__(self, other). Try adding two instances of class Box. What message is produced? Then override the method __add__ so that it adds the contents of the current box and the box described by other, returning a new box with the sum. Now what happens when two boxes are added together? Other methods can be used to provide indexing or slicing operations.

15. When using multiple inheritance, what happens if the same method is inherited from both parents? Which one is selected when the function is invoked using an instance of the child? If the child overrides the method, how can it invoke the method in the parent class?

16. A particularly troublesome form of multiple inheritance is called *diamond inheritance*. In this situation, one parent class is inherited by two child classes. Each of the child classes is then used as a parent to a new class:

```
class A (object):
  def __init__ (self):
     self.value = 0
  def getValue (self):
```

```
        return self.value

    class B (A):
        . . .
    class C (A):
        . . .
    class D(B, C):
        . . .
```

Notice that class A is a "grandparent" to class D in two ways, both through class B and class C. A curious question is, then, how many copies of the data fields defined in class A does an instance of class D possess? Write a small simple program to answer this question—that is, a program that will produce one answer if an instance of class D has only one data field and a different answer if an instance of class D has two data fields.

CHAPTER 8

Functional Programming

Programming a computer is a complicated task, and like most complicated tasks, there are many different ways to think about the process. The term *language paradigm* is sometimes used to describe the mental model that the programmer envisions as he or she is creating a program. The model we have used to this point is termed the *imperative paradigm*. This model views the computer as a combination of processor and memory. Instructions (such as assignment statements) have the effect of making changes to memory. The task of programming consists of placing statements in their proper sequence, so that by a large number of small transformations to memory, the desired result is eventually produced.

You might be surprised to learn that this is not the only possible way to think about the process of computation. In this chapter and the following, two alternative models are described. Each differs from the imperative paradigm not in the way the computer operates, but in the way that the programmer *thinks* about the tasks of programming.

THE FUNCTIONAL PROGRAMMING PARADIGM

The term *functional programming* does not imply simply programming with functions; it is used to describe an alternative to the imperative programming paradigm. As the *functional programming* name suggests, the creation of functions is an important part of the paradigm. But simply defining a few functions does not mean that you are programming in a functional style. For example, many functions were defined in earlier chapters, yet we did not call those functional programs.

The key characteristic of a program developed in the functional programming style is that it creates new values by a process of *transformation*. Generally, values are represented as lists, or dictionaries. This simple description requires further explanation. The traditional imperative style of programming produces complex values by modification—by making a large number of small changes to an existing data structure (for example, creating a dictionary of values, and then systematically setting each value independently of the others). Since small changes can often be accompanied by small errors, and small errors may produce only a minimal effect, debugging imperative programs can be frustratingly difficult.

By emphasizing *transformation*, rather than *modification*, functional programs work on a larger scale. Transformations are often more uniform and much simpler to write and debug. Errors, when they do occur, tend to be larger and thus easier to find and eliminate. The difference between a functional and an imperative style is best illustrated by examples, as we will present shortly.

Mapping, Filtering, and Reduction

The process of transformation can be subdivided into several common forms. The three most common varieties of transformation are mapping, filtering, and reduction.

A *mapping* is a one-to-one transformation. Each element in the source is converted into a new value. The new values are gathered into a collection, leaving the original collection unchanged. For example, suppose that you begin with the list [1, 2, 3, 4, 5] and map using the transformation x*2+1. The result would be the list [3, 5, 7, 9, 11].

A *filtering* is the process of testing each value in a list with a function and retaining only those for which the function is true. If you begin with the list [1, 2, 3, 4, 5] and filter with a function that returns true on the odd values, the result would be the list [1, 3, 5].

A *reduction* is the process of applying a binary function to each member of a list in a cumulative fashion. If you begin with the list [1, 2, 3, 4, 5] and reduce using the addition operation, the result would be $((((1 + 2) + 3) + 4) + 5)$, or 15.

Each of these three basic tasks is provided by a function in the Python library. Notice that the definition of each of these functions refers to invoking another function as part of the process. The function used in this case is passed as an argument. A function that uses another function that is passed as an argument is sometimes referred to as a *higher order* function.

Lambda Functions

When a function is required as an argument, one possibility is to simply pass the name of a previously defined function:

```
def even(x):
    return x % 2 == 0

>>> a = [1, 2, 3, 4, 5]
>>> print filter(even, a)
[2, 4]
```

However, because the functions that are passed as argument to maps, reductions, and filters are often simple and are usually used nowhere else, it is inconvenient to require the programmer to define them using the standard def keyword. An alternative is a mechanism to define a nameless function as an expression. This type of expression is termed a *lambda*. The following example illustrates the syntax:

```
lambda x, y : x + y
```

The body of the lambda function must be a simple expression. Because it must be written on one line, it cannot contain any complex logic, such as conditional statements or loops. Generally a `lambda` is passed as argument to `map`, `filter`, or `reduce`. The following illustrates the application of each of these functions:

```
>>> a = [1, 2, 3, 4, 5]
>>> print map(lambda x : x * 2 + 1, a)
[3, 5, 7, 9, 11]
>>> print filter(lambda x: x % 2 == 0, a)
[2, 4]
>>> print reduce(lambda x, y: x + y, a)
15
```

Notice that the original list, held in the variable named a, remains unchanged. The functions `map`, `filter`, and `reduce` produce new lists that are transformations of the argument.

The function `filter` requires an argument that is itself a function that takes only one argument and returns a Boolean value. A one-argument function that returns a Boolean result is termed a *predicate*.

List Comprehensions

An even simpler form of functional programming is provided by a *list comprehension*. Instead of defining a list by a sequence of elements, lists can be characterized by a process. This process is described by a series of keywords:

[*expr* **for** var **in** *list* **if** *expr*]

Here var is a variable name, and list is an existing sequence. The optional if part requires an expression that evaluates to `true` or `false`. Only those elements that evaluate to `true` are examined. To construct the new sequence, each element in the original list is examined. If it passes the if expression test, the initial expression is evaluated and the resulting value added to the new list. In this fashion, the list completion combines aspects of both a filter and a map. The following example illustrates the use of a list:

```
>>> a = [1, 2, 3, 4, 5]
>>> print [x*2 for x in a if x < 4]
[2, 4, 6]
```

List comprehensions are often simpler to read than the equivalent expression formed using filter and map, in part because lists do not require an explicit lambda function. However, both forms are useful, and a Python programmer should be familiar with both.

List comprehensions are often used as the body of a function. The function definition provides a convenient syntax and a way to provide names to arguments. The list comprehension is an easy-to-understand way to write the body of the function:

```
>>> def listOfSquares(a):
    return [x*x for x in a]
>>> listOfSquares([1, 2, 3])
[1, 4, 9]
```

The range of the list comprehension need not be a simple identifier. For example, if a is a list of numbers, the following will print every other element of the list:

```
>>> [a[i] for i in range(0,len(a)) if i%2 == 0]
[1, 3, 5]
```

Operations on dictionaries are often performed by selecting values from the range of keys, and then returning the items with the selected key:

```
>>> d = {1:'fred', 7:'sam', 8:'alice', 22:'helen'}
>>> [d[i] for i in d.keys() if i%2 == 0]
['alice', 'helen']
```

EXAMPLE: COMPUTING AN INTERSECTION

The difference between an imperative approach and a functional approach can be illustrated using a simple example. Suppose you have two lists (call them a and b), and you need to construct a third list containing their intersection. That is, the third list should have only those elements that are found in both lists. We will assume that both lists represent sets in which no value is repeated more than once.

An imperative approach would construct a new empty list, and in a doubly nested loop test each element in the first against each element in the second. This might be written as follows:

```
intersect = [] # build an empty set
for x in a:
  for y in b:
      if x == y:
            intersect.append(y)
# intersect now represents the final set
print "intersection is ", intersect
```

A slightly better, but still imperative, approach would simply loop over the first set and test each element in the second. The single loop will be much faster than the double loop of the first example:

```
intersect = []    # build an empty set
for x in a:
  if x in b:
      intersect.append(x)
print "intersection is ", intersect
```

If you were thinking in a functional programming fashion, you would notice that the intersection is a subset of the elements in either set. This naturally suggests the result can be formed using filter. All that is necessary is an argument that will determine whether or not each element should be retained. Using lambda, this can be written as follows:

```
intersect = filter(lambda x: x in b, a)
```

In one simple expression, this replaces a loop and a conditional test that previously required several lines. Because the code is simpler, it means fewer opportunities exist to make a mistake. It is relatively easy to look at the expression, understand what it is doing, and verify that it is correct.

The list comprehension form is even shorter. There is no need for the `lambda` expression, as the `if` keyword is performing a similar task:

```
intersect = [ x for x in a if x in b ]
```

Or, as a function:

```
def intersect(a, b):
    return [x for x in a if x in b]
```

Notice the features that make this solution characteristic of functional programming. Most important, rather than making a succession of small changes to a value, the function is building the result as a transformation of one or more values to produce a new value.

EXAMPLE: PRIME NUMBER SIEVE

Because lists are recursive, functional programs that manipulate lists are often written in a recursive fashion. This can be illustrated using the problem of finding prime numbers with the sieve of Erastosthenes. This technique, first described by the Greek mathematician Erastosthenes in 300 BC, works as follows: Start with a list of the numbers from 2 to some limit, written in order. Select the first element, which will be a prime number. Then strike out (that is, remove) all the values that are a multiple of the number. Repeat until the list is empty.

We describe the thought process you might follow in creating a program written in the functional programming style to perform this task. It is easy enough to create a list of values from 2 onward using the `range` function:

```
>>> a = range(2, 16)      # produce a list from 2 to 15
>>> print a
[2, 3, 4, 5, 6, 7, 8, 9, 10, 11, 12, 13, 14, 15]
```

Accessing the first element is easy; it is simply `a[0]`. The remainder of the list with the first element removed is also easy; it is `a[1:]`. What about the task of striking out those elements that are multiples of the first element? A test to see if one value is divisible by another can be formed using the remainder, or `mod` operator, `%`. If the remainder is zero, then the value is divisible. You can verify this with a few examples:

```
>>> print 5 % 2 == 0
False
>>> print 6 % 2 == 0
True
```

Using this idea, a filter to eliminate all multiples of the first element can be written as follows:

```
>>> print filter(lambda x: x % a[0] != 0, a[1:])
[3, 5, 7, 9, 11, 13]
```

Alternatively, you could use list comprehensions:

```
>>> print [ x for x in a[1:] if x % a[0] != 0]
[3, 5, 7, 9, 11, 13]
```

Having determined how to filter out multiples of a given value, the definition of the `sieve` function is then a straightforward recursive function:

```
def sieve(a):
   if a:      # that is, if a is non-empty
       return a[0:1]+sieve(filter(lambda x: x % a[0] != 0, a[1:]))
   else:
       return [ ]
```

Remember that a list is considered to be true inside an *if* statement if it is not empty. Testing the value a is shorthand for testing `len(a) != 0`. Notice how the body of the function closely parallels the definition. To form a sieve, you remove the first element, then strike out multiples of the element, and recursively invoke `sieve` on the remainder. The first element, the one you earlier removed, is known to be prime. So you add that value to the result of the recursive call on `sieve`. The expression `a[0:1]` returns a list containing the first element, as opposed to `a[0]`, which would return the first element itself. Keeping the first element in list form allows the use of the + operator to append the two lists. The alternative would have been to write `[a[0]]`, explicitly extracting the first element and then placing it into a list.

You can test the `sieve` function by passing it the list of integers from 2 onward:

```
>>> sieve(range(2, 20))
[2, 3, 5, 7, 11, 13, 17, 19]
```

EXAMPLE: INSERTION SORT

As noted in the prime sieve, the design of a program in the functional style often proceeds by defining the characteristic of the desired solution, rather than the step-by-step process used to produce the solution. For this reason, the paradigm is often called an example of *declarative programming*. This can be illustrated by an example. Suppose you wanted to program the process of performing an *insertion sort*. An insertion sort works by repeatedly inserting a new value into a sorted list. Therefore, a subtask of insertion sort is to perform a single insertion.

What are the characteristics of an insertion? If we have a sorted list, named *a*, and a new element *x*, an insertion can be defined as follows:

if *a* is empty, then [*x*] is an insertion,
otherwise if $x < a[0]$, then [*x*] + *a* is an insertion,
otherwise append *a*[0] to the insertion(*x*, *a*[1:])

This yields the following recursive function:

```
def insertion (a, x):
   if not a:        # that is, if a is empty
       return [ x ]
   elif x < a[0]:
       return [ x ] + a
   else:
       return a[0:1] + insertion(a[1:], x)
```

Having defined an insertion, the process of `insertionSort` is simply a matter of performing an insertion on each element in turn. One way to do this would be with another recursive function:

```
def insertionSort (a):
   if a:
       return insertion(insertionSort(a[1:]), a[0])
   else:
       return [ ]
```

This function can be read in the following fashion. An `insertionSort` of an empty list is simply the empty list. Otherwise, an `insertionSort` is formed by inserting the first element (that is, `a[0]`) into the list yielded by performing an `insertion Sort` on the remainder.

Repeatedly performing the same operation should make you think of the functions `apply` and `reduce`. Can either of those be used in this situation? The function insertion would at first not seem to be a candidate for reduction, since the arguments are two different types. However, an alternative form of `reduce` makes this possible. This form takes three arguments: the original list, the reduction function, and an identity element that will be used as the first element to start the process. Using an empty set as the identity, we can rewrite the `insertionSort` as follows:

```
def insertionSort2(a):
   return reduce(insertion, a, [ ])
```

If you imagine the execution of this function on a small list, you can see how the result is produced. Imagine starting with the list [3, 2, 1]. The result will be generated by this expression:

```
insertion(1, insertion(2, insertion(3, [ ])))
```

The innermost expression will insert 3 into the empty list. The value 2 will then be inserted into the resulting list. Finally, the value 1 will be inserted. The result will be a new list into which every element has been inserted.

EXAMPLE: QUICKSORT

The sorting algorithm `quicksort` provides another illustration of how a problem can be described as a transformation. The `quicksort` algorithm is a recursive algorithm that works by selecting some element, termed the pivot; dividing the original list into three parts, namely those that are smaller than the pivot, those equal to the pivot, and those larger than the pivot; and recursively sorting the first and third, appending the results to obtain the final solution.

Once you have described the `quicksort` algorithm in this fashion, the solution is a simple transliteration:

```
def quicksort(a):
  if a:
      # there are various ways of selecting the pivot
      # we simply choose the middle element
      pivot = a[len(a)/2]
      return (quickSort([x for x in a if x < pivot]) +
      [x for x in a if x == pivot] +
      quickSort([x for x in a if x > pivot]))
  else:
      return [ ]
```

We have illustrated higher-order functions by passing lambda expressions to functions such as `filter` and `map`. The flip side is to write a function that accepts a function as argument. For example, you might want a sorting function that allows the user to provide the comparison test as an argument, rather than using the < operator. The `quicksort` algorithm rewritten to allow the comparison test to be passed as argument is as follows:

```
def quicksort(a, cmp):
  if a:
      pivot = a[len(a)/2]
      return (quicksort([x for x in a if cmp(x, pivot)],cmp)+
      [x for x in a if x == pivot] +
      quicksort([x for x in a if cmp(pivot, x)], cmp))
  else:
      return [ ]
```

This version of `quicksort` could be invoked as follows:

```
>>> a = [1, 6, 4, 2, 5, 3, 7]
>>> print quicksort(a, lambda x, y: x > y)   # sort descending
[7, 6, 5, 4, 3, 2, 1]
```

SIMPLE REDUCTIONS

Many common tasks can be implemented as a form of reduction. The easiest form of reduction is the sum of the elements in a list:

```
>>> a = [1, 2, 3, 4, 5]
>>> print reduce(lambda x, y: x + y, a)
15
```

If you want to give this a simple name, you can wrap the call on `reduce` inside a function definition:

```
def sum(a):
    return reduce(lambda x, y: x + y, a)
```

To form the product of a list, you need the three-argument form of `reduce`. The third argument is an identity, the value used to begin the series of applications. For multiplication, the identity is 1:

```
>>> print reduce(lambda x, y: x * y, a, 1)
120
```

But much more can be done with `reduce`. Consider computing the length of a list. Admittedly, you would probably never do it this way, since a built-in function named `len` can be used for this purpose. But this is a good exercise in thinking about a problem as a reduction. What is the length of an empty list? Zero—which fortunately is the default value. For a function, you need a `lambda` that takes two arguments, ignores the second, and simply adds 1 to the first:

```
>>> print reduce(lambda x, y: x + 1, a)
5
```

How about computing the average of a list? It's simply a combination of a sum and dividing by the length:

```
def average(a):
    return sum(a)/len(a)
```

Reductions need not be arithmetic. Imagine performing a reduction using the function that appends an element to the end of a list, using an empty list as the identity. The result is a copy of a list:

```
>>> print reduce(lambda x, y: x + [y], a, [ ])
[1, 2, 3, 4, 5]
```

This might not seem particularly useful. But if we substitute another list for the empty list as the third argument, the result is a function that appends two lists:

```
def append(a, b):
    return reduce(lambda x, y: x + [y], b, a)
>>> print append([1, 2, 3], [5, 6, 7])
[1, 2, 3, 5, 6, 7]
```

Perhaps more interesting is the effect if the function appends to the front rather than to the back. The result is a reverse of a list:

```
>>> print reduce(lambda x, y: [y] + x, a, [ ])
[5, 4, 3, 2, 1]
```

We have just scratched the surface of the types of operations that can be performed using functional techniques. Once you start to think about how a problem can be addressed using techniques such as mapping, filtering, and reduction, you will find many other applications.

COMPUTING VARIANCE OF A LIST

The computation of the variance of a list of numbers illustrates how a longer function can be computed in a series of steps that are each functional. A variance of a list is defined as the sum of squares of differences of each number from the mean (average). To compute the variance, the average is first computed. As noted earlier, this is simply the sum of the elements divided by the number of elements. Next, the difference of each element from the average is computed as a mapping. A second mapping computes the squares. Finally, to compute the variance, the sum of the squares is computed and divided by the length:

```
def variance(a):
  average = sum(a)/len(a)    # compute average
  difs = map(lambda x: x—average, a)
  sqs = map(lambda x: x * x, difs)
  return sum(sqs)/len(a)
```

Notice how each step in the program is a transformation that acts on an entire collection as a whole, without the need to write a loop. By eliminating explicit loops, the program is both shorter and easier to understand. This makes functions written in a functional style much easier to debug and correct.

COMBINING FUNCTIONAL AND OBJECT-ORIENTED PROGRAMMING

It is possible to write programs entirely in a functional fashion. However, it is more common to combine functional programming features with other techniques. An individual function might be written in a functional fashion, while the remainder of a program is imperative.

Chapter 7 introduced the class, which is central to yet another paradigm, object-oriented programming. It is common for a class to include individual methods (functions) that are themselves written in a functional fashion. To become a skilled Python programmer, you need to learn the mechanics of all these techniques, and you should be able to identify situations in which it is appropriate to use one approach or another.

ITERATING OVER MULTIPLE LISTS*[1]

The function map can optionally take more than one list. The function in the first argument must itself take as many arguments as there are lists. The following, for example, will return the pairwise sum of two lists:

---

[1] Sections marked with an asterisk indicate optional or advanced material and can be skipped on first reading.

```
>>> print map(lambda x, y: x + y, [1, 2, 3], [9, 8, 7])
[10, 10, 10]
```

If either list is shorter than the other, the shorter list is padded with elements of value None.

List comprehensions can also in general have any number of for and if keywords. The effect is to loop over *all combinations* of the possible values. This can be illustrated by an expression that produces tuple pairs:

```
>>> print [(a, b) for a in [1, 2, 3] for b in [7, 8, 9]]
[(1, 7), (1, 8), (1, 9), (2, 7), (2, 8), (2, 9), (3, 7), (3, 8),
(3, 9)]
```

If conditions can work with all variables that have been defined by a *for* clause. The following saves only those tuples for which the sum of the two numbers is even:

```
>>> print [(a, b) for a in [1, 2, 3] for b in [7, 8, 9] if (a+b)%2==0]
[(1, 7), (1, 9), (2, 8), (3, 7), (3, 9)]
```

The production of all pairs of values is sometimes termed an *inner product*. Occasionally it is necessary to run down two equal-length lists in *parallel*. This is sometimes termed a *dot product*. A common Python idiom to perform this task is the built-in function named zip. The following illustrates the effect of zip:

```
>>> zip([1, 2, 3], [7, 8, 9])
[(1, 7), (2, 8), (3, 9)]
```

Tuple assignment can be used inside a list comprehension to break apart the elements formed by a zip:

```
>>> print [a+b for (a,b) in zip([1, 2, 3],[4, 5, 6])]
[5, 7, 9]
```

EXERCISES

1. Write a lambda function for each of the following:
   a. Take one argument and return true if it is nonzero.
   b. Take one argument and return true if it is odd.
   c. Take two arguments and return their sum.
   d. Take two arguments and return true if their sum is odd.
   e. Take three arguments and return true if the produce of the first two is less than or equal to the third.

2. Let *a* be the list of values produced by range(1, 11). Using the function map and a lambda argument, write an expression that will produce each of the following:
   a. A list of squares of the values
   b. A list of cubes of the values
   c. A list where each element is larger by one than the corresponding element in the original list

3. Let *a* be the list of values produced by `range(1, 11)`. Using the function `filter` and a `lambda` argument, write an expression that will produce each of the following:
    a. A list of the even values in *a*
    b. A list of the values in *a* divisible by 3

4. The expression `reduce(lambda x, y: x-y, range(1, 5))` produces the result `-8`. Explain the meaning of this value—that is, what computation it represents.

5. Explain the following execution of the function `filter`. Hint: Remember how integer values are interpreted when a Boolean is required.

    ```
    >>> filter(lambda x: x, [4, 0, 6, 3, 0, 2])
    [4, 6, 3, 2]
    ```

6. What happens if you `reduce` over an empty list? What if you use the optional third argument form of `reduce`?

7. Using `reduce`, write a function named `ave(lst)` that will return the average of a list of numbers.

8. Let *a* be the list of integer values. Explain what the following expression is returning:

    ```
    reduce(lambda x, y: x and y, filter(lambda x: x % 2 == 0, a))
    ```

    What would the function be returning if the `lambda` used the `or` operator instead of the `and` operator?

9. Using what you learned from the previous question, write a function named `forAll` that takes two arguments. The first argument should be a list. The second argument should be a predicate, a one-argument function that returns a Boolean result. The function `forAll` should return `true` if the predicate returns true when applied to all elements of the list.

10. A lambda is simply a value. This means that lambda can be, for example, stored in a list. The following shows one such example. What will be the result for the expression `d[1](2)`?

    ```
    d = [lambda x: x+1, lambda x: x*2, lambda x: x ** 3]
    ```

11. Let *a* be the list of values produced by `range(1, 11)`. Write a list comprehension that will produce each of the following:
    a. The values in *a* that are less than or equal to 5
    b. The squares of the values in *a*
    c. The cubes of the values in *a* that are less than or equal to 5
    d. The squares of those values in *a* that are even

12. Write three versions of a function that will take a list as an argument and return a list containing the cubes of the elements that are evenly divisible by 2. First write the function using standard loops and *if* statements. Then write the function using a combination of `filter` and `map`. Finally write the function using a list comprehension. Which form is shorter? Which do you think is easier to understand?

13. Using a combination of filter and the built-in function `len`, write a function that will take a list and a function as two arguments, and then return a count of the number of elements of the list for which the function returns `true`.

14. In an earlier chapter, you learned that functions defined using the `def` keyword create their own *scope*. This means that parameters as well as variables assigned within the

function have local scope, and changes to these values do not alter the value of similarly named variables at the global level. Write an example function that will show that `lambda` functions also produce their own scope. The `lambda` cannot contain assignments, but the names of the parameters can be the same as values in the surrounding scope. Show that the use of a parameter does not alter a similarly named value in the surrounding scope.

15. Write a function that takes a list and a function as arguments, and using a list comprehension returns a list containing the *positions* of the elements in the list for which the function returns `true`.

16. Write a function named `evenFilter` that takes as an argument a dictionary of elements indexed by integer keys. Using only a list comprehension, return the values of the elements associated with the keys that are evenly divisible by 2:

```
>>> data = {1:"one", 2:"two", 5:"five", 6:"six"}
>>> print evenFilter(data)
["two", "six"]
```

17. A `lambda` function is just a value. If you want, you can assign this value to a variable:

```
f = lambda x : x * 2 + 1
```

You can then use this variable like a function:

```
>>> print f(3)
7
```

What are some of the ways that a function defined in this fashion is similar to a function defined using the *def* statement? What are some ways that they are different?

18. Define the difference of two lists as a list comprehension. The difference consists of the elements in the first list that are not part of the second.

19. Using the difference function you wrote in the previous question, define a function that returns the union of two sets that are represented by lists. A union contains all elements that are found in either list, but if the same element is found in both lists, it is included only once.

20. Using the function `ave` for computing the average of a list that you wrote in an earlier question, write a function named `topStudent` that will take a dictionary indexed by name and holding a list of exam scores. The function should return the list of names for those students who have an average greater than 90 percent. The following shows an example of the input for this function:

```
{'sam':[.85, .90, .94], 'alice':[.74, .96, .34]}
```

21. The following four expressions represent a series of steps in the development of an expression to produce a well-known sequence. Examine the value of the last expression and identify the sequence. Then explain what each of the three previous expressions is doing—that is, what values they each produce.

```
range(2, 25)
[ range(2, i) for i in range(2, 25)]
[ [ x for x in range(2, i) if i % x == 0] for i in range(2, 25)]
[ i for i in range(2, 25) if len([x for x in range(2, i) if i%x==0])==0]
```

22. At times you'll want to include an *if* statement in a `lambda`. Of course, since the body of a `lambda` must be an expression, this is difficult—but not impossible. Recall that the logical operators `and` and `or` return the first value that can be interpreted as a Boolean `true`. Can you see this by executing the following expressions? Using this idea, explain how the following `lambda` very nearly produces the smaller of the two arguments. There is one case for which this will not work. Can you figure out what this might be?

```
>>> (3 < 4) and 5
5
>>> (4 < 3) or 7
7
>>> f = lambda x, y: ((x < y) and x) or y
>>> f(5, 6)
5
>>> f(7, 9)
7
>>> f(0, 3)
3
```

By the way, the conventional workaround for this problem is to wrap part of the results in a list, and then access the first element of the list. The following shows this. Explain why this solves the problem for the special case identified earlier. (Note that this is not considered to be a paragon of clarity in Python programming.)

```
>>> f = lambda x, y: (((x < y) and [x]) or [y])[0]
>>> f(0, 4)
0
```

Object-Oriented Programming

Chapter 8 introduced the notion of a programming *paradigm,* which refers to the mental model, or metaphor, that describes the task being performed by the programmer. The simplest paradigm is the *imperative* model. In imperative programming, you view computation as a process of making small changes to memory, until, by a long sequence of small changes, the desired result is produced. The *functional* paradigm, described in Chapter 8, views the task of computation as a process of *transformation.* By performing a sequence of transformations on a value, the desired result is produced.

This chapter introduces a third paradigm, the *object-oriented* model. In the object-oriented paradigm, a program is viewed as a collection of computing agents, each of which provides a *service* that can be used by the others.

The functional programming model requires the ability to create functions, but the paradigm is much more than the simple use of this mechanism. In a similar fashion, the object-oriented paradigm is built on the mechanics of defining classes, creating instances of those classes, and using inheritance, concepts that were all introduced in Chapter 7. However, the object-oriented *paradigm* refers to the model of computation built on top of these facilities, and not just the mechanics of defining classes.

COMMUNITY

As noted in Chapter 7, a *class* is an encapsulation mechanism, a way to bundle together a number of data values and functions. Properly designed, these items should be united in some purpose—that is, the class, by means of the functions it defines, is providing a *service* that can be used by other objects.

A program written in the object-oriented style can be viewed as a *community* of interacting agents. Each member of the community has a part to play, a service that it provides to other members of the community. Objects interact with each other by invoking functions defined within the class. In the object-oriented literature, this is termed *message passing.*

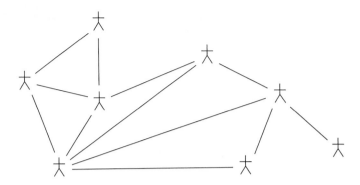

The idea of message passing can be compared to the way problems are solved in the real world. Consider the task of sending flowers to a friend who lives in another city. To do this, you interact with a local florist. In object-oriented parlance, you *pass a message* to the florist. The florist is an agent providing a service that you are using. This florist will, in turn, pass the message to a florist in the city where your friend lives. That florist will have acquired flowers for the arrangement by dealing with a wholesaler, who will interact with growers, delivery persons, and so on. So an entire community is working cooperatively to get the flowers to your friend, and the objects in this community interact by passing messages to each other.

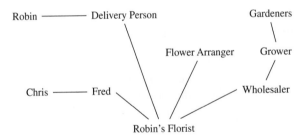

Object-oriented programming has become the dominant paradigm in recent years, largely because the metaphor of messages being passed to service providers is similar to problem-solving techniques used by programmers in their everyday lives. Because of this, intuition and skills from life experiences can readily be applied to object-oriented programs.

In programming languages, objects embody the idea of a service provider. A data structure (an object used to manage a collection of values) is a simple example of a service being provided by an instance of a class. An object can, for example, provide the services of a stack. To do so, the object provides the user with methods to push an item on to the top of the stack, access the topmost element in the stack, and remove an item from the stack. You might, in some project, require the use of two or more stacks. To address this issue, object-oriented languages divide the task of object creation into two parts, the *class* and the *instance*.

A class is like a cookie cutter or a template. It is a design specification, a repository for behavior. The class itself does not provide behavior beyond object creation.

Using the class, the programmer can create one or more instances of the class, termed *objects*. An object is a realization of the class. It is a working entity. All instances of the same class will have their own data fields but will have the same functionality.

An example will illustrate some of the mechanisms of class design and creation. The following creates our stack class, using a list as the underlying storage area:

```
class Stack(object):
  def __init__ (self):
      self.storage = [ ]
  def push (self, newValue):
      self.storage.append(newValue)
  def top (self):
      return self.storage[len(self.storage) - 1]
  def pop (self):
      result = self.top()
      self.storage.pop()
      return result
  def isEmpty (self):
      return len(self.storage) == 0
```

To create an instance of this class, you use the class name as if it were a function:

```
>>> # create two stacks
>>> stackOne = Stack()
>>> stackTwo = Stack()
```

Once created, you access the functionality provided by the class (that is, pass a message to the object) using the dot operator, as in the following:

```
>>> stackOne.push(12)
>>> stackTwo.push('abc')
>>> stackOne.push(23)
>>> print stackOne.top()
23
>>> stackOne.pop()
>>> print stackOne.top()
12
>>> print stackTwo.top()
'abc'
```

Using the Stack: An RPN Calculator

Another class might use the services of the stack class. For example, suppose we are building a calculator that performs operations in reverse Polish notation (RPN), which means that operations are performed by pushing arguments onto a stack and then performing operations using the topmost elements of the stack. For example, the calculation conventionally written as 2 * (3 + 7) would be written in RPN as 2 3 7 + *. It would be evaluated by pushing the values 2, 3, and 7 onto the stack, and then performing the addition with the topmost two elements, pushing the result onto the stack. Finally, the multiplication would be performed using the top two elements on the stack, leaving the result sitting in the stack.

The heart of our RPN calculator is a class for performing calculations and managing the stack. We will simplify the design of this class by using lambda functions to specialize a common function for performing binary operations:

```python
class CalculatorEngine(object):
    def __init__ (self):
        self.dataStack = Stack()
    def pushOperand (self, value):
        self.dataStack.push(value)
    def currentOperand (self):
        return self.dataStack.top()
    def performBinary (self, fun):
        right = self.dataStack.pop()
        left = self.dataStack.pop()
        self.dataStack.push(fun(left, right))
    def doAddition (self): self.performBinary(lambda x, y: x+y)
    def doSubtraction (self): self.performBinary(lambda x, y: x-y)
    def doMultiplication (self): self.performBinary(lambda x, y: x*y)
    def doDivision (self): self.performBinary(lambda x, y: x/y)
    def doTextOp (self, op):
        if (op == '+'): self.doAddition()
        elif (op == '-'): self.doSubtraction()
        elif (op == '*'): self.doMultiplication()
        elif (op == '/'): self.doDivision()
```

The user of the calculator engine can either explicitly call the appropriate function (doAddition, doSubtraction, and so on) or invoke the function doTextOp. However, forcing the end user to pass messages to the calculator engine is not very friendly. A better design would create another class whose only purpose is to provide a useful user interface. This function will request a line of input, use split to break the line into parts, loop over the elements of the list invoking the appropriate function from the calculator engine, and finally print the value remaining on top of the stack. Execution of the function halts if the user enters a blank line:

```python
class RPNCalculator(object):
    def __init__ (self):
    self.calcEngine = CalculatorEngine()

def eval (self, line):
    words = line.split(" ")
    for item in words:
        if item in '+-*/':
```

```
          self.calcEngine.doTextOp(item)
      else: self.calcEngine.pushOperand(int(item))
  return self.calcEngine.currentOperand()

def run (self):
  while True:
      line = raw_input("type an expression: ")
      if len(line) == 0: break
      print self.eval(line)
```

The following is an example illustrating the use of the `calculator` function:

```
>>> calc = RPNCalculator()
>>> calc.run
type an expression: 3  4  +
7
type an expression: 3  4  +  2  *
14
type an expression: 3  4  2  +  *
24
type an expression:
>>>
```

The program at this point is not very robust in reaction to errors in the input. In the exercises at the end of the chapter, we will suggest ways in which this could be improved.

Separating the Model from the View

Notice that the calculator application is constructed out of three separate classes: the stack, the calculator engine, and the calculator itself. Each class is providing a distinct service that can be considered independent of the others. As noted earlier, they work as a *community* to complete the operations of the calculator application. The stack is simply implementing a simple data structure and knows nothing about how it is being used. The calculator engine encapsulates the logic concerning how the stack is being used to perform arithmetic instructions, but it knows nothing about the user interface. The final class, the `RPNCalculator`, provides the user interface, but it knows nothing about the logic of the task at hand.

Separating the application into several classes offers many advantages. One advantage is that it makes the program easier to understand, as each class has only one purpose and can be examined and studied in isolation. Another important reason is software reuse, since general-purpose classes, such as our stack, can be easily carried from one project to the next.

The division between the calculator engine, which has no user interaction, and the calculator, which interacts with the user but has no knowledge of the calculator function, deserves more investigation. This division is common enough to be recognized as a principle of good design and has been given a name. The *view* is the object that interacts with the end user, and the *model* is the logic that actually implements whatever task is being performed. Placing these in separate classes is known as *separating the model from the view*, and the separation offers many practical advantages.

One advantage is that many views can exist for the same model. For example, we might want to implement a graphical user interface (GUI). (We will examine GUIs in Chapter 12.) The interface can be implemented as a new class that embodies only user interaction issues and not interaction issues on the calculation itself. Thus, separating the model from the view makes it easier to reuse existing code, as well as make changes to one part of an application without affecting other sections.

As you practice object-oriented programming skills, you should look for opportunities to separate each new application into classes that provide services to other parts of the system. Recognize situations such as the separation between model and view, and design your program using good software practices.

An Infix Calculator

While the use of the function `string.split` to divide the line into tokens simplified the development of the RPN calculator, it also introduced some problems. First, it required that spaces be placed around every number and every operator. Second, many people find the RPN notation difficult to understand. We can solve both problems by adding yet another layer on top of our calculator application. The class `InfixCalculator` will read an expression written in normal arithmetic notation, including parentheses, and translate the expression into RPN. After translating the expression, the RPN calculator will then be invoked to evaluate the expression.

The process of finding a meaning in a textual string is called *parsing*. The Python interpreter uses parsing, for example, as the first step in determining the meaning of each expression. The technique we will use here is termed *operator-precedence parsing*. It has the advantage of being very simple; however, it works only for simple arithmetic expressions. The parser in the Python interpreter is much more robust and complicated.

The idea behind operator precedence parsing is to maintain a stack of pending operators. These are operators for which the argument to the left of the operator is known, but the right argument is not. Operands are copied into the output buffer as soon as they are recognized. As soon as both arguments for an operator are recognized, the operator is also copied into the output.

Examining a few examples will help you uncover what needs to be done. To handle a simple expression such as 3 + 4, the value *3* would be copied to the output buffer. Next, the operator + would be saved in the operator stack, since the right argument is not yet known. The value *4* is copied into the output. As a final step, all operators from the operator stack are copied into the output. The result is the expression 3 4 +, which is the RPN for this input.

Next, consider the input 3 + 4 * 7. As before, the value *3* is copied to the output, the operator + is pushed on the stack, and the value *4* is copied to the output. The next symbol is the operator *. To determine whether or not the operator in the operator stack should be processed, the precedence of the operator * is compared to that of the operator currently on top of the stack. Since the * has higher precedence, it is simply pushed onto the stack. The result is then the RPN expression 3 4 7 * +.

Contrast this with the processing of the input 3 * 4 + 7. Here, when the precedence of the second operator, the +, is compared to the first, the *, we find the precedence of the value on the stack is higher. Therefore, the operator in the stack is popped and copied to the output. This results in the expression 3 4 * 7 +.

Finally, let us consider the impact of the use of parentheses. When a left parenthesis is encountered, it is simply pushed onto the stack. A parenthesis has a low precedence, so it will never be popped from the stack by an operator. When the corresponding right parenthesis is encountered, all operators from the stack above the left parenthesis are simply copied to the output.

The program that embodies these ideas is shown next. You should simulate the execution of the program on a few examples to convince yourself it is doing the right thing.

```python
class Calculator(object):
    def __init__ (self):
        self.calcEngine = RPNCalculator()
        self.opStack = Stack()

    def eval (self, line):
        self.outLine = ''
        i = 0
        while i < len(line):
            if line[i] == '(':
                self.opStack.push('(')
            elif line[i] == ')': self.doParen()
            elif line[i] in '+-*/':
                self.doBinary(line[i])
            elif line[i] in '0123456789':
                self.outLine += line[i]
            i = i + 1
        while not self.opStack.isEmpty():
            self.doOp(self.opStack.pop())

    def run (self):
        while True:
            line = raw_input("type an expression: ")
            if len(line) == 0: break
            print self.eval(line)

    def doParen (self):
        while self.opStack.top() != '(':
            op = self.opStack.pop()
            self.doOp (op)
        self.opStack.pop() # remove the left paren
```

```
def doOp (self, op):
    self.outLine += (' ' + op + ' ')

def prec (self, op):
    if op == '/' or op == '*': return 2
    elif op == '+' or op == '-': return 1
    return 0

def doBinary (self, topop):
    self.outLine += ' '
    if self.opStack.isEmpty(): self.opStack.push(topop)
    else:
        nextop = self.opStack.top()
        if self.prec(topop) <= self.prec(nextop):
            self.doOp(nextop)
            self.opStack.pop()
        self.opStack.push(topop)
```

The separation of reading the line of input from evaluating the line using the function `eval` means that this class, too, could be used as a component in a larger application. In Chapter 12, this will be illustrated by adding a GUI to our calculator. As with the Infix calculator program, our interest in presenting the operator precedence algorithm is not so much the program itself (although it is one of the classic computer algorithms that all students should know), but rather the way in which this program reflects an object-oriented design.

The calculator program makes use of a stack to hold operators as part of the parsing process. To do this, it uses the services of the `stack` class. It also uses the RPN calculator to produce the actual result after parsing. The RPN calculator is used to evaluate an expression written in RPN notation. To do this, it also uses the services of the `stack` class. The original calculator need not know that the RPN calculator is using a stack; it only knows the service that is being provided. Each member of the community is providing a simple service that is defined by the interface (functions) they provide to the other objects in the program.

DISCOVERING OBJECTS

We have emphasized the view that objects are *entities* that provide *services*. This simple but key insight provides a heuristic that can be used to help you identify what should and should not be an object when you're designing a new application. To apply this heuristic, start by writing one or more stories that describe the execution of your new application from the user's point of view. These stories are often termed *scenarios* or *use-cases*.

Next, go through your scenarios and highlight each noun with one colored pen, and each verb with a different colored pen. The verbs represent the tasks to be done—the *what*. But in an object-oriented world, a task can be performed only if somebody does it—the *who*. The nouns define (as a first approximation) the entities in the community that make up your application. Match each action (verb) with an agent (noun)—that is, match each what with a who.

A useful tool in this process is the Class-Responsibility-Collaborator (CRC) card. Only the first two, class and responsibility, are discussed here. Write the name of each class (noun) on an index card. Below this, write a short English language description of the responsibilities of this class.

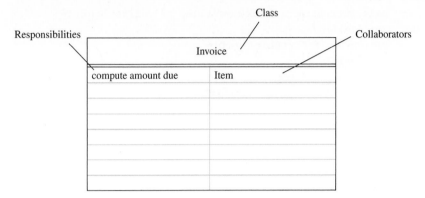

A collection of scenarios and CRC cards is a good starting place for the process of designing a new application. Walk through the scenarios, and for each action (verb) make sure you have identified an agent (represented by a CRC card) responsible for performing the action.

Once you are satisfied that you have captured all the actions necessary to make your application work as you expect, the CRC cards can be used as a basis for coding the classes in your application.

DUCK TYPING

In the object-oriented paradigm, classes are characterized by the services they provide. A consequence of this view is that any value can be replaced by another value, as long as the replacement provides the same service—that is, the same actions using the same names. This is true even if the implementation of the service is radically different.

This can be illustrated by an alternative implementation of a stack. This implementation uses a *linked list*. While common in many other programming languages, the linked list approach would typically not be used in Python since the built-in list type is both faster and easier.

A linked list is formed using an auxiliary data type called a *link*, which holds a value and a reference to another link:

```
class Link(object):
    def __init__ (self, v, n)
        self.value = v
        self.next = n
```

When a new element is pushed on the stack, it is stored in a new link. When the value is removed from the stack, the current first link is skipped over. This approach is embodied in the following implementation of a stack:

```
class LinkStack(object):
   def __init__ (self):
        self.firstLink = None
   def push (self, newValue):
        self.firstLink = Link(newValue, self.firstLink)
   def top (self):
        return self.firstLink.value
   def pop (self):
        result = self.top()
        self.firstLink = self.firstLink.next
        return result
   def isEmpty (self):
        return self.firstLink == None
```

To change our program to use a `LinkStack` rather than a `Stack`, we need to change the statement that constructs the value. Because both classes implement the same interface, the rest of the program is oblivious to the change.

In an abstract sense, we have created a "type" that represents the concept of the stack, and both classes implement this type. However, this is only an abstract characterization, and no actual entity represents this type. This idea is often called *duck typing*, after the folk saying, *If it walks like a duck, and talks like a duck, then it probably is a duck*. Duck typing is found in dynamically typed object-oriented languages, such as Python. (Another programming language with similar features is Smalltalk.) Strongly typed languages, such as Java and C++, use an entirely different approach to typing.

ENCAPSULATION AND PROPERTIES

We have emphasized that the hallmark of object-oriented programming is the view that an object is providing a service that can be used by other objects. The features of this service are defined by the functions, or methods, defined by the class that created the object. The user of the service need know only the names of the operations and the correct arguments. For example, the user of the `stack` class need know only the names `push`, `pop`, `top`, and `isEmpty`. The user of the `stack` need not know that the underlying values are stored in a list. This is termed *encapsulation*, or *information hiding*, and it is one of the most important means for controlling complexity.

An important design guideline for object-oriented programming says that one object should never directly modify a data field in another object. Doing this breaks the encapsulation barrier the class is intended to preserve. But often a class seems to exist only as a repository of data—that is, the purpose of the class is to hold a data value. These two seemingly conflicting goals are resolved through the intervention of methods whose sole purpose is to provide access to or allow modification of data values. These functions are called *getters* and *setters*.

For example, suppose we want to define a simple class to represent a time duration, where a period of time is defined by hours, minutes, and seconds. A class definition that shows getters and setters for each unit can be written as follows:

```
class TimeDuration(object) :
    def __init__ (self, h, m, s):
        self._hour = h
        self._min = m
        self._sec = s
    def setHour (self, h): self._hour = h
    def setMinute (self, m): self._min = m
    def setSecond (self, s): self._sec = m
    def getHour (self): return self._hour
    def getMinute (self): return self._min
    def getSecond (self): return self._sec
```

Here the actual data values are being stored in field names that begin with underscores. While nothing in the Python language prevents direct access to these data fields, the underscore is a convention widely followed in the Python programming community to indicate that the name is purely internal to the class.[1] To access or set the data field, the getter or setter should be invoked:

```
>>> t = TimeDuration(3, 20, 15)
>>> print t.getHour()
3
>>> t.setHour(4)
>>> print t.getHour()
4
```

The getter and setter convention offers many advantages. The presence of these functions documents the fact that the data fields might potentially be changed. Furthermore, it is sometimes desirable to perform something other than simply using the data field—for example, you might want to print a message on a log each time a value is changed. Setters often check the validity of the new value before making a change. The setter function can throw an exception, for example, if the new value is not proper. The encapsulation within a function of the action makes this easy to do.

Nevertheless, the function call syntax can sometimes complicate the readability of a program. For this reason, a mechanism called a *property* hides the function call syntax, permitting the appearance of direct access to a data field while actually performing the actions of the getter and setter functions.

---

[1] You have undoubtedly encountered a variety of names that begin or end with underscores as you have explored the Python universe, starting with the __init__ method used for initializing a newly constructed object. The general rule of thumb is this: a name that begins with an underscore should never be used directly, but is instead intended for internal system-level or class-level manipulation.

To create a property, a class invokes a built-in function. This function takes two arguments: The first is the name of the getter function, and the second is the name of the setter function. The value None can be used in place of either argument to create a field that can read but not set, or set but not read. The following illustrates this use:

```
class TimeDuration(object):
    def __init__ (self, h, m, s):
        self._hour = h
        self._min = m
        self._sec = s
    def setHour (self, h): self._hour = h
    def setMinute (self, m): self._min = m
    def setSecond (self, s): self._sec = m
    def getHour (self): return self._hour
    def getMinute (self): return self._min
    def getSecond (self): return self._sec
    hour = property(getHour, setHour)
    min = property(getMinute, None)
    sec = property(None, setSecond)
```

Attempting to use a value incorrectly will produce an error:

```
>>> t = TimeDuration(3, 20, 32)
>>> t.hour
3
>>> t.hour = 4
>>> print t.hour
4
>>> print t.sec
AttributeError: unreadable attribute
>>> t.min = 42
AttributeError: can't set attribute
```

You should use properties whenever you have a value that can be set or used outside the class boundaries and you want to avoid the function call syntax.

EXERCISES

1. How does the RPN calculator respond to each of the following errors in input?
   a. 3 4+ error, no space between 4 and plus
   b. 3 + error, not enough operands
   c. 3 4 5 + error, not enough operators

2. Modify the RPN calculator to pop the final operand from the stack and produce an error message if the stack is then not empty. What changes do you need to make to the calculator engine? Which of the errors from question 1 can now be caught?

3. Modify the RPN calculator to place the evaluation of the expression in a try block, catching the error and printing a message. Which of the errors from question 1 can now be caught?

4. Suppose you wanted to add the modular division operator, %, to the RNP calculator. Can you do this making changes only to the class RPNCalculator, without modifying the class CalcEngine?

5. Suppose you are designing the software for a vending machine. What should the interface for your system be? You need to handle two classes of users: One type of user is depositing coins and requesting items from the machine. The other category of user is restocking the inventory of the machine. Specify the actions for each. Then design a system to support those actions. Does it make sense to divide your implementation into separate classes to manage features such as counting the money and managing the inventory?

6. Suppose you are designing the software for an ATM (Automatic Teller Machine). Write at least three different scenarios describing the use of your system. From these, create CRC cards to describe the various classes that might be used to implement your design. Walk though your scenarios to make sure that all activity is matched to a class.

7. Suppose you are designing software for an automated video rental kiosk. This system allows the user to browse movie clips, select a limited number of movies to rent, check and verify a credit card, and finally dispense movies that the user has selected. Create at least three different scenarios for the use of this system. From these, develop a design that includes at least four different classes. Create the CRC cards for your design.

8. Rewrite the class Link to use properties so that both the link and value fields are read-only.

9. Functions, including methods, are simply values that happen to be stored in a name space so that they can be accessed in the appropriate way. When a method does nothing more than invoke another function with the same arguments, an alternative to defining the method is simply to name the attribute with the value of the correct function. For example, the method named push in the class stack could be written as follows:

```
class Stack(object):
    def __init__ (self):
        self.storage = [ ]
        self.push = self.storage.append
    def top (self): . . .
```

First, verify that this does indeed work, and that the push method can be used with an instance of stack as before. Next, compare and contrast this style of definition with the conventional style. Can you see any advantages of one over the other?

Scopes, Name Spaces, and Modules

As projects become large, a major challenge for the programmer is the management of details. Most often, these details are manifest as a proliferation of names (names of variables, names of functions, and names of modules). If too many details are involved, no one person can remember them all. Worse, the same names can, perhaps unintentionally, collide. A collision occurs when one name is used for two or more entirely different purposes. Collisions can be fatal, because one section of code may depend on a value being held in a variable with a particular name. If that variable is overridden with a different value, chaos can ensue. The control of complexity ultimately amounts to managing access to names.

Most programming languages, including Python, manage names chiefly through the use of *name spaces*. A name space, or scope, is an encapsulation, or a packaging, of names. As with all encapsulations, the scope works by creating levels of abstraction. The scope can be viewed from the "outside" as a single entity, or it can be viewed from the "inside" as a collection of names and values. Furthermore, different scopes can hold values with the same name without danger of collision. This feature allows the programmer to use short and easy-to-remember names without worrying that the names will conflict with those of other variables in a different scope.

Our discussion of name spaces is divided into three major topics: First, we introduce the *LEGB rule* for simple variables. The second topic is *qualified names*, including class variables. Finally, we discuss the idea of *modules* and show how to create your own module.

THE LEGB RULE

In Chapter 3, you learned how to write function definitions. You learned that variables assigned within the body of a function are implicitly made local. Parameters also have *local scope*, which means that they have meaning only within the body of the function. If a global variable has the same name, the two values are distinct.

The following example illustrates two of the four levels in the *LEGB rule*. The *L* stands for local, such as the variable named *x* that is assigned within the function.

The *G* stands for global, which is the scope for variables defined at the top level, such as the variable *x* that is holding the value 42.

```
>>> x = 42
>>> def afun():
...     x = 12
...     print x
>>> aFun()
12
>>> print x # function has not changed the global variable
42
```

The other two levels, *E* and *G*, represent *enclosing* function definitions, and the dictionary of *built-in* functions. The LEGB rule says that when Python is looking for a meaning to attach to a name, it searches the scopes in this order: Local, Enclosing, Global, and Built-in.

The enclosing level is perhaps the least frequently encountered. It occurs when one function is defined inside another. Each function definition creates a new scope for variables assigned at that level. But functions can also access variables from the surrounding context. This somewhat contrived example will make this easier to understand:

```
def a(x):
  def b(y):
      print x + y
  y = 11
  b(3)
  print y # note that y is unchanged
>>> a(4)
7
11
```

When the function a is invoked, the variables *x* and *y* are characterized by the Python interpreter as local to the function. When the nested function b is invoked, it creates its own local scope, containing a new variable with the name *y*. This variable *y* has value 3, whereas the variable that was local contained a value 11. The body of b can access both local variables, such as *y*, and variables that are local to surrounding functions, such as the variable *x*.

Scopes are sometimes described by a series of *nested* boxes. To find a match for a given variable, the boxes are examined from the inside out until the name is found.

Lambda functions (introduced in Chapter 8) are simply a shorthand method for defining functions. They also create their own local scope, which is distinct from the surrounding function scope. In the following, the variable named *x* created inside the lambda is distinct from the variable named *x* that is the parameter for the surrounding function:

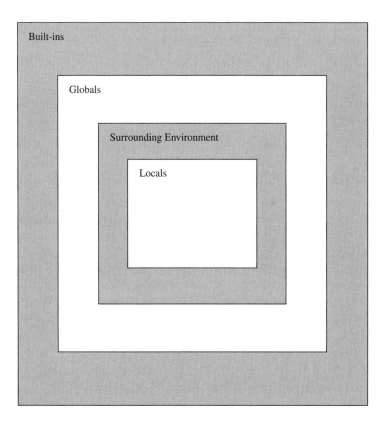

```
def a(x):
  f = lambda x: x + 3
  print f(3)
  print x # see that x is unchanged
>>> a(4)
7
4
```

The last level of the LEGB rule is the built-in scope that contains functions that are initially part of any Python program. These include functions such as `open` (for opening files) or `zip` (for combining two lists into one). Because these are simply names in the final scope level, they can be overridden in a different scope. For example, the programmer is free to write his own function named `open`. However, this action should be taken with great care, as most users will expect the names in the built-in scope to refer to the standard functions. Overriding the function named `open` would prevent access to the standard function from within the new scope.

The dir Function

A function named `dir` (for directory) can be used to access a list of the names in the current scope. If you print the value returned by this function at the topmost level, you will get the global scope. If you print the value within a function, you will get the local scope for that function. Here's an example:

```
>>> z = 12
>>> def dirtest():
...    x = 42
...    print dir()
>>> print dir()
['__builtins__', '__doc__', '__name__', 'dirtest', 'z']
>>> dirtest()
['x']
```

If you provide an argument to the `dir` function, you can discover the scope for the object. This works for functions, classes, and modules. Here's an example:

```
>>> dir(dirtest)
['__call__', '__class__', '__delattr__', '__dict__',
'__doc__', '__get__', '__getattribute__', '__hash__',
'__init__', '__module__', '__name__', '__new__',
'__reduce__', '__reduce_ex__', '__repr__', '__setattr__',
'__str__', 'func_closure', 'func_code', 'func_defaults',
'func_dict', 'func_doc', 'func_globals', 'func_name']
>>> dir(math)
['__doc__', '__file__', '__name__', 'acos', 'asin', 'atan',
'atan2', 'ceil', 'cos', 'cosh', 'degrees', 'e', 'exp', 'fabs',
'floor', 'fmod', 'frexp', 'hypot', 'ldexp', 'log', 'log10',
'modf', 'pi', 'pow', 'radians', 'sin', 'sinh', 'sqrt', 'tan',
'tanh']
```

The Global Statement

In general, the programmer has very little control over the scope level for variables; however, there are two exceptions to this rule: the *global* statement and the *from* statement for modules. The latter will be discussed as part of the larger exploration of modules. The *global* statement, which you first encountered in Chapter 3, tells the Python compiler that the indicated name is to refer to the variable in the global scope rather than the default, which would be the variable in the local scope. Here's an example:

```
def fun():
  global x
  x = 42 # now changes global, not local variable
>>> x = 12
>>> fun()
>>> print x
42
```

Notice that the *global* statement is necessary only if a variable is the target of an assignment. If a variable is simply being used, then the LEGB rule already specifies that the global variable will be accessed:

```
def fun():
   global x
   x = x + y # both x and y are global
>>> x = 3
>>> y = 4
>>> fun()
>>> print x
7
```

The fact that *access* to global variables is easy within functions but that *modification* is difficult (requires an explicit statement) is a purposeful design decision. The use of global variables can make programs difficult to understand, since assigning a global variable explicitly breaks an encapsulation barrier. There are times when this is necessary, so it should be possible, but the language forces the programmer to think about the issue each time this feature is used.

Class Scopes

Classes create a new scope in much the same fashion as function definitions. However, a curious feature is that class scopes are not part of the LEGB rule. The effect is that methods defined within a class can see their surrounding scope, but they cannot see the class scope. Normally classes are defined at the top level, so the surrounding scope for the method definitions is the global level. However, nothing in the language prevents a class from being defined inside a function. In this case, the surrounding scope for the methods is the surrounding function, not the class:

```
def silly():
  x = 12
  class A:
       x = 42
       def foo(self):
            print x
            print self.x
  return A()
>>> anA = silly() # create an instance of our inner class
>>> anA.foo()
12 # prints x local to silly, not x in class A
42 # prints x in class scope
```

The LEGB rule is why methods must go through the self variable to reference other methods or values defined at the class level.

Two different types of variables can be defined within a class scope. Variables that are simply defined at the class level are shared by all instances of the class. The initialization of these variables is performed only once—the first time the class statement is executed. Variables defined using the variable self are unique to each instance of the class. The following example illustrates class variables being used to count the number of instances of the class that have been created:

```
class CountingClass:
   count = 0
   def __init__ (self):
             count = count + 1

>>> a = CountingClass()
>>> b = CountingClass()
>>> print 'number of initializations:', CountingClass.count
number of initializations: 2
```

Scopes, Names, and References

Note that scope is a property of a *name*, not a property of a *value*. Two names can refer to the same value in Python, and they can frequently have different scopes. This is illustrated by the following example:

```
class Box(object):
   def __init__ (self, v): self.value = v

def newScope (x):
   y = x
   y.value = 42

>>> a = Box(3)
>>> newScope(a)
>>> print a.value
42
```

The variable *a* has global scope. When passed as an argument to the function newScope, it is assigned to the variable *x*. This variable is then used to assign to variable *y*. At this point, all three variables, *a*, *x*, and *y*, refer to the same object. But *x* and *y* have local scope. Nevertheless, a change to the internal state of the variable (in this case, changing the value attribute) will have an effect on the value referenced by the global variable *a*.

QUALIFIED NAMES

A *qualified name* is denoted by a period following a base, as in object.attribute. To determine the meaning of a qualified name, the meaning of the base is first determined using, for example, the LEGB rule. Once the base is known, the attribute is then determined in reference to the base. Several different types of names can be qualified. These include the following:

- **Classes** The attribute must be a variable defined within the class body.
- **Instances or objects** The attribute is a data field used to store the state of the object or a method defined for the object.

- **Instances of built-in types (such as list or dictionary)** The attribute can be a data field or, more commonly, a function (method) defined as part of the type.
- **Modules** The attribute is a data value or function defined in the module.

Qualified names serve much the same purpose as name scopes. Insisting that names be qualified by a base limits the proliferation of names in the broader scope. Similarly, the same name can be used in more than one qualified fashion and will refer to the attribute appropriate to the base.

Much of the mechanism associated with name scopes is built using simple dictionaries. For example, the current local name scope can always be found using the function `locals()`, and the current global scope using the function `globals()`. Classes store their name space in a field named `__dict__`, as do modules. All of these values can be examined by the programmer, although modifications to these values should be performed only with great care.

```
class A(object):
   x = 1
   def foo(self):
       return 'foo'
   def bar(self):
       return X
```

```
>>> print A.__dict__
{'__module__': '__main__', 'bar': <function bar at 0x4b470>,
'__dict__': <attribute '__dict__' of 'A' objects>, 'x': 1,
'foo': <function foo at 0x4b3f0>, '__weakref__': <attribute
'__weakref__' of 'A' objects>, '__doc__': None}
```

MODULES

Modules have been used since Chapter 3, yet we have not explained what a module is or showed you how to create your own modules. Now, with the benefit of an understanding of name spaces, you can do both.

The construction of a module is very simple. A module is simply a Python file, exactly the same as the program files you have been building since Chapter 2. What is different is the handling of the names in the module. This occurs during the execution of the *import* statement.

The *import* statement scans a file and executes each statement in the program, in exactly the same fashion that occurs when the file is given as an argument to the Python interpreter. The only difference is that rather than using the standard local dictionary, the names of all values defined within the module are stored in their own dictionary. This dictionary is held by a value of type `module`. Referencing a qualified name, `modName.x`, is in fact shorthand for the dictionary reference `modName.__dict__['x']`.

You can see this by examining the type associated with a module name after executing the *import* statement:

```
>>> import string
>>> print type(string)
<type 'module'>
>>> print string.__dict__['split']
<function split at 0x6b270>
```

It is now easy to explain the meaning of the *from* statement in terms of name spaces. When a *from* statement is encountered, the effect is first to import the specified module, constructing the module dictionary. The given attribute from this dictionary is then *copied* into the local dictionary. Thereafter, the attribute can be used without qualification, exactly as if it had been defined in the local space:

```
from modName import attribute
```

The difference between a simple import and a from import can have an important effect on execution time. Suppose you are using only the function `bar` from module `foo`. One approach would be to import the module:

```
import foo
```

You could then use the function `bar` by means of the qualified name, `foo.bar()`. However, each time you use this expression, two run-time lookups are performed. The first finds the meaning for the variable `foo` in the current name space. Next, a run-time lookup is performed to find the data field named `bar` in the dictionary associated with the value `foo`. If, on the other hand, you import just a single function, such as

```
from foo import bar
```

then the function `bar` is placed in the local name space. The function can then be invoked, without qualification, as `bar()`. Discovering the meaning of this name requires only one search, since the name is found in the local name space.

Most of the time, the difference in execution is not noticeable. However, if imported functions are used within a loop and executed many times, the difference in execution can be significant.

Avoiding Name Space Collisions When Importing Modules

It is possible to use a wildcard character (*) to import everything from a module into the current name space. However, this should be used with care, because any name in the current environment that matches a name in the imported name space will be overridden. For example, suppose you have sometime stored in a variable named *e* and then import everything from the `math` module:

```
>>> e = 42
>>> from math import *
>>> print e
2.71828182846
```

The `math` module defines the value *e* (the base of the natural logarithms). This definition has now replaced the earlier value associated with the name.

One way to avoid name space collisions when performing an import is to use the optional `as` clause on the *from* import statement. This clause allows the programmer to import a value but give it a new name in the local space:

```
>>> e = 42
>>> from math import e as eConst
>>> print e
42
>>> print eConst
2.71828182846
```

Creating Your Own Module

Creating your own module is surprisingly easy. A module is exactly like a Python program: it's simply a list of Python statements in a file. The difference is that the module is loaded using an *import* statement, rather than by being given directly to the Python interpreter.

Normally files that are used as modules contain only class and function definitions. However, this is just convention, and nothing in the language prevents the user from placing other types of statements in the module. All the statements will be executed when the module is loaded by the *import* statement.

The following illustrates a typical module. Here the module simply defines three functions for common data structures (a *stack*, a *queue*, and a *set*):

```
#
# Module for simple collection classes
#

class Stack(object):
    def __init__ (self):
        self.storage = [ ]

    def push (self, newValue):
        self.storage.append(newValue)

    def top (self):
        return self.storage[len(self.storage)-1]

    def pop (self):
        result = self.top()
        self.storage.pop()
        return result

    def isEmpty (self):
        return len(self.storage) == 0

class Queue(object):
```

```
    def __init__ (self):
        self.storage = [ ]

    def add (self, newValue):
        self.push = self.storage.append(newValue)

    def front (self):
        return self.storage[0]

    def removeFront (self):
        result = front()
        del self.storage[0]
        return result

    def isEmpty (self):
        return len(self.storage) == 0

class Set(object):
    def __init__ (self):
        self.storage = [ ]

    def add (self, newValue):
        if not newValue in self.storage:
            self.storage.append(newValue)

    def contains (self, testValue):
        return testValue in self.storage

    def remove (self, testValue):
        i = self.storage.find(testValue)
        if i:
            del(self.storage[i])
```

Testing the Name Space within a Module

Frequently, a program can be used either as a stand-alone application or as a module for a larger system. For example, the calculator program developed in Chapter 9 works as an application using a *textual* interface. However, we can also reuse the code for this application in another system that uses a graphical user interface (GUI), as you will see in Chapter 12.

When this occurs, you'll usually not want to execute some statements when the program is loaded as a module. Fortunately, the name of the current module is held in an internal variable called __name__. The top-level program executed by the Python interpreter is given the name __main__. Testing this value provides a means to execute statements conditionally. In our calculator program from Chapter 9, for example, we could replace the final statements with the following:

```
# only execute if we are being run as top level program
if __name__ == "__main__":
  calc = Calculator()
  calc.run()
```

Now the commands that begin the application will be executed only when the program is selected as the top-level command from the Python interpreter, not when the file is loaded as a module.

Module Reuse

The biggest feature that distinguishes modern software development from earlier approaches is an increased emphasis on *software reuse*. Rather than expecting that every program will be written entirely with new code from the first line to the last, applications are now almost always constructed from reusable *software libraries*. These libraries can be as simple as our data structure module described earlier, or much more complicated systems for performing network connections or parsing XML files.

One of the features that distinguishes Python is that it provides an extremely rich set of existing modules that can be reused in any new application. You have seen a number of these already. A few more will be used in the case studies in the second part of this book. Many more are documented on the Python Web site, at www.python.org.

Equally important, Python makes it easy, almost trivial, to create your own modules. A module is nothing more than a Python program stripped of the main driving statements.

As you advance in your Python programming skills, you will learn about many more useful modules. You should also strive to acquire a mindset that recognizes and values reusable code in your own programs. When you find a set of classes or functions that you think are general enough to be used for two or more different applications, package them as a module and use the same code in each of the new programs. Doing so will make you more productive and will make your programs more reliable and error-free.

EXERCISES

1. Consider the following program fragment. Imagine that execution has reached the *print* statement. Assign a letter from LEGB to each of the following identifiers according to whether the name is local, from an enclosing scope, global, or built-in.

```
a = 7

def fun(b):
  c = 17

  def morefun(d):
    e = 12
```

```
    print a + b + c + d + e

  morefun(3)

fun(5)
```

2. Try creating a simple function, such as the following, and print out the values in the locals dictionary. What values do you see? Are you surprised at any of the entries in this diction- ary? What values are stored in the dictionary returned by the function `globals()` at the point where the locals dictionary is being displayed?

```
a = 7

def fun(b):
  c = 17

  print "locals and globals inside the function"
  print locals()
  print globals()

fun(5)
print "locals and globals at the local level"
print locals()
print globals()
```

3. Try creating a nested function, such as the following, and print out the values in the locals dictionary. What values do you see? Are you surprised at any of the entries in this dictionary?

```
a = 7

def fun(b):
  c = 17

  def morefun(d):
    e = 12
    print locals()
    print globals()

  morefun(3)


fun(5)
```

4. Try creating a simple class, such as the following. What values are stored in the class dictionary, which can be accessed as the attribute __dict__ following the class name?

```
a = 7

class see:
  "a simple class definition"
  b = 12
  def fun(self, c):
    d = 17

a = see()
```

```
a.fun(12)
print see.__dict__
```

5. Try creating a class that inherits from another class, such as the following. What values are stored in the class dictionary?

```
a = 7

class see:
    "a simple class definition"
    b = 12
    def fun(self, c):
        d = 17

class more(see):
    "an inherited class"
    e = 17 # or 17 + see.b

a = more()
a.fun(12)
print more.__dict__
```

6. Try creating a simple module, such as the one described in the section "Creating Your Own Module." After loading the module, examine the module dictionary. This value can be accessed as the __dict__ attribute following the module name. Do any values in this dictionary surprise you? What purpose do you think these additional values serve?

7. If you look at the value of the dictionary returned by globals(), you will find a key named __builtin__. What do you think this represents? What type of value is this? How can you find the elements stored in this value?

8. If you call the function dir on a value of type class you will find a number of fields that begin with two underscores. As we have noted elsewhere, these typically indicate fields that are manipulated internally. Among the fields for a class are the following: __bases__, __dict__, __doct__, __module__, and __name__. Experiment with different class definitions and, by examining the values for these fields, see if you can figure out what they represent.

9. If you create an instance of a class, you can also invoke the dir function on this value. Fields in this dictionary include __class__ and __dict__. Experiment with different class definitions and see if you can figure out what these represent.

CHAPTER 11

Advanced Features

This chapter explains a few of the more advanced aspects of Python. These features are not commonly employed in most programs, but you might find them useful in special situations.

KEYWORD ARGUMENTS

All the examples used up to this point in the book have matched actual argument values to parameters according to their position—that is, the first argument is assigned to the first parameter, the second to the second, and so on. However, you can also pass function arguments by explicitly naming each parameter and specifying a value. In this case, the order of the arguments is unimportant and need not match the order of the parameters:

```
def printInfo (name, age, gender):
    print 'Name: ', name, 'Age: ', age, 'Gender: ', gender
>>> printInfo('sam smith', 32, 'male')
Name: sam smith Age: 32 Gender: male
>>> printInfo(name='robin jones', age=18, gender='female')
Name: robin jones Age: 18 Gender: female
>>> printInfo(age=12, gender='male', name='chris brown')
Name: chris brown Age: 12 Gender: male
```

If you omit any named parameters a `TypeError` will be produced:

```
>>> printInfo(name='randy jones', age=22)
Traceback (most recent call last):
File "<stdin>", line 1, in ?
TypeError: printInfo() takes exactly 3 non-keyword arguments (2 given)
```

You can mix positional and keyword arguments in the same call, providing the positional arguments are listed first:

```
>>> printInfo('robin smith', gender='female', age=23)
Name: robin smith Age: 23 Gender: female
```

Default Parameter Values

Parameter names in a function definition can optionally be followed by an assignment. The value to the right of the assignment is termed the *default value* and will be assigned to the parameter if the call does not provide an alternative argument value:

```
def incr (x, y = 1):
   return x + y

>>> incr(7)
8
>>> incr(7, 3)
10
```

The expressions appearing in default parameters are evaluated only once, at the time the function is defined. They are not reevaluated each time the function is called:

```
>>> a, b, c = 4, 5, 6
>>> def incr(x, y=b): return x + y
>>> b = 12 # change the value of b
>>> incr(2) # uses the value b had when function defined
7
```

Variable Length Argument Lists

If an asterisk (*) is placed in front of the last argument name, all remaining parameters are placed into a tuple and passed to this argument. This allows functions to take a variable number of arguments:

```
def many(name, *values):
   print name, values

>>> many("zero")
zero ()
>>> many("one", "abc")
one ('abc',)
>>> many("two", "abc", 23)
two ('abc', 23)
>>> many("three", "abc", 23, 3.1415)
three ('abc', 23, 3.1415000000000002)
```

If the last argument is preceded by two asterisks, all the remaining keyword arguments (those that have not already been matched to a parameter) are placed into a dictionary that is passed through the argument. Note that the keys in this dictionary are strings representing the argument names:

```
def echo(**args):
   for e in args.keys(): print e,":",args[e]
```

```
>>> echo(a=3)
a : 3
>>> echo(a=3, b='abc', c=3.14)
a : 3
c : 3.14
b : abc
```

You can combine the variable positional argument with the variable keyword argument, as long as the latter is written last. Any remaining positional parameters will be assigned to the first, while any remaining keyword arguments will be assigned to the latter:

```
def silly(name, number, *vargs, **kargs):
  print name, ':', number
  print vargs
  print kargs
>>> silly('one', 32)
one : 32
()
{}
>>> silly('two', 42, 3.14, 42, x=32, z='z')
two : 42
(3.1400000000000001, 42)
{'x': 32, 'z': 'z'}
```

Apply and Call

As noted in Chapter 6, a function is simply a value like any other value. Functions can be assigned to a variable, passed as argument, or returned from a function. The function `apply` takes as argument a function and a list of arguments. The function is invoked binding the elements of the list to the function parameters. The resulting value is then returned as the result of calling `apply`:

```
def sum(x, y): return x + y

>>>> apply(sum, [7, 3])
10
```

Keyword arguments can be passed in a dictionary supplied as the third argument. Note that the dictionary represents the variable names as strings:

```
>>> apply(sum, [], {'y':4, 'x':12})
16
```

OBJECT OVERLOADING

Any legal Python operation can be applied to a user-defined type. The programmer can provide a behavior for the operation by defining a function with the appropriate name. It is only when the interpreter is unable to find a function with the appropriate name that an error will be generated. Because the functions are used internally, they follow the two-underscore prefix and suffix convention.

For example, suppose you want to create a `Box` object that stores a numeric value. Two `Box` objects can be added, resulting in a new `Box` that holds their sum. You could achieve this behavior by writing the following class:

```
class Box (object):
    def __init__ (self, v):
        self.value = v
    def __str__ (self):
        return 'Box [' + str(self.value) + ']'
    def __add__ (self, right):
        return Box(self.value + right.value)


>>> print Box(3)
Box[3]
>>> print Box(3) + Box(4)
Box[7]
```

This example also illustrates the use of the function `__str__`, which is internally invoked to convert a user-defined object into a string. When two instances of a `Box` are added, the function `__add__` is invoked. In this case, the function is creating a new `Box` that holds the sum of the argument values.

Other operators are implemented in a similar fashion. The following table lists a few of the more common operators and their functional equivalents:

Operation	Equivalent Function
a + b	__add__ (a, b)
a − b	__sub__ (a, b)
a * b	__mul__ (a, b)
a / b	__div__ (a, b)
a % b	__mod__ (a, b)
a & b	__and__ (a, b)
-a	__neg__ (a)
len(a)	__len__ (a)
a.b	__getitem__ (a, b)
a.b = c	__setitem__ (a, b, c)
str(a)	__str__ (a)
if a	__nonzero__ (a)
int(a)	__int__ (a)
a(b, c, d)	__call__ (a, b, c, d)

REGULAR EXPRESSIONS AND STRING PROCESSING

The method `find` is used to find a fixed string embedded within a larger string. For example, to locate the text "fis" within the string "existasfisamatic," you can execute the following:

```
>>> s = 'existasfisamatic'
>>> s.find('fis')
7
```

The length of the search string (in this case, 3) gives you the size of the matched text. But what if you were searching for a floating-point constant? A number has not only an indefinite number of digits, but it also may or may not have a fractional part, and it may or may not have an exponent. Even if you can locate the start of the string (by, for example, searching for a digit character), how do you determine the length of the matched text?

The solution is to use a technique called *regular expression notation*. Regular expression notations were being used by mathematicians and computer scientists even before computers were common. The particular notation used by the Python library derives from conventions originating with the Unix operating system. In Python, the regular expression package is found in the module named `re`.

Expression	Description
Text	Matches literal
^	Start of string
$	End of string
(. . .)*	Zero or more occurrences
(. . .)+	One or more occurrences
(. . .)?	Optional (zero or one)
[chars]	One character from range
[^chars]	One character not from range
pat | pat	Alternative (one or the other)
(. . .)	Group
.	Any character except newline

The regular expression notation will at first seem cryptic; but it has the advantage of being short, and, with practice, you'll find it easy to understand and remember. The most common regular expression notations are shown in the table above. Symbols such as ^ and $ are used to represent the start and end of a string. Parentheses can be used for grouping, and the * and + signs are used to represent the idea of one or more, or zero or more, respectively. Square brackets denote *character classes*, a single character from a given set of values. Dashes help simplify the description of a range of characters—for example a-f represents the set *abcdef*, and A-Z can be used to match any capital letter.

Let's see how to define a regular expression for floating-point literals. The basic unit is the *digit*. This is a single character from a range of possibilities (sometimes termed a *character class*). Square brackets are used to surround the list of possible characters. So this could be written as [0123456789]. However, when the characters are part of a sequential group of ASCII characters, the regular expression library allows you to list simply the starting and ending points, as in [0-9]. (Other common sequences of characters are the lowercase letter, a-z, and the uppercase letters, A-Z.) Since our floating-point number begins with one or more digits, we need to surround the pattern with parentheses and a plus sign, as in ([0-9])+.

Next, we need a pattern to match a decimal point followed by zero or more digits. Literal characters generally represent themselves, but the period has a special meaning, so it must be escaped, which looks like this: \.([0-9])*. If we want to make it optional, we surround it with a question mark, as in (\.([0-9])*)?.

Finally, we have the optional exponent part, which is followed by an optional sign, and a number consisting of one or more digits: ([eE]([+-])?([0-9])+)?. Putting everything together gives us our final pattern:

```
([0-9])+(\.[0-9]*)?([eE]([+-])?([0-9])+)?
```

Having defined the regular expression pattern, we must then compile it into a *regular expression object*. The regular expression object is an internal form used for pattern matching. The following illustrates this process:

```
>>> import re
>>> pat = re.compile("([0-9])+(\.[0-9]*)?([eE]([+-])?([0-9])+)?")
```

(Make sure you qualify the name compile with the prefix re, because another function named compile is included in the standard library, and it completes a totally different task.) The pattern then supports a number of different search operations. The simplest of these is named search. This operation takes as argument a text string and returns a match object. Again, make sure you qualify the name. A match object supports various different operations. One is to test whether or not the match was successful:

```
>>> text = "the value 2.45e-35 is close to correct"
>>> mtcobj = pat.search(text)
>>> if mtcobj: print "found it"
found it
```

However, the match object can also tell you the starting and ending positions of the matched text:

```
>>> print mtcobj.start(), mtcobj.end()
10 18
>>> text[mtcobj.start():mtcobj.end()]
2.45e-35
```

A table in Appendix A lists the most common operations found in the regular expression module.

ITERATORS AND GENERATORS

The *for* loop has this general form:

```
for ele in collection:
```

In earlier chapters, you saw how different types of collections can be used with a *for* loop. If the collection is a string, the loop iterates over the characters in the string. If it is a list, the elements in the list are generated. If the collection is a dictionary, the elements refer to the keys for the dictionary. Finally, if the collection is a file, the elements produced are the individual lines from the file.

It is also possible to create a user-defined object that interacts with the *for* statement. This happens in two steps. In the first step, the *for* statement passes the message __iter__ to the collection. This function should return a value that understands the *iterator protocol*. The iterator protocol consists of a single method, named next, that is expected to produce values in turn until the collection is exhausted. Once exhausted, the function must raise a StopIteration exception.

The following two classes illustrate this behavior. The first class maintains a collection of values stored in a list. When an iterator is requested, it creates an instance of another class named SquareIterator. The SquareIterator class cycles through the values in the list, returning the square of every element.

```
class SquareCollection (object):
    def __init__ (self):
        self.values = [ ]
    def add (self, v):
        self.values.append(v)
    def __iter__ (self):
        return SquareIterator(self)


class SquareIterator (object):
    def __init__ (self, c):
        self.container = c
        self.index = 0
    def next (self):
        if self.index >= len(self.container.values):
            raise StopIteration
        result = self.container.values[self.index] ** 2
        self.index += 1
        return result

>>> s = SquareCollection()
>>> s.add(3)
```

```
>>> s.add(4)
>>> s.add(2)
>>> for e in s: print e
9
16
4
>>>
```

If the __iter__ method is not defined, the *for* statement tries an older and simpler protocol. It generates a series of index values, from 0 onward, and invokes the method __getitem__. This method either returns a value or raises an exception. The loop continues until the exception is raised. Here is a simple class that illustrates this behavior. Notice that this time the class does not hold any actual values, only the upper limit for execution:

```
class SquareTo (object):
    def __init__ (self, m):
        self.max = m
    def __getitem__ (self, i):
        if i >= self.max:
            raise StopIteration
        return i ** 2
```

Executing a for loop with an instance of this class produces a sequence of squares:

```
>>> for e in SquareTo(5): print e
0
1
4
9
16
>>>
```

The iterator technique is useful for collection classes, but it can be awkward in other situations. A useful abstraction that is layered on top of iterators is the idea of a *generator*. A generator is a function that can be suspended in the middle of execution and restarted from the point of suspension. To suspend a function, simply use the statement yield instead of the statement return. A suspended function can be restarted until it executes a normal return or until it runs out of statements to execute (that is, "falls off the end").

The following is an example generator. This function produces values from the Fibonacci sequence until they exceed the limit provided by the argument:

```
def genfib (n):
    a = 0
    yield a
    b = 1
    yield b
```

```
    while b < n:
        a, b = b, a+b
        yield b
```

When used in a *for* statement, the generator runs through its values:

```
>>> for e in genfib(20): print e
0
1
1
2
3
5
8
13
21
>>>
```

Behind the scenes, the generator is producing a value that satisfies the iterator protocol. You can see this by capturing the value and executing the method next that it supports.

```
>>> x = genfib(3)
>>> x.next()
0
>>> x.next()
1
>>> x.next()
... # so on, until
>>> x.next()
Traceback (most recent call last):
File "<stdin>", line 1, in ?
StopIteration
>>>
```

MODULE RELOAD

As described in Chapter 10, when an *import* statement is executed, the associated module is executed and the resulting name space is stored in a variable with the module name. However, if the programmer tries to import the same module twice, the second import has no effect. This can be seen by creating a simple module that has a side effect, such as printing a value. Create a file named *printMe.py* with nothing more than a *print* statement:

```
print 'Print me!'
```

If you try to import the file more than once, only the first will have any effect:

```
>>> import PrintMe
Print Me!
>>> import PrintMe
>>>
```

If you want to re-execute an already imported module, you must use the state-ment `reload`. The argument for this statement is the previously created `module` object:

```
>>> reload(PrintMe)
Print Me!
<module 'PrintMe' from 'PrintMe.pyc'>
>>>
```

This feature is chiefly used when debugging a module, as it permits the pro-grammer to make changes to the module file, and then reload the file to see the effects of the change.

DOCUMENTATION STRINGS

In addition to comments, Python supports an alternative mechanism for provid-ing documentation on functions, classes, modules, and methods. This is called a *docstring*. Syntactically, a docstring is simply a string that appears immediately after the line containing the `def` in a function or method, or the keyword `class` in a class description, or at the beginning of a file for a module. For illustration, consider the following simple module stored in a file name *docStringTest.py*:

```
'''This is a module
to illustrate the docstring
facility'''

class Aclass (object):
  'you can describe a class here'

  def aMethod (self):
      "this method returns 3"
      return 3

def aFun (x, y):
  "this function multiplies x and y"
  return x * y
```

The comments contribute marginally to the readability of the code, but probably no more so than would comments that used the # syntax. However, the advantage of docstrings is that they are recognized by the Python interpreter and stored along with the objects as an attribute named __doc__. This attribute can be read at run-time:

```
>>> import docStringTest
```

```
>>> print docStringTest.__doc__
This is a module
to illustrate the docstring
facility
>>> print docStringTest.Aclass.__doc__
you can describe a class here
>>> print docStringTest.Aclass.aMethod.__doc__
this method returns 3
>>> print docStringTest.aFun.__doc__
this function multiplies x and y
>>>
```

   While most programmers are unlikely to spend the time creating docstrings for
their own code, it is fortunate that the creators of the modules in the standard distribution have done so. You can discover basic information about most built-in functions
and modules simply by printing their docstrings:

```
>>> print abs.__doc__
abs(number) -> number
Return the absolute value of the argument.
>>> print range.__doc__
range([start,] stop[, step]) -> list of integers
Return a list containing an arithmetic progression of integers.
range(i, j) returns [i, i+1, i+2, . . . , j-1]; start (!) defaults to 0.
When step is given, it specifies the increment (or decrement).
For example, range(4) returns [0, 1, 2, 3]. The end point is omitted!
These are exactly the valid indices for a list of 4 elements.
>>> import random
>>> print random.randint.__doc__
Return random integer in range [a, b], including both end points.
>>>
```

PART 2

Case Studies

GUI Programming with Tkinter

These days, most computer users have little difficulty interacting with computer programs by means of a graphical user interface, or GUI. Conventions in GUI programming that are now commonplace include such items as windows, menus, buttons, text boxes, and scrollbars. The Python language does not provide a standard library for creating GUI components, but a number of different libraries have been adapted to work with Python.

This chapter explores *Tkinter*, the most commonly used Python library. The Tkinter library was developed in conjunction with the Tcl programming language. Since then, the Tcl/Tkinter facility has been ported to a number of different platforms and languages. The Tkinter module is now normally found as part of every Python installation.

TKINTER EXAMPLE: VARIATIONS ON HELLO, WORLD!

The traditional first example for any GUI library is a window that displays a hopelessly cheerful message. Using the Tkinter module, this can be performed as follows:

```
import Tkinter

root = Tkinter.Tk()
root.title("Hello example")
```

```
root.geometry("200x100")

w = Tkinter.Label(root, text="Hello, world!")
w.pack()

root.mainloop()
```

Let's examine this program line by line. The *import* statement loads the Tkinter library. As with most windowing systems, Tkinter is based around the concept of nested rectangular regions called *windows* or *frames*. The highest level frame is termed the *root frame* and is returned as the value of the function `Tk()`. The function `title` sets the title of this region, and the function `geometry` takes a string that represents the size of the window as a width and height pair.

Within the root window is a label, which is among the simplest form of GUI *widget* (or component). A label takes a simple text message. The Tkinter library is somewhat unusual in that many of the arguments for the functions defined in the library employ *keyword arguments*, rather than the more conventional *placement arguments*. See Chapter 11 for a discussion of keyword arguments.

The function `pack` makes the label component visible, while the function `mainloop` initiates the windowing main loop. The program halts when the user clicks the close box for the main window. The illustration at the beginning of this section shows what this program looks like on a Macintosh. The graphical components follow the conventions of the underlying operating system, and hence will have a different look on different platforms.

Because the Tkinter library defines a large number of symbolic values as well as functions, it becomes tedious to preface each with the name *Tkinter*. By using the `from` form of the *import* statement, the definitions in the module become part of the local name space and the prefix can be omitted. In this fashion, the program becomes slightly less wordy:

```
from Tkinter import *

root = Tk()
root.title("Hello example")
root.geometry("200x100")

w = Label(root, text="Hello, world!")
w.pack()

root.mainloop()
```

This convention will be used in the remaining examples.

EVENT-DRIVEN PROGRAMMING

GUI systems are an example of *event-driven programming*, sometimes termed *reactive systems*. In normal programming, the flow of control is dictated by the programmer, and the end user normally has very little control over execution. In event-driven programming, the end user specifies the actions to perform using features such as buttons, text boxes, and scrollbars. The program then *reacts* to the user's actions, performing whatever is required. For this reason, event-driven programs are also sometimes termed *asynchronous* programs.

The Tkinter library attaches actions to graphical components using a technique called a *callback*. The programmer specifies a function to be invoked, attaching this to a graphical component when the component is created. Later, when the end user interacts with the component (by pressing a button, for example), the function is invoked.

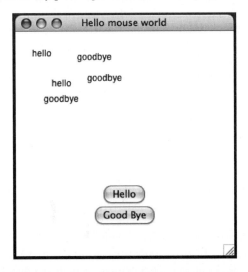

This can be illustrated with a slightly more complicated version of the hello world program. This version features two buttons and also reacts to mouse clicks in the region of the window. When the mouse is clicked, the text "hello" is printed at the location of the mouse click. By clicking the buttons, the user can change the text of the message.

```
from Tkinter import *
root = Tk()
root.geometry("300x300")
root.title("Hello mouse world")
canvas = Canvas(root)
text = "hello"

def sayHello():
  global text
  text = "hello"

def sayGoodbye():
  global text
  text = "goodbye"
```

```
def buttonPressed(evt):
    if evt.widget == canvas:
        canvas.create_text(evt.x, evt.y, text=text)

hellob = Button(root, text="Hello", command=sayHello)
goodbyeb = Button(root, text="Good Bye", command=sayGoodbye)
root.bind("<Button-1>", buttonPressed)

canvas.pack()
hellob.pack()
goodbyeb.pack()

root.mainloop()
```

The structure of the program is similar to that of the first example. The root window is placed into the variable named `root`. On the root window is a *canvas*, a type of component that understands a number of graphical operations. In addition to the canvas, our application will have two more components, both instances of the class `Button`. The constructor for each of these buttons requires as argument the name of a function that will be invoked when the button is clicked. Because the button cannot be created until these functions are known, the assignment statement that creates the button must appear after the function definitions. Similarly, the action for the button click is specified by a callback function given as argument to the function `root.bind`. (The arguments to the function root.bind are, inconsistently, given by a positional argument while the button uses a keyword argument.) Various different arguments for the bind function can be used to attach commands to a variety of mouse motions.

The functions for the button click change the value of the global variable named `text`. The argument for the button event requires an argument that will be given a value of type `event`. The event object records such information as the widget in which the event occurred, and the x and y locations for the event. Because this function is invoked for all mouse down events, even the button clicks, an *if* statement is used to verify that the mouse was clicked inside the canvas. In this case, it prints a text message at the given x and y coordinate.

The program ends by making the components visible, and then it starts the event loop. As the user clicks the various components, the display is updated.

SLIDERS, FONTS, AND OTHER VARIATIONS

We can illustrate a few more of the capabilities of Tkinter by adding a slider at the bottom of the screen that can be used to change the size of the text, and a drop down menu that can be used to change the font.

Let's start with the slider. Two types of sliders are available in Tkinter: scrollbars and scales. Scrollbars are used exclusively with lists and canvases, and scales are used for any numeric display. The constructor for the scale takes the lower and upper bounds for the range of values, an orientation, and the name of a callback function. Because the word `from` is a keyword in Python, the lower bound is set by an argument named `_from` (note the underscore). The callback function is presented with a string argument, which is the value of the scrollbar. The functions `set` and `get` can also be used to set or retrieve the value of the slider. A slider typically spans the entire width of the window, and this can be indicated by an argument in the `pack` command:

```
size = 10 # variable that will be set by slider

def updateSize(svalue): # call back for slider
  global size
  size = int(svalue)

slide = Scale(root,from_=5,to=24,orient=HORIZONTAL,command=updateSize)
slide.set(12)

slide.pack(fill=X)
```

To change the size of the text being printed, simply alter the `text` printing command as follows:

```
canvas.create_text(evt.x, evt.y, text=text, font=("Times", size))
```

We will next add features to alter the font using menu commands. As with the size, we create a `global` variable to hold the font name and some callback functions to change the value held by this variable:

```
fontname="Times"

def settimes():
  global fontname
  fontname = "Times"

def sethelvetica():
  global fontname
  fontname = "Helvetica"

menubar = Menu(root)
fontMenu = Menu(menubar)
fontMenu.add("command",label="Times", command=settimes)
fontMenu.add_command(label="Helvetica", command=sethelvetica)
menubar.add_cascade(label="Font", menu=fontMenu)
```

Next, two new menus are created. The one stored in menu bar will be the top level menu, while the one stored in the variable `fontMenu` will be a *cascaded* menu, displayed when the font menu is selected. The two menus will each have a callback function attached to it. The `create_text` command is now changed to use the font name stored in the `global` variable. As a final step, the top level window must be told to use the new menu bar. This is accomplished using the following command typically just before calling the function `mainloop`:

```
root.config(menu=menubar)
```

With these two changes, the user can dynamically alter both the font and the size of the text displayed.

TELEPHONE DATABASE UPDATED

The next example improves the telephone database application originally presented in Chapter 5, giving it a GUI. As in the Chapter 5 application, this example will use the `shelve` module to provide persistence to values between sessions. The GUI for this application is shown here:

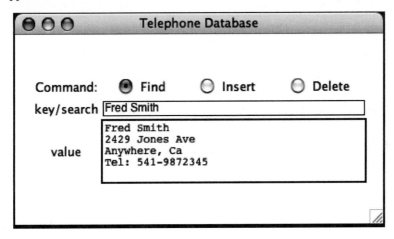

The command to be performed is indicated by a series of *radio buttons*. A radio button allows only one command to be selected at a time. When the button is clicked, a variable is changed and a callback function is invoked. The key field used for indexing or inserting a value into the database is specified by a widget of type `Entry`, while the text of the value stored is a widget of type `Text`.

This example also uses a more complicated layout manager, called a *grid layout*. The *pack* layout, used in the earlier examples, placed widgets one on top of another, top to bottom. The grid layout allows the programmer to specify the location of widgets within a grid of components. Each component is assigned a row and column number within this grid. Components are allowed to span several grid cells. For example, the `entry` component spans three different cells.

```
import shelve
from Tkinter import *
```

```python
data = shelve.open("database")
root = Tk()
root.geometry("400x200")
root.title("Telephone Database")

# make some of the widgets
cmd = IntVar()
lab = Label(root, text="Command:")
kl = Label(root, text="key/search")
ke = Entry(root, width=40)
vl = Label(root, text="value")
ve = Text(root, width=40, height=5)

def doRadio():
  c = cmd.get() # get the command number
  if c == 1: # search
      ve.delete("1.0", END)
      if data.has_key(ke.get()):
          ve.insert(END, data[ke.get()])
      else:
          ve.insert(END,"no information for key" + ke.get())
  elif c == 2: # insert
      data[ke.get()] = ve.get("1.0", END)
      ve.delete("1.0", END)
      ve.insert(END, "database has been updated")
  else: # delete
      del data[ke.get()]
      ve.delete("1.0", END)
      ve.insert(END, "entry has been deleted")

# finish making widgets
r1=Radiobutton(root,text="Find",variable=cmd,value=1, command=doRadio)
r2=Radiobutton(root,text="Insert",variable=cmd,value=2,command=doRadio)
r3=Radiobutton(root,text="Delete",variable=cmd,value=3,command=doRadio)

# lay out the grid
lab.grid(row=0, column=0)
r1.grid(row=0, column=1)
r2.grid(row=0, column=2)
r3.grid(row=0, column=3)
kl.grid(row=1, column=0)
ke.grid(row=1, column=1, columnspan=3)
vl.grid(row=2, column=0)
ve.grid(row=2, column=1, columnspan=3)
```

```
# loop over main program, save database after user quits
root.mainloop()
data.close()
```

Do not try to mix pack and grid layout commands. Doing so invariably results in the windowing system falling into a loop. If you believe you need to mix the two styles, place the grid items into a *frame* (see next section), and then pack the frame into the outer window.

Only a few statements in the program are different from those in earlier examples. The radio buttons communicate with their callback function by means of a global variable of type `IntVar`. An `IntVar` can be set and read. Similar widgets, named `StringVar` and `DoubleVar`, are used for storing and retrieving string and floating point values, respectively.

Insertions and deletions in the text component are specified by a string that indicates a row and column location. The initial location is given by the string `1.0`. This indicates the zero character in the first line. The end of the text area is described by the symbolic constant `END`. Specifying these two values to the `delete` command will erase the value stored in the component. Alternatively, specifying these two values in the `get` method will return the entire text string.

Finally, for the first time, we see a statement appearing after the call on `mainloop`. This statement will be executed after the user has halted the program by clicking the close button on the main window. In this case, the statement is closing the `shelve` database.

ADDING A DIALOG

Clicking the Insert radio button changes the entry stored in the database under the given key. This has the effect of erasing anything stored previously under the key. This might be the intended behavior, but it might not. If there is an existing entry, it might be prudent to ask the user whether or not he intended to overwrite it.

In the GUI convention, this type of action is performed by a dialog, as shown here. A *dialog* is a special type of window that appears when the system requires more information from the user before it can proceed. Execution halts until the necessary information is supplied in the dialog.

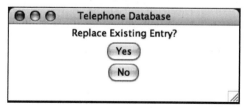

We can implement a dialog by creating a special class for the window:

```
class YesNoDialog (Toplevel):
    def __init__ (self, par, t, var):
```

```
        Toplevel.__init__(self, par)
        self.geometry("300x300")
        self.parent = par
        self.var = var
        f = Frame(self)
        lab = Label(f, text=t)
        byes = Button(f, text="Yes", command=self.ok)
        bno = Button(f, text="No", command=self.notok)
        lab.pack()
        byes.pack()
        bno.pack()
        f.pack()
        self.wait_window(self)
    def ok (self):
        self.var.set("yes")
        self.parent.focus_set()
        self.destroy()
    def notok (self):
        self.var.set("no")
        self.parent.focus_set()
        self.destroy()
```

This class inherits behavior from a Tkinter class named `Toplevel`, which is used to created top-level windows. The constructor for the dialog takes as argument the parent window (in our case, the root window), the text to be displayed, and an instance of `StringVar` through which the result will be passed back to the application. A `Frame` is created to hold the components of our dialog. Our dialog consists of a label and two buttons: Yes and No. When an instance of the dialog is created, it suspends execution of the main window and shifts focus to itself by means of the function `wait_window`. After the user clicks one of the buttons, the string variable is set, the focus is returned to the parent class, and the dialog is destroyed.

To create a dialog, the programmer first creates a string variable, and then creates an instance of class `YesNoDialog`. The constructor for the latter will not complete until the user has responded to the dialog. After this, testing the value of the string variable will indicate the user's response:

```
yesNoVar = StringVar()
YesNoDialog(root, "Overwrite existing entry?", yesNoVar)
if yesNoVar.get() == 'yes':
    . . .
```

CALCULATOR PROGRAM

The final example program updates the calculator program originally discussed in Chapter 9, placing a graphical user interface on top of the calculator engine. Once again we will use a grid component, and a number of buttons. In this example we have placed the GUI creation in the constructor for a class, in keeping with the object-oriented theme of the calculator program created in Chapter 9.

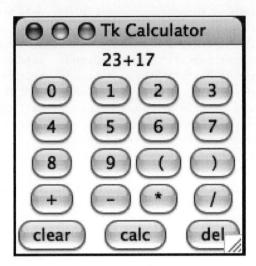

Because the majority of the buttons differ from each other only in the text they specify, they are defined here with callback functions using *lambda expressions*. The lambda can, in turn, invoke a method in the class, passing the character for the button as an argument to the method. The alternative would have required defining a separate method for each button.

The Clear and Del buttons both manipulate the string variable used by the label. The Calc button is slightly larger than the others. When clicked, the Calc button passes the text in the label to the calculator engine developed in Chapter 9. (Here we assume that the calculator program has been repackaged as a module named Calc. Modifications to remove the two lines that start the textual application were described in Chapter 10.) The value returned by this function is then placed into the label variable. This is in keeping with the themes of community and software reuse developed in that chapter.

Having written the calculator program, we have no reason to reinvent the program, so we can simply use it as a service provided to the CalcGui class.

```
from Tkinter import *
import Calc

root = Tk()
root.title("Tk Calculator")

class CalcGui (object):
   def __init__ (self):
        # load the calculator engine
```

```
self.calcEngine = Calc.Calculator()
# now create the gui
self.labelString = StringVar()
lab = Label(root, textvariable=self.labelString)
b0 =Button(root,text="0",command=lambda: self.buttonAction('0'))
b1 =Button(root,text="1",command=lambda: self.buttonAction('1'))
b2 =Button(root,text="2",command=lambda: self.buttonAction('2'))
b3 =Button(root,text="3",command=lambda: self.buttonAction('3'))
b4 =Button(root,text="4",command=lambda: self.buttonAction('4'))
b5 =Button(root,text="5",command=lambda: self.buttonAction('5'))
b6 =Button(root,text="6",command=lambda: self.buttonAction('6'))
b7 =Button(root,text="7",command=lambda: self.buttonAction('7'))
b8 =Button(root,text="8",command=lambda: self.buttonAction('8'))
b9 =Button(root,text="9",command=lambda: self.buttonAction('9'))
blp=Button(root,text=" (",command=lambda:self.buttonAction('('))
brp=Button(root,text=" )",command=lambda:self.buttonAction(')'))
bplus=Button(root,text="+",command=lambda:self.buttonAction('+'))
bminus=Button(root,text="-",command=lambda:self.buttonAction('-'))

btimes=Button(root,text="*",command=lambda:self.buttonAction('*'))
bdivide=Button(root,text="/",command=lambda: self.buttonAction( '/'))
bclear= Button(root, text="clear", command=self.doClearButton)
bcal = Button(root, text="calc", command=self.doCalcButton)
bdel = Button(root, text="del", command=self.doDelButton)
lab.grid(row=0, column=0, columnspan=4)
b0.grid(row=1, column=0)
b1.grid(row=1, column=1)
b2.grid(row=1, column=2)
b3.grid(row=1, column=3)
b4.grid(row=2, column=0)
b5.grid(row=2, column=1)
b6.grid(row=2, column=2)
b7.grid(row=2, column=3)
b8.grid(row=3, column=0)
b9.grid(row=3, column=1)
blp.grid(row=3, column=2)
brp.grid(row=3, column=3)
bplus.grid(row=4, column=0)
bminus.grid(row=4, column=1)
btimes.grid(row=4, column=2)
bdivide.grid(row=4, column=3)
bclear.grid(row=5, column=0)
bcal.grid(row=5, column=1, columnspan=2)
bdel.grid(row=5, column=3)
```

```
    def buttonAction (self, c):
        self.labelString.set(self.labelString.get() + c)

    def doClearButton(self):
        self.labelString.set("")

    def doCalcButton(self):
        self.labelString.set(self.calcEngine.eval(self.labelString.get()))

    def doDelButton(self):
        self.labelString.set(self.labelString.get()[:-1])

if __name__ == "__main__": # only do if invoked as application
    c = CalcGui()
    root.mainloop()
```

MORE INFORMATION ON TKINTER

You can learn more about Tkinter by using the Python system itself and the online
help facility, as discussed in Appendix A. Appendix A also includes a bare-bones
description of the more basic Tkinter functions. For a more comprehensive tutorial,
search the Internet using the words "Python Tkinter" to reveal a number of sources
for information on using the Tkinter system in Python.

A larger collection of useful widgets has been developed on top of Tkinter and
packaged as the *Python Megawidgets* library. These can be obtained from http://
pmw.sourceforge.net.

Alternative GUI toolkits for Python include the Python Gimp Toolkit, PyGTK
(www.pygtk.org) and the Python Open GL Toolkit, PyOpenGL (http://pyopengl
.sourceforge.net). The Jython system is a Python interpreter written entirely in Java
(www.jython.org/Project/). Because it is a Java program, it can access the Java windowing toolkits (both Python AWT and Swing). You can also add a GUI to a program
by using a web browser, which is explored in a series of examples in Chapters 13–15.

EXERCISES

1. Try changing the size of the buttons in the hello world program using the options
   width=n and height=n. What is the effect? The description of the slide widget
   showed how to make the component as wide as the window using the argument pad=X
   with the pack command. What happens if you do this with a button?

2. Another option for the pack command is side=*loc*, where *loc* is LEFT, RIGHT, TOP,
   BOTTOM, or CENTER. Experiment using this option on the buttons from the hello world
   example and explain their effect.

3. Write a simple temperature conversion utility that consists of an entry field and two buttons. When the button labeled Celsius is clicked, the entry field is converted from Fahrenheit to Celsius. Conversely, when the button labeled Fahrenheit is clicked, the value is converted from Celsius to Fahrenheit.

4. Rewrite the temperature conversion utility to use a scale and a label. The user selects a temperature in Celsius using the scale, and the equivalent temperature in Fahrenheit is shown in the label.

5. The text of a button can be set using a `textvariable=var` option, rather than the `text=str`. This causes the current value of a `StringVar` to be the text displayed on the button. Modify the hello world program so that the text displayed at button down events can be set by an entry box.

6. As in question 5, rewrite the hello world program so that the text displayed when a mouse down event occurs can be changed dynamically. However, this time add a menu bar and menu items so that the text can be selected from a variety of alternatives specified by a menu item.

7. Rewrite the application from question 6 so that one of the menu items produces a dialog box in which the user can enter the text to be displayed on mouse down events.

8. Rewrite the hello world program that reacts to mouse events to use a grid layout rather than the pack layout. Place the two buttons side-by-side under the canvas widget.

9. Keypress events are captured in a similar fashion to mouse presses, by binding the root window using the selector `<KeyPress>` and a callback function. The callback is given a single argument of type `Event`. The field named `char` in this object holds the value of the key that was pressed. Create an application that captures keypresses and displays the value as a string in a `Label` widget.

10. Add a search feature to the telephone database. When the Search radio button is clicked, the text in the key field is used as a search pattern. The first entry in which the search pattern occurs is printed. If no entry in the database matches the search pattern, a message is printed.

11. Using a grid layout, rewrite the yes/no dialog to place the buttons next to each other under the text message.

12. Using the different selectors for the `bind` method (see Appendix A), write a simple application that prints the location of mouse down, mouse motion, and mouse enter, and exit actions. Each event requires a different callback function. The function should simply print a message in a label box, indicating the type of event that has occurred.

13. Try adding the following two lines to the constructor for the `dialog` class. What do you predict they will do?

```
self.bind("<Return>", self.ok)
self.bind("<Escape>", self.notok)
```

14. Generalize the yes/no dialog by adding a pair of optional parameters that describe the text of the buttons. The optional values should be *yes* and *no*, but the user could replace these with *true/false*, *zero/or*, or any other binary choice.

CHAPTER

Case Study:
Web-Based Applications

This chapter begins the first of three case studies that explore one of the major application areas for Python programs: using Python in support of web-based programming. The application in this chapter is purposely simple, a rewriting of the *Eliza* application explored in Chapter 4. In this chapter, however, the application is initiated from a web page using a web browser that serves as the graphical interface for the program.

In the next chapter, we will develop a simple blog (a web log). A blog is a vehicle for an author (the *blog writer*) to share ideas and opinions with many readers. In the third case study in Chapter 15, we will develop a *wiki*, a vehicle for many authors to cooperate in the publication of information.

CLIENT/SERVER COMPUTING

All three case study applications are initiated from commands embedded in a web page. Since web pages can be shared, this style of operation means that users can be anywhere in the world; all they need is a web browser connected to the Internet.

The computer on which the user (the web browser) is running is different from the computer in which the Python program is executed. This style of execution is known as *client/server computing*. The client/server model is a simple way to allow sharing between two or more computers across a network. The end user runs an application, such as a web browser, on the *client* machine. This application sends a request for information (for example, a request for a web page) to another computer, the *server*. The server bundles the response for the information, such as the web page, and sends it back to the client. The client computer then formats and displays the response.

A client/server application can be viewed in several parts: the code that runs on the client machine, the code that runs on the server machine, and the commands that are transferred between the two.

Web pages are normally represented by *files* stored in a particular location, often a directory named *public_html*. A special application named the *web server* runs on the server machine. This application accepts the request for a web page and returns the file containing the commands for the web page.

Programs that are intended to be run in response to commands originated at web servers are often called *cgi-bin* programs. The term *cgi-bin* stands for Common Gateway Interface-binary and describes the protocol that such programs use to communicate with each other. Cgi-bin programs frequently must be stored in a particular directory, such as a directory in the *public_html* area named *cgi_bin*. The details vary from system to system depending upon how the web server has been configured. Consult your system administrator for details on your particular installation.

HTML FORMATTING COMMANDS

Web pages are simply text files. What makes them unique is that they are stored in a particular location (typically public_html) that is known to the web server. Web pages are written using commands that are read by the web browser to determine formatting, or how the pages appear on your screen. These commands are written in *HyperText Markup Language (HTML)*. The source script for a typical web page can look similar to the following, which would produce the image shown below:

```
<html>
<head>
<title>An Example Web Page</title>
</head>
<body>
<h1>A Simple Web page!</h1>
<p>
Hello. This is a simple web page
</body>
</html>
```

Notice that the source for the web page consists of a series of commands, called *tags*. Some of these tags come in matched pairs. For example, the tag <h1> creates a heading. The end of the heading is indicated by the tag </h1>.

Many applications allow a user to create web pages without knowing the HTML commands used to represent the information. Browser applications often include these features, so that the browser application can be used to format and create web pages as well as view them. Often these applications allow the user to *toggle* between the graphical view and the HTML code view. You can experiment with such a system to see how HTML commands are used to describe a variety of different representations.

This chapter does not describe HTML commands, but several uncomplicated commands are used here. Many readers will already be familiar with HTML, and numerous tutorials are readily available on the web or in books.

FORM-BASED WEB PAGES

One of the simplest varieties of interaction with a web page is constructed using *forms*. A form allows the programmer to place graphical elements, such as text boxes and buttons, on a web page. The form then specifies the name of a program that should be executed on the server side to handle the values entered into the form. The form for our Eliza application is shown here:

```
<html>
<title>Eliza Program</title>
<body>
<h1>Phreds Phrendly Pseudo-Psychiatric Couch</h1>
<p>
<form action = "/cgi-bin/cgiwrap/~lisa/eliza.py" method="GET">
<p>
Hello. What can we do for you today?
<p>
<input type="text" name="line" size="80">
<br>
<input type="submit" value="submit new entry">
</form>
</body>
</html>
```

The HTML commands shown will produce a web page that looks like the following:

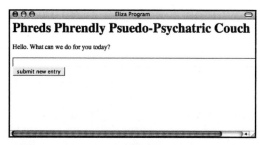

The `action` entry in the `form` tag is telling the web browser the name of the program to run in response to the command. The text shown here uses *CGIWrap*, a popular tool for running cgi-bin scripts in a university setting. This command will run the program named eliza.py (a Python program) that is in the directory belonging to a programmer named lisa. You should consult your system administrator for the commands that are appropriate to your web server installation.

The program eliza.py is a Python program that must produce HTML commands. The fact that two languages are being mixed in the same file is a frequent source of confusion for new Python users. The HTML commands are simply generated by a series of *print* statements. The Eliza program can be written as follows:

```
#!/usr/local/bin/python
import cgi
import string

def getReply (line, words):
  # find a reply based on the words
  # . . . as in Chapter xx
  return "Tell me more. "

print "Content-type: text/html"
print
print "<html><body>"
print "<title>Eliza Program</title>"
print "<h1>Couch</h1>"

form = cgi.FieldStorage()

            # figure out our reply
line = form['line'].value
print '<p><i>' + line + '</i>'
reply = getReply(line, string.split(line))

print '<p> <form action = "/cgi-bin/cgiwrap/~lisa/eliza.py"
method="GET">'
print '<p><i>' + line + '</i>'
print '<p>' + reply
print '<p> <input type="text" name="line" size="80">'
print '<br> <input type="submit" value="submit new entry">'
print '</form> </body>'
print '</html>'
```

The comment on the first line is a convention that tells the web server the correct utility program (in this case, the Python Interpreter) to run to process this file. Once again, the exact location of the Python Interpreter can vary from system to system, so you should ask your system administrator for the correct form of this instruction. This is followed by a pair of *import* statements for the libraries to include, and a function definition. The function definition is taken from Chapter 4 and is not repeated here.

The initial *print* statements, after the imports and the function definition, simply produce the HTML header commands. Compare this with the header commands in the original HTML script. Preceding this is a line with the text `Content-type: text/html`. This line informs the web browser that the remainder of the output should be interpreted as HTML commands.

The `cgi` module provides a simple way to get hold of the contents the user placed in the cgi fields. These values are placed into a dictionary by the command `cgi.FieldStorage()`. The program shows how to access the text written in the text box marked (in the original form) with the name `line`.

The processing of this line of input is exactly the same as the processing of the line of input in the Eliza program examined in Chapter 4. A response is produced and presented to the user and at the same time requests a new line of input. So that the user can continue the conversation indefinitely, *print* statements are used to produce a new form. This new form matches exactly the form used in the original web page. If the user now types a new response, the same program will be invoked, which will produce a new web page, and so on, *ad infinitum*.

TRIPLE-QUOTED STRINGS

Notice how the cgi-bin program begins with a series of *print* statements. These can be reduced to a single statement using a special form of string constant. A *triple-quoted string*, as the name suggests, begins and ends with three quotation marks. However, unlike other string literals, a triple-quoted string is allowed to span multiple lines. It is also allowed to include other quotation characters (both single and double).

The starting *print* statement for the application could be written using triple quotes as follows:

```
print '''Content-type: text/html
<html><body>
<title>my-blog</title>
<h1>Couch</h1>'''
```

The entire four lines of output are represented by a single string. A similar string can be used to print the standard text that terminates the web page. Another common use for triple-quoted strings is to represent literal values that include both single and double quotation marks:

```
line = '''He said: "don't do it!" '''
```

DEBUGGING CGI-BIN PROGRAMS

Because cgi-bin programs are normally both invoked and viewed through a web browser, they can be annoyingly difficult to debug. The following tricks can help save you many hours of frustration.

First, although the command `cgi.FieldStorage` will make sense only when run from a web browser, the majority of the rest of the application is simply a Python program. This means it can be run from the Python Interpreter, like any other Python program. To avoid error messages from the cgi commands, simply replace these commands with a comment, and substitute a *dummy assignment* during the process of debugging. This might look like the following:

```
# remove the user of the cgi module for now
# form = cgi.FieldStorage()
# line = form['line'].value
# the following is simply a dummy value
line = "You look like my mother"
```

Now the program can be run directly from the command line:

```
python eliza.py
```

Doing this will allow you to discover the vast majority of syntax and logic errors before you ever start trying to connect the program to the web browser.

Even when your Python program runs without compiler error messages, it can still have errors that are difficult to detect when the program is implemented. This is partly because the output must be expressed as HTML commands. This can complicate the common debugging trick of writing out values using *print* statements. A simple solution is to use the HTML tags for preformatted text, `<pre>` and `<\pre>`. Anything that appears between these two tags is simply displayed by the web browser. So a typical session might have commands such as the following:

```
# debugging commands, I need to find out these values
print '<pre>'
print 'the value coming in is' + form['line'].value
print '</pre>'
```

Run-time error messages are sent to `sys.stderr`, which is sometimes ignored by web browsers. These messages can be diverted into the standard output using the command

```
sys.stderr = sys.stdout
```

Placing this line before some commands that you suspect might be producing an error, and placing the entire contents within a `pre` command (so that any output is displayed) can be very effective:

```
print '<pre>'
sys.stderr = sys.stdout
. . . # some Python commands you suspect might produce an error
print '</pre>'
```

Now any error messages that are produced will be formatted as HTML commands by the browser.

EXERCISES

1. Explore various HTML commands. What does the command `<i>text</i>` do? How about the `<b>text</b>` command? How do you produce a numbered list in HTML? A bulleted list?

2. Write a form that asks the user for a name, and then invokes a Python program that produces the lyrics for the name game song. The name game, you will remember, takes a name, such as "sally," and places it in a rhyme such as the following: "Sally Sally bo Bally! Banana fanna fo Fally! Fee fi mo Mally! SALLY!"

3. Explore using triple quotes in interactive mode. What can you do with triple quotes that you cannot do with single or double quotes?

4. Explore various other types of HTML form elements. These include buttons, text lines, text boxes, check boxes, radio button, and pull-down menus.

## CHAPTER 14

Case Study: A Simple Blog

In this case study, we continue our exploration of applications that use the Internet and employ a web browser for their graphical interface. We will create a simple blog for a programmer named Tina. Unlike the Eliza program examined in the previous chapter, the blog will allow multiple different actions to occur. To illustrate an alternative way to structure an application, rather than using a single Python program, each of these actions will be represented by a separate Python program.

The term *blog*, short for web log, is a vehicle for an author (the *blog writer*) to share his or her ideas and opinions with many readers. This can be contrasted to a *wiki*, described in Chapter 15, which is a vehicle for many authors to cooperate in the publication of information on the web. Simple blogs can be a form of public, online diary, with readership limited to the author and a few friends. At the other extreme, popular blogs become like newspaper columns, with loyal readers looking forward to regular (sometimes daily) postings. Blogs vary greatly in the quality of presentation, as well as writing. Complicated blogs can incorporate pictures, sound, movement, and complex layout, while simple blogs can comprise a series of text entries.

In this chapter, we will create a relatively simple blog and suggest a number of improvements that readers can make on their own.

BLOG CREATION

As with the Eliza program, execution for our blog begins with a web page. The web page has a simple appearance, as follows:

The text for this web page is as follows:

```
<html>
<title>Tina Smith's Web Log</title>
<body>
<h1>Welcome to Tina's World</h1>
<p>
From this page you can read Tina's blog and,
if you are on Tina's machine, you can create new entries.
<p>
<form action = "/cgi-bin/cgiwrap/~tina/tinablog/read.py" method="GET">
<input type="submit" value="Read Tina's Blog">
</form>
<p>
<form action = "/cgi-bin/cgiwrap/~tina/tinablog/newentry.py" method="GET".
<input type="submit" value="Submit New Entry">
</form>
</body>
</html>
```

As you read in the previous chapter, forms are used to specify a program to be executed when a button has been clicked. In this application, each button is described by its own form. This allows the two buttons to invoke different forms. The first button can be clicked to read entries in the blog, and the second is clicked to create a new entry. Each form is matched to a Python program that will be executed to process the contents of the form. These Python programs must exist in a specific directory (frequently called *cgi-bin*) in Tina's web page area. To simplify the management of these programs, Tina has placed them in a subdirectory named *tinablog*.

We will explore the second program first. The program, newentry.py (shown next), uses a module you have not seen before. The module os provides information about the operating system on which a Python program is being executed. In this case, we want the program to work only if it is running on Tina's personal machine. (In the exercises, we will suggest various other ways to keep other people from making new entries.)

```
#!/usr/local/bin/python
import cgi
import os

print '''Content-type: text/html

<html>
<body>
<h1>Tina's Personal Web Log</h1>'''

if os.environ['REMOTE_HOST'] == "tina.stateuniversity.edu":
```

```
# read the existing database
print '''Type the new entry here:
<p>
<form action = "/cgi-bin/cgiwrap/~tina/tinablog/submit.py" method="GET">
Subject: <input name="subject" size="40">
<p>
<textarea name="text" rows="10" columns="80">
Erase this and put your new text here.
</textarea>
<input type="submit" value="submit new entry">
</form>'''

else:
    print "<p>sorry, Tina only allows submissions from her machine"

print '''</body></html>'''
```

Assuming that the program is running on Tina's machine, a new form is created. This form allows the user to type a subject and the text for a new entry. These commands produce a web page that looks like the following:

When Tina clicks the Submit New Entry button, the program submit.py is executed. This program has the following definition:

```
#!/usr/local/bin/python
import cgi
import os
import time
import shelve

print '''Content-type: text/html
```

```
<html>
<body>
<h1>Tina's Personal Web Log</h1>'''

if os.environ['REMOTE_HOST'] == "tina.stateuniversity.edu":
  # get the form values and the database
  form = cgi.FieldStorage()
  dbase = shelve.open("database")
  # place the value into the database
  dbase[str(time.time())] = (form['subject'].value, form['text'].value)
  # print a reassuring message
  print "<p>Your message has been added to Tina's blog"
else:
  print "<p>sorry, Tina only allows submissions from her machine"

print '''</body></html>'''
```

In addition to using the os module to restrict execution to Tina's machine, this program uses another new module named time. The time module provides access to various functions dealing with times and dates. In this case, we will use the current time (a value accessed by time.time()) as the key for the database. Since keys must be *immutable* (not changeable), the value returned by the time function is converted into a string. Using time as a key ensures that no two entries will use the same key and makes it easy to sort the entries in chronological order.

The shelve module, described in Chapter 5, is used to provide a persistent storage area. The subject and the text are combined into a *tuple* that is stored in this database. If everything works successfully, a reassuring message is presented to the user:

The final Python program for the blog application is used to read and display the previously entered contents of the blog. This program simply loads the database produced by the shelve module and formats each entry:

```
#!/usr/local/bin/python
import cgi
import shelve
```

```
import time

print '''Content-type: text/html

<html>
<title>Tina's wonderful web log</title>
<body>
<h1>Tina's Wonderful Web Log</h1>'''

form = cgi.FieldStorage()
dbase = shelve.open("database")

for entry in dbase.keys():
  # get time entry was placed
  t = float(entry)
  # get text of entry
  (subject, text) = dbase[entry]
  # now print it out
  print "<hr><h2>", subject, "</h2>"
  print "<p><i>" + time.ctime(t) + "</i>"
  print "<p>", text
  print "<p>"

print '''<hr>
This program was written by Tina Smith, 2005.
</body></html>'''
```

A method in the `time` module can be used to convert the time value (which is
stored as a floating-point value) into a more human-readable string. The database
entry is separated into the subject and text portions, and each is displayed with appropriate formatting strings. Output from Tina's blog might look as follows:

In the exercises, we will suggest several different variations you might want to make for this simple blog. In programming these exercises, you would be well advised to reread the suggestions presented in the previous chapter on debugging cgi-bin programs.

EXERCISES

1. Tina's blog ensures that only Tina can make new entries by not allowing input unless it comes from a specific machine. This is both too restrictive, since Tina might work on many different machines, and not restrictive enough, since several different users might work on Tina's machine. An alternative is to use a password. A password can be simply a text box on the original page. Instead of checking the machine, check the contents of the password box and permit the entry only if it matches a specific value.

2. The new entry page will fail if the user does not type any text in the subject area. This can be easily checked by seeing if the form has an entry for the value `subject`. Add this to the program, and if no subject was typed, use the default text (`no subject`).

3. Many blogs allow only the author to create new entries, but anybody else can make a comment entry. Add the ability to make comments by adding a Comment button that will produce a new web page that allows the user to enter comment material. This information will then be stored in a third entry in the database. Comments should then be displayed along with the original entry.

4. The current implementation displays the entire blog in one large file. An alternative would be to display only the subject lines, making each into a button that when clicked displays only the given entry. Show how to implement this feature.

5. Having implemented the ability to display just one blog entry as described in question 4, show how to add a feature that will allow users to search for a blog entry that contains a given search string. Do this by creating a new text line for the search text, and then examining each blog entry in turn using a method such as `string.find()`. If the search string is found in the entry, then display it.

## CHAPTER 15

Case Study: A Wiki Web

A *wiki* is designed to allow many individuals to share in the creation of a common database of information. The most famous wiki is Wikipedia (http://wikipedia.org), a free online encyclopedia containing articles on almost every imaginable topic. Anybody with a web browser can connect to Wikipedia and create a new entry that describes a topic of interest. Similarly, anybody can edit an article to correct errors (either grammatical or factual) or add further information. A community of readers for Wikipedia periodically examines recently altered articles to weed out inappropriate content, but such deletions are rare in comparison to the vast amount of useful information that is added.

The Wiki Web application we develop in this chapter is much simpler and closer in spirit to the original wiki (the first wiki ever written) at http://c2.com/cgi/wiki. Wiki information is organized using *pattern words*, each of which is written as a single word with embedded capital letters—for example, *PatternWord*. (This convention grew up in the context of the study of ideas termed *design patterns*, hence the name. However, the idea of the wiki has since transcended its original use in the design pattern community.) Each pattern word is matched to a page, similar to a web page, that describes the idea or concept. These descriptions can themselves contain pattern words, which automatically become hyperlinks to their associated page. The result is a collection of tightly interconnected web pages that mirror the way that information is connected.

The first page of our wiki will be named, by convention, FrontPage. It looks something like this:

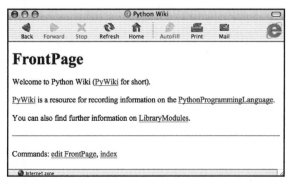

Notice how the pattern words on the page have been rendered as hyperlinks. Two special links are at the bottom of the page—one for editing the current page and one for producing an index of all the current pages. If the user clicks a hyperlink, such as the PyWiki link, a new page will be produced, as shown:

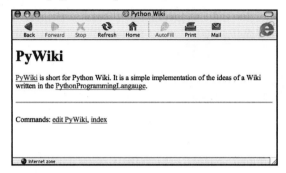

Pattern words can be written before the associated pages have been described. For example, suppose no entry for PythonProgrammingLanguage exists. Clicking that link will produce the following:

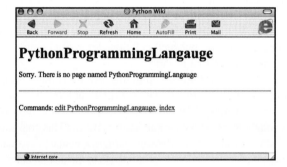

By clicking the Edit link at the bottom of the page, the user can produce a form that will allow the creation of a new page.

By typing in the text area, the user can create his or her own description of the topic PythonProgrammingLanguage. Simple conventions are used for formatting. A blank line will be formatted as the start of a new paragraph. A line consisting of two dashes (—) will be formatted as a horizontal bar.

When the user has finished typing, she can click the Submit Changes button to open the following window:

The last window displays when the user types the `index` command. This produces a window containing all currently recognized pattern words in the wiki:

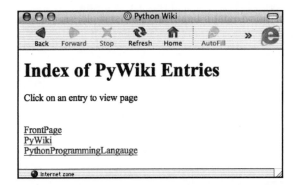

The key feature of the wiki is that anybody with a web browser can enter changes and, by doing so, add information to the wiki. The result is an ever-changing and growing document that captures knowledge from an entire community of users, rather than simply one individual.

IMPLEMENTING OUR WIKI

The implementation of our wiki begins with a web page, like the previous two case studies. In this case, the web page will simply provide a link to the first Python program:

```
<html>
<body>
<h1>Python Wiki</h1>
<p>
```

```
Click <a href="/cgi-bin/cgiwrap/~lisa/pywiki/wiki.py">here</a>
to enter the world of Python Wiki.
</body>
</html>
```

As in the previous chapter, the Python program must be placed in a cgi-bin directory. We have grouped the several Python scripts that will be used in this application into a directory named *pywiki*. A subdirectory in this directory, named *db* (for database), will contain files for each of the pattern words.

The file *wiki.py* is the heart of the application. It is a program with a simple structure, although it uses a few features we have not yet explored:

```python
#!/usr/local/bin/python
#
# pyWiki main page
#
import re
import cgi

# create regular expression patterns to match input lines
pat1 = re.compile('^$') # empty line
pat2 = re.compile('^-$') # line of dashes
pat3 = re.compile('([A-Z][a-z0-9]+([A-Z][a-z0-9]+)+)') # pattern word

print '''Content-type: text/html

<html>
<title>Python Wiki</title>
<body>'''
# get our page number
form = cgi.FieldStorage()
if form.has_key('page'):
  page = form['page'].value
else:
  page = 'FrontPage'

print '<h1>' + page + '</h1><p>'
# try to open file
try:
  fileName = "db/" + page
  f = open(fileName, 'r')
  for line in f:
      line = line.rstrip()
      if pat1.search(line): print '<p>'
      elif pat2.search(line): print '<hr>'
      elif pat3.search(line):
```

```
            print pat3.sub(r'<a href="wiki.py?page=\1">\1</a>', line)
      else: print line
except:
    print '<p>Sorry. There is no page named ' + page
else:
   f.close()


# no matter what, give opportunity to edit it
print '<hr><p>Commands: <a href="edit.py?page=' + page +
'">edit ' + page + '</a>, <a href="index.py">index</a>'
print '''</body></html>'''
```

The new feature used in this program is the *regular expression* package, found in the module named `re`. Regular expressions were discussed briefly in Chapter 11.

Ignoring the regular expressions, the structure of the program is very simple. It prints the standard prolog for all web pages. It then looks to see if any cgi form value exists with the name `page`. If not, the default value `FrontPage` is used. A *try* block then attempts to open a file with the given name in a directory of files named *db*. If this fails (typically because the file does not exist), a message is produced telling the user that no information can be found. If the file open succeeds, the file is read, and each line is individually formatted. At the end, a pair of *print* statements are used to produce HTML commands for invoking a script named `edit.py` and for ending the web page.

Notice the particular form for the *anchor* `<a>` in the HTML commands produced at the end. This line is producing an anchor that might look as follows:

```
<a href="edit.py?page=PiWiki">edit PiWiki</a>
```

The information following the question mark is an argument that is being passed to the script edit.py. The value of this argument is accessed using the same `cgi` `.fieldStorage` mechanism used to access values entered in a form.

REGULAR EXPRESSIONS

As we explored in Chapter 11, regular expressions are a technique for defining patterns used in the process of searching a text string. A pattern can be a simple string—for example, searching for the starting location of the string *sip* in the word *Mississippi*. Or a pattern can be much more complex, such as finding the location of the first double letter that is followed by a vowel and then followed by another double letter.

The variables `pat1`, `pat2`, and `pat3` in our wiki program represent three different regular expression patterns. The first pattern is `^$`. This matches the start of a string followed by the end of a string—that is, an empty string. Since the strings in question are going to be lines read from a file, this will match an empty line. The second pattern is `^-$`. This matches lines consisting of two dash marks and nothing

more. The third pattern, used to find pattern words, is by far the most complex. It is
`([A-Z][a-z0-9]+([A-Z][a-z0-9]+)+)`.

Let's analyze this pattern in steps. The pattern `[A-Z]` matches a capital letter.
The pattern `[a-z0-9]+` matches a run of one or more lowercase letters or numbers.
The pattern `([A-Z][a-z0-9]+)+` represents one or more capital letters followed
by a sequence of one or more lowercase letters. Appending the latter to the former
produces a pattern that matches *two* or more capital letters followed by lowercase
letters—that is, a pattern word. These are surrounded by an additional set of parentheses to form what is termed a *group*.

The regular expression module (named `re`) provides a number of useful functions for manipulating strings using regular expressions. The function `re.compile`
translates a string representing a regular expression into an internal form called a
pattern. The function `pat.search`, where `pat` is a pattern, returns a value that is
nonempty if a pattern can be matched in a string. Here we are simply using the result
of this function in a conditional statement; however, the value can also be used to find
the starting and ending position of the match.

The loop at the heart of our program examines each line of the file in turn. If an
empty line is found, an HTML paragraph start tag (`<p>`) is printed. If a pair of dashes
is found, a horizontal line tag (`<hr>`) is printed. The third pattern, looking for pattern
words, is more complicated.

The function `pat.sub` is used to replace all non-overlapping occurrences of a
pattern with another value. The first argument in the pattern with another value is the
replacement string, while the second is the string to be examined. The replacement
string can be a simple string, or it can include values of the form */n*, where *n* is a number. The form */n* is used to indicate groups from the matched string. In this case, we
are using the value `\1` to find the text of the pattern word. A pattern word is replaced
by an HTML anchor of the form:

```
<a href="wiki.py?page=PatternWord>PatternWord</a>
```

Notice how the pattern word appears twice in the replacement. If none of the
three patterns match in a line, the line is simply printed. The remainder of the application is similar to the case studies presented in the previous chapters.

THE EDIT PAGE

If the user clicks the Edit link at the bottom of a wiki page, the following application
is invoked:

```
#!/usr/local/bin/python
#
# PyWiki edit page interface
#
import cgi
```

```
print '''Content-type: text/html
<html>
<title>Python Wiki</title>
<body>'''

# get our page number
form = cgi.FieldStorage()
if form.has _key('page'):
   page = form['page'].value
else:
   page = 'FrontPage'

print '<h1>Edit Page ' + page + '</h1>'

print '''<p>Use the following form to make your changes
<p><form action="/cgi-bin/cgiwrap/~budd/pywiki/submit.py" method="GET" border=2>
<textarea name="content" rows="20" cols="80">'''

# keep text if we know it
try:
   fileName = "db/" + page
   f = open(fileName, 'r')
   for line in f.readlines():
        print line.rstrip()
except:
   print 'place your explanation of ' + page + ' here'

print '''</textarea>
<br><input type="submit" value="submit changes">'''
print '<input type="hidden" name="page" value="' + page + '">'
print '</form>'

print '''</body></html>'''
```

This Python program is very similar to those we have seen in the preceding two chapters. It produces standard HTML for a header. This is followed by a form that includes a text box in which the user can make changes. This text box is initialized either with the current text of the file that describes the pattern word (if the file exists) or by a sentence of instructions (if the file does not yet exist). The application ends by emitting the standard HTML instructions for the end of a page.

When the user clicks the Submit Changes button, the following application is invoked:

```
#!/usr/local/bin/python
#
# wiki submit edits interface
```

```
#
import cgi

print '''Content-type: text/html

<html>
<title>Python Wiki</title>
<body>'''
# get our page number
form = cgi.FieldStorage()
if form.has_key('page'):
  page = form['page'].value
else:
  page = 'missing page'
if form.has_key('content'):
  content = form['content'].value
else:
  content = ''

print '<h1>Change Page ' + page + '</h1>'

# open file and make changes
try:
  fileName = "db/" + page
  f = open(fileName, "w")
  f.write(content)
  print '<p>Your changes have been entered'
except:
  print '<p>Your changes failed for some reason'

print '<p>Click <a href="/cgi-bin/cgiwrap/~budd/pywiki/
wiki.py?page=' + page + '">here</a>'
print 'to see updated contents of page ' + page

print '''</body></html>'''
```

This program simply saves the entered text, producing either a simple message indicating everything was successful or a warning message if for some reason the file could not be written.

THE INDEX APPLICATION

All that remains is the application that produces an index of those pattern words that currently exist in the database. Here's the application:

```
#!/usr/local/bin/python
#
# wiki index interface
# produce index page of all entries
#

import glob

print '''Content-type: text/html

<html>
<title>Python Wiki</title>
<body>
<h1>Index of PyWiki Entries</h1>
<p>Click on an entry to view page<p>'''

# files, read file names, strip off directory name
files = [x[3:] for x in glob.glob('db/*')]
files.sort()
for name in files:
    print '<br><a href="wiki.py?page='+name+'">'+name+'</a>'

print '''</body></html>'''
```

The `glob` module is useful for finding file names in a directory. The argument string represents a directory name, with the `*` character representing a wild card, which can be matched by anything. The result will be a list of file names that match the string.

In our application, file names have a one-to-one correspondence with pattern words. The command `x[3:]` is used to strip off the first three characters—that is the text *db/*. This list of names is sorted, so that the patterns are in alphabetical order. A loop is then used to produce HTML tags that will, when clicked, link the user to the appropriate page.

That's it. With four small Python programs, we have created our completed Wiki Web application. The following exercises will help explore some of the ideas introduced in this chapter.

EXERCISES

1. One problem with the pattern word convention is that it can frequently make the English in a sentence sound awkward. For example, the pattern word may be a singular noun that is used in a sentence that requires a plural noun. One solution is to separate the pattern word used as an identification and the representation of the word in the text. This could be done as a pattern such as this: {PatternWord!textual form}. When a pattern such as this is found, the link is made to the pattern word, but it is printed using the alternative form:

> `<a href="wiki.py?page=PatternWord">textual form</a>`. Modify the wiki.py program to recognize words using this format.

2. Some wikis allow the user to enter HTML commands directly, such as using `<i>text </i>` to italicize text. Other wikis do not allow this. What is the behavior of the wiki described in this chapter? Can you think of arguments for and against this decision?

3. Add a pattern that looks for embedded URLs of the form *http://web page* and turns them into anchor tags.

4. Another common feature of wikis is a command to view recently changed pages, listed in order of their modification. To produce this, maintain a file named recentChanges. Each time a file is changed, append a line to this file containing the file name and date. Then implement a program that will be run in response to a command to view the recent changes. This program will take each line of the recent changes file and format it as a link to the correct wiki page.

A Sudoku Solver

Sudoku is a popular logic puzzle. Each Sudoku puzzle is represented by a nine-by-nine grid, subdivided into 9 three-by-three cells. Several cells are initially filled by values between 1 and 9. The objective is to fill the remaining cells with digits so that no digit is ever repeated in any column, row, or three-by-three block. An example Sudoku is shown below.

				9		5	8	2
					2			
8	7			1	5	6		
2								5
	5	8				3	4	
7								9
		5	1	3			2	7
			6					
9	3	7		5				

This chapter presents a simple Sudoku solver—a computer program written in Python that will solve simple Sudoku puzzles, such as the one shown here. More complex examples of the genre require more subtle heuristics than those described here, although near the end of the chapter, you'll read about some of the ways that this program could be improved. The purpose of this example is to illustrate *functional programming techniques*—in particular the use of *list comprehensions* in Python as an example of the ideas of functional programming.

REPRESENTATION

[[0,0,0,0,9,0,5,8,2],
[0,0,0,0,0,2,0,0,0],
[8,7,0,0,1,5,6,0,0],
[2,0,0,0,0,0,0,0,5],
[0,5,8,0,0,0,3,4,0],
[7,0,0,0,0,0,0,0,9],
[0,0,5,1,3,0,0,2,7],
[0,0,0,6,0,0,0,0,0],
[9,3,7,0,5,0,0,0,0]]

Let's start by defining a representation for the puzzle. As is typical in Python, a two-dimensional matrix is represented by a list in which each element is itself a list. The representation of the puzzle shown earlier is presented at left.

To make the program more general, the values will be read from a data file. Each line in the data file will consist of nine characters, with 0 used to represent a blank space. The task of reading such a file and creating the initial list can serve as a useful example comparing the task of writing list comprehensions (to which you were introduced in Chapter 8) to ordinary Python code. A first cut at a function to read the puzzle data might look like this:

```
def readPuzzle (f): # f is input file
    puzzle = []
    for line in f.readLines():
        row = []
        for ch in line.rstrip():
            row.append(int(ch))
        puzzle.append(row)
    return puzzle
```

You can read the logic of this function as follows:

1. Create an empty list for the final result.
2. Read the input file line by line.
3. Create an empty row for this line of the puzzle.
4. After stripping off the trailing newline character (an artifact of textual input), read the line character by character.
5. Convert each character into an integer, and add it to the row list.
6. After reading the entire row, add the row list to the puzzle list.
7. After reading each line of the input file, return the resulting puzzle list.

Any time you see the pattern

```
newlist = [ ]
for . . . :
  newlist.append( . . . )
```

it means the situation is ripe for replacement with a list comprehension. As you learned in Chapter 8, the list comprehension succinctly encodes the creation of a new list through a process of *transformation*, by moving the loop from the outside to the inside of the expression. The inner loop of this function can be replaced by the following:

```
[ int(ch) for ch in line.rstrip()]
```

The list comprehension is shorter, eliminates one unnecessary variable, and clearly indicates that the objective of the process is to create a list, and that the list will contain integer values formed by transforming each character in the line.

Having transformed the inner loop, we can now do the same to the outer loop, resulting in the following function definition:

```
def readPuzzle (f):
return [ [int(a) for a in list(line.rstrip())] for line in f.readlines()]
```

Once you learn to read list comprehensions, the resulting function is considerably shorter, faster, and easier to understand.

ACCESSING PUZZLE DATA

Having decided on the representation of the puzzle, the next step is to define functions that will return an individual row, an individual column, and an individual block. Each of these will return a list containing the indicated data. Both the column and block are converted into a list; for example, the center right block of the puzzle is represented by the list [0,0,5,3,4,0,0,0,9]. The methods to compute these values will take the puzzle matrix as argument, since in a moment we will introduce a second matrix and will eventually want to perform the same data access on both.

A slight complication exists, in that Python indexes lists starting from 0, so the set of legal index values is 0 through 8, while the set of data values of interest is 1 through 9. This just means we need to be careful to distinguish *index* data from *matrix* data. The global values r9 and r19 help keep this distinction clear. The first is the set of index values (starting with zero), while the second is the set of data values (starting with one).

```
import sys

r9 = range(9)
r19 = range(1,10)

def readPuzzle(f):
  return [ [int(a) for a in list(line.rstrip())] for line in f.readlines()]

def row(i, grid):
  return grid[i]

def column(j, grid):
  return [grid[i][j] for i in r9]

def block(i,j, grid):
  return [grid[(i/3)*3+a][(j/3)*3+b] for a in range(3) for b in range(3)]

def missing(lst):
  return [x for x in r19 if x not in lst]

def possible(i,j):
  if puzzle[i][j]: return []
```

continued

```
        else:
            return [x for x in r19 if x in missing(row(i, puzzle)) and
                x in missing(column(j, puzzle)) and x in missing(block(i,j, puzzle))]

def makePossibles():
    return [[possible(i,j) for j in r9] for i in r9]

def drop(lst, i):
    return [lst[j] for j in range(len(lst)) if i != j]

def flatten(lst):
    return [x for y in lst for x in y]

def checkAllBut(x, lst, pos):
    return x not in flatten(drop(lst, pos))

puzzle = readPuzzle(open(sys.argv[1]))
changed = True
while changed:
    changed = False
    possibles = makePossibles()
    for i in r9:
        for j in r9:
            if len(possibles[i][j]) == 1:
                puzzle[i][j] = possibles[i][j][0]
                changed = True
            for x in possibles[i][j]:
                if (checkAllBut(x, block(i, j, possibles), (i%3)*3 + j%3) or
                    checkAllBut(x, column(j, possibles), i) or
                    checkAllBut(x, row(i, possibles), j)):
                        changed = True
                        puzzle[i][j] = x
for i in r9: # print solution
    print puzzle[i]
```

THE POSSIBLES MATRIX

The first step in solving Sudoku is to compute the set of possible values for each square. Let's call this the *possible set*. Since values cannot be repeated in any row, column, or block, the set of possibles is determined by starting with the values 1 through 9, and then eliminating any value that occurs elsewhere in the row, column, or block. We can once again use a list to represent the set of values. The initial possible sets for the center right block of our Sudoku are shown on the following page.

[1,7,8]	[1,6,7]	[]
[]	[]	[1,6]
[1,2,8]	[1,6]	[]

The computation of the possibles matrix illustrates another hallmark of a functional program: the creation of general-purpose functions that can be mixed and matched with each other to produce a variety of effects. The function missing takes as argument a list and returns the list containing the values from 1 to 9 that are not in the argument list.

```
def missing (lst):
return [x for x in r19 if x not in lst]
```

By separating the computation of the missing data from the collection of the row, column, or block data, we make it possible to mix these operations, by passing different arguments to the function. This is illustrated by the function possible, which computes the possible set for a specific (i,j) pair. A value is possible if it is in the missing set for both the row and the column and the block. If the puzzle block is already filled, the possible set is empty. The function makePossibles uses the function possible to create a matrix of all the possible sets.

A SOLUTION HEURISTIC

If a possible set contains a single element, then that value must be the correct value for the cell. However, this fortuitous event does not occur very often; this would make the puzzle far too easy. Another pattern can also be used to infer a value. If a value occurs in a possible set and does not occur in any other possible set in the same block (or row or column), then the value must be the correct answer for that cell. This situation occurs in the set of possibles shown in the example at the top of the page. Here the value 2 occurs only in the lower-left cell. Since no other cell in the block contains a 2, we know this must be the location for this digit. (This will subsequently lead to identifying 8 as the solution of the upper-left cell, then 7 as the value in the upper-middle cell.)

To detect this situation, we first need to construct the set of possibles from a row, column, or block without a specific element. This is accomplished by the function named drop. Again, because drop is separated from the computation of the row, column, or block data, the same function can be used with each. Next, the resulting data is a list of lists. To tell whether a value is or is not found in the data, we need to reduce this to a list of values. This is called *flattening a list*. For example, flattening the list [[1,2],[3,2,4]] produces the list [1,2,3,2,4]. This task is performed by the function flatten. With these two tools, the test to determine whether a value x does not occur in, for example, the possibilities for row i and column j can be determined as follows:

```
x not in flatten(drop(row(i, possibles), j))
```

We need to perform a similar task for each row, column, and block. We can factor out the common task into a function named checkAllBut. This function takes a single element, a list, and a position. It removes the position from the list and checks that the element does not occur in the list. By changing the arguments passed to this function, we can use the same logic to test both rows, columns, and blocks.

We now have all the pieces needed to make our puzzle solver. The main program computes the set of possibles, and then loops over each cell. If the possibles set has just one element, then it must be the correct value. Otherwise, each element in the possibles set is examined, and for each the function checkAllBut is invoked three times: once to check row data, once to check column data, and once to check block data. If any of these works, then the value is correct.

Of course, changing the values in the puzzle will change the values in the possible sets. Using paper and pencil, puzzlers simply erase the values from the given sets, and then rescan the entire grid to see if any new moves are enabled. For example, in the block described at the top of the previous page, the placement of the 2 then leads to the discovery of the placement for the 8, which then leads to the placement of the 7. Since the grid must be scanned multiple times anyway, our approach will be to recompute the possibles matrix on each scan and keep a flag to determine whether any changes have been made during the scan. If a scan is made with no changed detected, then either the solution has been found or we have reached the limit of this solution heuristic.

IMPROVEMENTS

This program implements just two simple heuristics for solving Sudoku puzzles, but this is not sufficient for many puzzles. You can add another heuristic called the *pairs test*: If two squares have the same pair of possible values, you can eliminate those values from all other squares in the same block. This situation occurs in the block shown below. We cannot yet determine which of the two lower squares will have a 1 and which will have a 5, but we know that these values will go into one or the other of these two squares, and therefore they cannot be found anywhere else in the block. Erasing the values from the other squares reveals that 3 must be the value for the middle square. This then leads to the discovery of the 8 in the square above, and so on.

4	[1,3,5,8]	[1,3,5,7,8,9]
[1,3,5,6,7,9]	[1,3,5]	[1,3,5,6,7,9]
[1,5]	2	[1,5]

Another heuristic is the *box line technique*. This moves in the forward, "must," direction, rather than in the backward "cannot," direction. Suppose we know from examination of the other values in a row or column that the value 9 must be in the third column above. Then we can eliminate the value from the first column, which may be enough to force a value. Further hints on solving even more difficult puzzles can be found by Googling the word *Sudoku* online.

BENEFITS

The purpose of this discussion has not been to discuss a Sudoku solver, since this program works only with very simple puzzles. Instead, the purpose has been to illustrate the idea of a functional program represented by list comprehensions in the Python language. The advantages of this style of programming are numerous. Functions tend to be short, faster than their more traditional alternatives, and easy to read. Furthermore, errors made in the development of list comprehensions tend to have a major effect. When it comes to debugging, big errors are much easier to find than small ones, so a change that causes the wrong result to be produced on almost every input is likely to be discovered very quickly. The result is a faster and more reliable program.

As a secondary issue, note that the approach to the solution described in this chapter is markedly different from the approach described in Chapter 6. Here we have started with the representation of the data, and moved upward toward a solution. This is often called a *bottom-up* approach. In most problems, programmers produce a solution using a combination of top-down and bottom-up development, sometimes working from the objective downward using refinement, and sometimes working from the representation upward using composition. When the two finally meet in the middle, a solution can be found.

## 17

CHAPTER

Using XML to Read an iTunes Database

Computers are used for both storage and communication of information. Instead of using a "natural language" to communicate verbally, computers pass information from one place to another. Information without context has very little structure and is therefore prone to misunderstanding.

Imagine two computers that need to compare information regarding items in an inventory and the quantity and cost of each. The information on each product could be represented in three successive lines of text, such as the following:

Toast O'Matic
42
12.95
Kitchen Chef Blender
193
47.43

Does this information help you immediately understand that currently 42 Toast O'Matics are in the inventory and that they cost $12.95 each? Now compare the above descriptions to the following *Extensible Markup Language (XML)* encoding of the same data:

```
<inventory>
<product>
<name>Toast O'Matic</name>
<onHand>42</onHand>
<price>12.95</price>
</product>
<product>
<name>Kitchen Chef Blender</name>
<onHand>193</onHand>
<price>47.43</price>
</product>
</inventory>
```

This example illustrates both the advantages and the disadvantages of the XML format. The advantage is that the information is more self-documenting. It is clear what each field represents, so you can read the information and immediately know what it means. Since the information appears as ordinary text, it can be read by both humans and computers. On the other hand, the XML description is longer and more difficult to process. You cannot simply use three "readLine" statements to extract the information on each product. Instead, a tool called a *parser* must be used to read the XML description.

Another advantage of the XML format is that it allows for evolution and change in the data format. For example, suppose that next week your firm decides to add a field in the inventory database to represent the product manufacturer. In the XML format, this would mean simply adding a new field, like so:

```
<product>
<name>Toast O'Matic</name>
<onHand>42</onHand>
<price>12.95</price>
<manufacturer>General Toaster, Inc</manufacturer>
</product>
```

Existing programs that extract information from the inventory will simply ignore the new field, while new programs can make use of this information. For reasons such as these, XML has readily become a de-facto standard for encoding data that is shared between programs.

Notice that XML looks very similar to the HTML language used for web pages (as discussed in Chapter 14). Both use *tags* to describe information. However, in XML tags must always include an ending element, while in HTML, the ending tag can often be omitted. Furthermore, HTML has a small set of predefined tags that are used for one purpose: namely, to communicate the layout of a web page. XML tags are *unstructured* and by themselves have no meaning until a program that reads the XML file provides one.

iTUNES DATABASE IN XML

You might use at least one database described using XML on your computer right now. If you use iTunes to organize your music collection, you should be able to find a file named *iTunes Music Library.xml* in your iTunes directory. This is simply a text file, so you should be able to examine it with a simple text editor (such as SimpleText or Notepad). The beginnings of this file might look something like the following:

```
<?xml version="1.0" encoding="UTF-8"?>
<!DOCTYPE plist PUBLIC "-//Apple Computer//DTD PLIST 1.0//EN"
"http://www.apple.com/DTDs/PropertyList-1.0.dtd">
<plist version="1.0">
```

```
<dict>
        <key>Major Version</key><integer>1</integer>
        <key>Minor Version</key><integer>1</integer>
        <key>Application Version</key><string>6.0.1</string>
        <key>Features</key><integer>1</integer>
        <key>Music
Folder</key><string>file://localhost/Users/budd/Music/iTunes/iTunes%20
Music/</string>
        <key>Library Persistent ID</key><string>E4D128BB1074A394</string>
        <key>Tracks</key>
        <dict>
            <key>123</key>
            <dict>
                <key>Track ID</key><integer>123</integer>
                <key>Name</key><string>Don't Know Why</string>
                <key>Artist</key><string>Norah Jones</string>
                <key>Composer</key><string>Jesse Harris</string>
                <key>Album</key><string>Come Away With Me</string>
                <key>Genre</key><string>Jazz</string>
                <key>Kind</key><string>AAC audio file</string>
```

The structure of this file is typical of XML documents. The first line identifies the version of XML used to encode the information. The second line identifies the document type, or DOCTYPE. Among the information provided by the DOCTYPE is the reference to a file (in this case, http://www.apple.com/DTDs/PropertyList-1.0.dtd) where the meanings of the various tags are described. You should enter this URL into your browser and examine the file it denotes. This *data definition file* gives the names of the tags that will be used in the remainder of the document.

The majority of the document is described as a plist, which is simply a list that's similar to the list data type in Python. The first element of this list is dict, a collection of key and value pairs, similar to the dictionary data type in Python. What follows is a series of keys and their associated values. Each key is a string; however, the values have different types: some are integers, some are strings, and one, the tracks field, is another dictionary.

The tracks dictionary is used to record information about each song (track) stored in the database. Information that is stored includes the name of the song, artist's name, composer, album, and other information.

We will use this file as our example to illustrate how Python programs can read and manipulate information stored in an XML database.

PARSING XML FILES USING THE DOCUMENT OBJECT MODEL

XML files are simply text files, so you could, if you wanted, simply read the file descriptions line by line using the standard file commands. However, reading the tag fields, separating the tag names from the enclosed data, and matching every opening tag with its associated closing tag are complex operations you would like to avoid, if possible. Fortunately, a number of XML parsers have been designed to simplify this process.

Two general approaches can be used for the task of processing an XML file, and two general libraries are in common use. One approach is to read the entire XML document into one huge structure, and then to break the structure apart to find the items of interest. Here the parser does its job, returning a value to the programmer. The programmer then manipulates the returned value. This is called the *Document Object Model (DOM) approach*. This is easiest if the document is small or must be shared with many sections of a program.

The second approach is to interact more dynamically with the parser. The parser alerts the program each time an item has been read. The program can then do with the item what it wants. The parser and the programmer's code run side by side, and no single representation of the entire XML file is ever built. This approach is preferable if the XML file is very large. Both types of parser will be illustrated in this chapter.

Our first program is shown in Figure 17-1.

Outside the function definitions (which we will describe shortly), the program itself is less than 10 lines of code. The function named `parse` is doing the majority of the real work.

You can start by experimenting with this function in *interactive mode*. After you have located your iTunes XML file, try entering the following three lines:

```
>>> import xml.dom.minidom
>>> itunesdb = xml.dom.minidom.parse("iTunes Music Library.xml")
>>> print(itunesdb.documentElement)
[<DOM Text node "\n">, <DOM Element: dict at 0x261d78>, <DOM Text node "\n">]
```

This short experiment illustrates one of the drawbacks of XML parsers. The parser does not know what part of the input is important, so it saves everything, including newline and space characters. In this case, the text that appears before and after the `dict` tag is unimportant. The function `removeText` (Figure 17-1) is a simple routine that removes these extraneous text nodes, leaving the elements of interest.

After removing the extra text nodes, the dictionary itself is the first (and only) node. If you examine the initial lines of the iTunes database, you can see that the structure of the database is a dictionary containing information about the database itself. One of the fields in this dictionary is named *Tracks*, which includes one track for each song in the database. That field itself holds a dictionary with entries for information such as the song name, artist, composer, and so on.

The function `readKeys` is used to reconstruct a Python dictionary from the XML representation. If you examine the database, you can see that an XML dictionary consists of a *key element* that is immediately followed by the *associated data value*. The parser returns the entire list of nodes as a single list. The method `readKeys` finds each key, saves the tag name, and then uses the next node as the value stored at the given

```
import xml.dom.minidom

def removeText (node):
   return [x for x in node.childNodes if x.nodeType != xml.dom.Node.TEXT_NODE]

def readInfo (tag, node):
   if node.nodeType != xml.dom.Node.ELEMENT_NODE: return None
   if node.tagName == 'string':
       return node.firstChild.data
   elif node.tagName == 'integer':
       return int(node.firstChild.data)
   elif node.tagName == 'date':
       return node.firstChild.data
   elif node.tagName == 'dict':
       return readKeys(removeText(node))
   return None

def readKeys (lst):
   i = 0
   dict = { }
   while i < len(lst):
       if lst[i].nodeType == xml.dom.Node.ELEMENT_NODE and lst[i].tagName == 'key':
           tag = lst[i].firstChild.data
           i += 1
           dict[tag] = readInfo(tag, lst[i])
       i += 1
   return dict

itunesdb = xml.dom.minidom.parse("iTunes Music Library.xml")
topnodes = removeText(itunesdb.documentElement)
topdict = readKeys(removeText(topnodes[0]))
trackdict = topdict.get('Tracks', {})

for track in trackdict:
   song = trackdict.get(track)
   print song.get('Name',''),':',song.get('Artist',''),':',song.get('Year','')
```

FIGURE 17.1 The DOM parser for the iTunes database

key. The function `readInfo` is used to perform the conversion between an XML node and the equivalent Python representation. Integers are converted using the function `int`, dictionaries are handled by a recursive call to `readKeys`, and all other values (such as strings and dates) are simply left as is.

Having converted the XML form into a Python structure, the entry with name *Tracks* is accessed to load the dictionary of songs. A loop is used to access each individual song, and a *print* statement generates some of the information about each song. Example output might look as follows:

Feelin' the Same Way : Norah Jones : 2002
Come Away with Me : Norah Jones : 2002
Shoot the Moon : Norah Jones : 2002
Que Creias : Selena : 1992
Missing My Baby : Selena : 1992
Las Cadenas : Selena : 1992
Siempre Estoy Pensando En Ti : Selena : 1992
All of Me : Billie Holiday : 1996
You Go to My Head : Billie Holiday : 1996
Nightingale : Norah Jones : 2002

The following exercises suggest various extensions that could be made to this program.

PARSING XML WITH THE SAX MODEL

The alternative to the DOM model is *SAX*, the *Simple API for XML*. The SAX model is structured around the idea of *events*, which are actions of interest to the programmer. For each event, the programmer can define code that will handle the event. For the XML parser, three major categories of events are used. The first occurs when the start of a tag has been recognized, the second occurs when the text between tags has been recognized, and the third and final event is the processing of an end tag. Each of these is handled by a method in the class `xml.sax.handler.ContentHandler`. To make a specialized type of parser, the programmer simply constructs a new class that inherits from this class and overrides the appropriate methods. Such a class is shown in Figure 17-2.

The class `ItunesHandler` defines internal data values that will be manipulated as the parser scans the XML file. As the start of each tag is recognized, the name of the tag is stored in an internal variable named `tag`. This value is set as blank at the end of the associated tag. Between these variables, the method `characters` is used to process the `tag` contents. If the `tag` is a key, the data is stored in the internal variable `keyText`. Otherwise, assuming that both tag and key are set, the information is saved in the internal variable named `info`.

Notice that the SAX parser ignores most data fields and simply processes those of interest—namely the keys associated with individual songs in the database. Using

FIGURE 17.2 The
SAX parser for the
iTunes library

```
import xml.sax.handler

class ItunesHandler (xml.sax.handler.ContentHandler):
   def __init__ (self):
       self.keyText = ""
       self.tag = ""
       self.info = {}

def startElement (self, name, attributes):
   self.tag = name

def characters (self, data):
   if (self.tag == "key"): self.keyText = data
   elif (self.tag and self.keyText):
       self.info[self.keyText] = data
       if (self.keyText == 'Album'):
           print self.info['Name'],':,'self.info['Artist']
       self.keyText = ''

def endElement (self, name):
   self.tag = ""

parser = xml.sax.make_parser()
handler = ItunesHandler()
parser.setContentHandler(handler)
parser.parse("iTunes Music Library.xml")
```

the fact that the Album entry is one of the last fields recorded for each song, when an Album is found, the information for the song is printed.

Just as you did with the DOM parser, you should experiment with the SAX parser, both in interactive mode and in simple programs, to see how each of the three methods is invoked as the XML file is processed.

EXERCISES

1. Examine the Document Type Definition (DTD) file described by the DOCTYPE entry in the iTunes database. What XML tags does it describe?

2. Assuming you have access to your own iTunes XML database file, how would you use a text editor to discover what information is stored for each track (song) in the database?

3. How would you write a Python program using the DOM parser to uncover the information?

4. Our application outputs just a small bit of information about each song before moving on to the next. The order in which values are printed will match that of the database. This

is not characteristic of most XML applications. Instead, most applications will gather a large amount of information and then produce *summaries* or *digests* in a different order. By starting from the DOM parsing application, rewrite the program to produce each of the following:

- Produce an alphabetized list of all songs in the database, and for each song list the composer and artist.
- Produce an alphabetized list of each album in the database, and for each album generate an alphabetized list of songs.
- Produce an alphabetized list of composers, and for each composer produce a list of all songs, artists, and albums containing work by the composer.

5. Compare the XML database described at the beginning of this chapter with the iTunes database. While both are legal XML, they differ in, for example, the way they treat data types (such as integers and strings). Describe these differences.

6. Compare and contrast the DOM and SAX model of parsing. How are they similar? How are they different? Can you imagine situations for which one would be preferable to the other? Combine your observations with the analysis you performed for question 5. Does the way the XML document describes information favor one approach over the other?

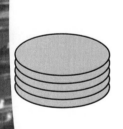

18

CHAPTER

Data Structures

A s you have probably noticed from the many example programs presented in this book, *collections* of values are part of almost any nontrivial computer program. The Python primitive types list, tuple, and dictionary are extremely flexible, and as a consequence, the Python programmer seldom needs to write his or her own classes for storing collections. Nevertheless, the formal study of collection classes, called *data structures*, is an important part of the discipline of computer science. This chapter presents a short introduction to this field.

LEVELS OF ABSTRACTION

As you learned in Chapter 3, *abstraction* is a mechanism used to manage complexity. Abstraction allows programs to emphasize certain features and to ignore others. In an atlas, for example, a map of a continent will note large-scale features, such as mountain ranges and rivers, and ignore smaller features, such as city streets. These features, however, become important in more regional maps, such as a city map.

Collections can be similarly considered at many different levels of abstraction. At the highest level, we can simply describe the *idea* or *concept* of a collection. Often this is done with a metaphor, appealing to the listener's experience with examples from everyday life. For example, we say that a *stack* is a collection organized by the principle that the only item that can be removed is the item most recently inserted— similar to the way that a stack of dishes are organized. A *queue*, on the other hand, is also organized by time of inclusion, but the item removed is the item that has been in the queue the longest. A line of people waiting to get into a theater is an appropriate mental image. This is termed the *abstract data type (ADT)* description of a collection.

At the next level, we can give names to collection operations, which is sometimes called the *interface level description*. We might say that to insert a value into a stack, you use the *push* operation, and to remove an item you use the *pop* operation. Notice that a person who wants to use a collection needs only the interface description. Most likely, for example, you'll include only the interface description of the dictionary data type in Python, and you'll not have any idea how it is actually implemented.

Finally, at the lowest level is the *implementation level description*. This tells you how the collection is actually stored and manipulated in the internal part of the system. These details ideally should be *encapsulated*, so that most users do not need to see them. But, of course, somebody (such as the module developer) must know about them.

This chapter examines all three levels: abstraction, interface, and implementation. However, the discussion of implementation techniques will, by necessity, be only cursory. Many textbooks consider the implementation of data structures in much more detail.

CONTAINERS AS ABSTRACTIONS

Traditionally, collections are divided into two categories based on how they are used: containers in which the *times of insertion* are important, versus those in which *values* are important. Of course, these two categories describe how the container is being *used*, not how it *operates*, so the same implementation (such as a list) can often be used in either fashion. Nevertheless, the division represents a time-honored starting place for the examination of containers.

```
class stack (object):
    def __init__(self):
        self.stack = []
    def push (self, value):
        self.stack.append(value)
    def pop (self):
        return self.stack.pop()
    def isEmpty (self):
        return len(self.stack) == 0

class queue (object):
    def __init__(self):
        self.queue = []
    def insert (self, value):
        self.queue.append(value)
    def remove (self):
        return self.queue.pop(0)
    def isEmpty (self):
        return len(self.queue) == 0
```

You have already read about the two most common abstractions in which the time of insertion is most important: the stack and the queue. Both can be easily constructed using a list as the underlying storage area for values. The stack appends the value to the end and uses the list method pop to remove an item, while the queue uses the pop method from the front.

You might want to use these classes, instead of using the list operations directly, for several reasons. Most important, the classes stack and queue restrict use so that only the provided operations can modify the collection. You are guaranteed that the item removed from a queue will be the item that has been in the queue the longest. If you simply use a list, there is no guarantee that another user—perhaps accidentally, perhaps maliciously—might not insert a new value into the middle of a collection.

Even when the list type is being used directly, programmers will often use abstraction names to describe how the type is being manipulated. A programmer might say, for example, that "this list is being used in a stack-like fashion" (or "being used as a stack"). So it is useful for all programmers to be familiar with the traditional names for these abstractions.

A combination data structure, termed a *deque* (short for double-ended queue, and pronounced "deck"), allows items to be inserted or removed from either end. This is also easily implemented using a list.

The other major category is collections in which the value of elements is more important than the time of insertion. In general, the big three operations for these containers are inserting a value, removing a value, and testing to see whether a value is held in the container. Variations on these operations, as well as other more minor operations, are particular to each category of abstraction.

```python
class bag:
    def __init__(self):
        self.storage = []

    def add(self, value):
        self.storage.append(value)

    def size(self):
        return len(self.storage)

    def test(self, value):
        for v in self.storage:
            if v == value: return True
        return false

    def __in__(self, value):
        return self.test(value)

    def remove(self, value):
        for i in len(self.storage):
            if self.storage[i] == value:
                self.storage.pop(i)
                return

    def __iter__(self):
        return iter(self.storage)
```

A *bag* is the simplest type of collection. A value can be added to a bag, a value can be removed from a bag, and a test can be performed to see if an item is found in the bag. The same item can appear in a bag more than one time. Again, these are easy to simulate using list operations. As described in Chapter 11, defining the method __iter__ allows a bag to be used in a *for* statement. Similarly, defining the method __in__ allows the test operation to be performed using the in operator.

An *ordered bag* (or sorted bag) maintains values in sorted order based on their value. Of the basic abstractions, this is probably the most difficult to implement using a list. The sort method can be used to order the elements; however, thereafter maintaining the order can be complicated. A useful help is the module bisect. The method bisect.bisect performs *a binary search*, which is similar to the way you play "guess the number." It starts in the middle and compares the element found there to the value you seek. If it is smaller, it searches the upper half; if larger, it searches the smaller half. Using a binary search on an ordered collection is much faster than the sequential loop used in the bag algorithm. The bisearch function returns the position where the item is found, or where it can be inserted without destroying the ordering. The latter can be larger than the set of legal index values, if the item being sought is larger than any existing value. For this reason, the remove and test methods must first examine the value returned by bisearch to see if it is legal.

```
import bisect

class sortedBag (object):
    def __init__ (self):
        self.storage = []

    def add (self, value):
        insertionPoint = bisect.bisect(self.storage, value)
        self.storage.insert(insertionPoint, value)

    def size (self):
        return len(self.storage)

    def test (self, value):
        insertionPoint = bisect.bisect(self.storage, value)
        return (insertionPoint < self.size() and
            self.storage[insertionPoint] == value)

    def remove (self, value):
        insertionPoint = bisect.bisect(self.storage, value)
        if insertionPoint < self.size():
            self.storage.pop(insertionPoint)

    def __iter__ (self):
        return iter(self.storage)
```

A *set* differs from a bag in two important respects. First, each item in a set is unique—that is, the same item cannot appear more than once in a set. This is usually enforced by the add method, which simply does not add a value if it is already in the collection. Second, sets incorporate new operations that combine one set with another. For example, an *intersection* returns the elements that are found in both sets, while a *union* represents the elements found in both sets. These concepts are familiar to most programmers from mathematics or the use of Venn diagrams.

```python
class set (object):
  def __init__(self):
      self.storage = []

  def add (self, value):
      if not self.test(value):
          self.storage.append(value)

  def size (self):
      return len(self.storage)

  def test (self, value):
      for v in self.storage:
          if v == value: return True
      return False

  def __in__ (self, value):
      return self.test(value)

  def remove (self, value):
      for i in len(self.storage):
          if self.storage[i] == value:
              self.storage.pop(i)
              return

  def union (self, aSet):
      newSet = set()
      for x in self.storage:
          newSet.add(x)
      for x in aSet:
          newSet.add(x)
      return newSet

  def intersection (self, aSet):
      newSet = set()
      for x in aSet:
          if x in self:
              newSet.add(x)
      return newSet
```

As an abstraction, a *dictionary* is very similar to the Python built-in class of the same name. A dictionary must support key/value pairs, inserting new values into the collection as a pair and accessing or removing values using the key.

A *priority queue* maintains values that have a precedence, or priority. Values can be inserted into the priority queue in any order, but when an element is removed, it is the value with highest priority. A simulation of a hospital waiting room, for example, might want to maintain a list of patients in priority based on the severity of their injury. A simple way to implement a priority queue is through a sorted list, although other techniques can be efficient.

TRADITIONAL IMPLEMENTATION TECHNIQUES

Although our simple implementations of data structure abstractions have been built on top of a list, this is not the only way. And, in fact, the list is a high level abstraction itself that must ultimately be implemented using more primitive features.

The exploration of data structure implementation techniques traditionally begins with an *array*, a fixed-length block of memory.

Because elements in the array are placed end-to-end, accessing a value is very fast. On the other hand, because the array is fixed length, it can be difficult to use for collections. A common solution is to make the block larger than necessary and store elements in the front. This is often termed a *dynamic array*, or in some languages, a *vector*. Two values then characterize the extent of the collection: the size (that is, number of elements in the collection) and the capacity (number of elements in the block of memory).

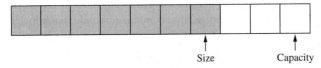

Size   Capacity

Adding an element in the middle of the collection is complicated by the fact that the existing values must be moved over to make room for the new value.

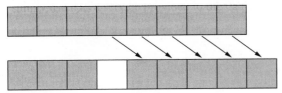

If many elements are added to the collection, the size will eventually reach capacity. At this point, a new block of memory with increased capacity is requested, and the values are copied into the new structure.

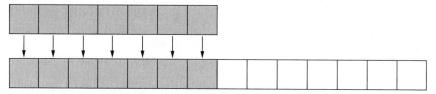

In Python, you can simulate an array using a list and the multiplication operator. For instance, the command

```
[ None ] * 10
```

creates a block of 10 elements, each holding the value `None`. Using this approach, the exercises at the end of the chapter will lead you through the design of a *vector abstraction*. (For Python users, this is purely an academic exercise, as the built-in `list` data type provides all these abilities and more. However, a programmer may not always have the privilege of working in Python. Hence, a working knowledge of how various data types are implemented is valuable information.)

An alternative implementation technique is called a *linked list*, in which each value is stored in a small structure. This structure contains both the value and a reference to the next element in a chain. The collection itself simply maintains a pointer to the first (or sometimes the first and the last) link in this chain.

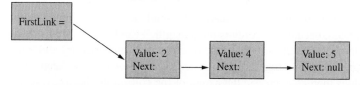

The advantage of a linked list is that adding a new element does not require sliding values around in a block. However, finding where a new value should be inserted requires walking down the list of links.

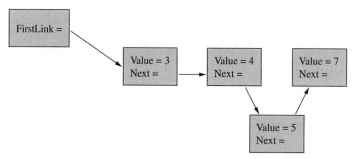

Chapter 9 noted that a linked list could be developed using a pair of classes. The class `Link` is used to store an individual link value:

```
class Link(object):
    def __init__ (self, v, n)
        self.value = v
        self.next = n
```

The class `LinkedList` maintains a pointer to the first `Link`. Operations on the list are performed by walking down the chain of links:

```
class LinkedList (object):
    def __init__ (self):
        self.firstLink = None
    def add (self, newElement):
        self.firstLink = Link(newElement, self.firstLink)
    def test (self, testValue): # see if test value is in collection
        pass
    def remove (self, testValue): # remove value from collection
        pass
    def len (self): # return size of collection
        pass
```

In the exercises at the end of this chapter, you will explore the development of this class. (Again, for the Python programmer, this is a purely academic exercise, since the `List` data structure is built-in. But the approach used here can be applied in many different languages.)

Both the vector and the linked list suffer from the problem that most operations (such as searching to see whether a value is contained in the collection) require a traversal of the entire structure. To address this problem, an programmer can use more complex data structures. One such possibility is a *binary search tree*, which is formed out of *nodes*, similar to the links in a linked list. However, each node can reference two possible child nodes (called the *left* and *right* children). In a binary search tree, the values in each node are larger than or equal to the values in the left children, and smaller than or equal to the values in the right children.

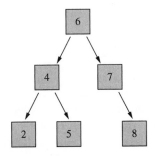

Inserting a value into or removing a value from a binary search tree requires only a traversal from top to bottom, which is much faster than examining every element as is required by a vector or linked list.

The implementation of a binary search tree uses a class termed a `Node`. Each `Node` holds a single value and a pointer to left and right subtrees:

```
class Node (object):
    def __init__ (self, v, l, r):
        self.value = v
        self.left = l
```

```
            self.right = r
```

The tree maintains a reference to the root node for the collection. In the exercises, you can explore the implementation of this data structure.

```
class BinarySearchTree (object):
   def __init__ (self):
        self.root = None
   def add (self, newValue):
    . . .
```

An even more complicated implementation technique is the *hash table*, which is a combination of an *array* and a *linked list*. The function hash() takes an immutable value in Python (number, string, or tuple) and returns an integer. You should try invoking this with different values to see the effect. Integer values simply return their own value as a hash, while for floats, tuples, and strings, the rules are more complicated. Because the arguments are immutable, the same argument will always return the same value.

To make a container, an array is first created. This array will hold links in a linked list. When an element is inserted, its hash value is computed and the remainder is determined when divided by the table size. The value is then placed into the linked list at the given location. The following shows a few example values assuming a hash table of size 5.

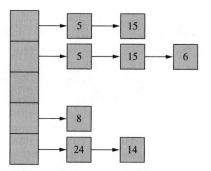

Notice that the elements do not appear to be ordered by their values in any particular way. Assuming that the lists do not become too long, insertions and removals from a hash table can be very fast. To assure good performance, you can increase the size of the table when a threshold of values has been reached (for example, when the number of elements is three times the size of the table).

Hash tables are typically used to implement the dictionary data type. Here each link in the linked lists will maintain both the key and values for the dictionary. The hash value for each entry is determined by the hash value of the key. This is why the list returned by the method keys() for a dictionary is not guaranteed to have any order, since it typically results from a simple walk through the hash table. Similarly, if a sufficient number of values are inserted into a dictionary, a new table may be created, resulting in the reorganization of the hash table. This usually results in the values being shuffled and is one more reason why the order of values returned by the method dict.keys() is not specified.

To implement a hash table, you would again use a pair of classes. Like the links in a linked list or the nodes in a binary search tree, the first class, `Association`, stores the values in the collection as well as a link field to the next association:

```
class Association (object):
    def __init__ (self, k, v, n):
        self.key = k
        self.value = v
        self.next = n
```

The `Hashtable` class stores a table of values and the number of elements currently being maintained in the table. Here we make a table that initially maintains 10 values:

```
class Hashtable (object):
    def __init__ (self):
        self.table = [None] * 10
        self.count = 0
    def add (self, newKey, newValue):
    def has_key (self, key):
    . . .
```

The implementation of some of the operations for a hash table is explored in the exercises.

This small chapter has only scratched the surface of the study of data structures. Much more information and analysis can be found in any textbook on the subject.

EXERCISES

1. Provide a class definition for a deque (double-ended queue), which allows insertions and removals from both ends of a queue. Your class should support the operations `addFront`, `addBack`, `removeFront`, `removeBack`, and `isEmpty`. You can use a list for the underlying implementation.

2. You can use the methods in a module named *time* to discover the current time. This can then be used to measure execution time. Use this technique to measure the difference between a linear search, such as is performed using our simple bag implementation, and the binary search of the `sortedBag` class. Create a collection with 10,000 random integers. Then measure the amount of time it will take to test whether 10,000 other random integers are found in the collection. Do the execution times for the simple bag and sorted bag differ?

3. Chapter 8 described the set operations using a functional rather than an imperative approach. Complete the implementation of the `set` data type using techniques such as list comprehensions.

4. If Python did not already have a `List` data type, you might need to implement a data structure such as the dynamic array or vector described in this chapter. In this exercise you will explore how this can be done. Begin by creating the following class definition:

```
class Vector (object):
    def __init__ (self):
```

```
    self.data = [ None ] * 5
    self.size = 0
    self.capacity = 5
def add (self, newValue): # add an element to the
collection
    pass
def insert (self, I, newValue): # insert at location
i
    pass
def remove (self, i): # remove value at location i
    pass
def test (self, testValue): # see if collection
contains element
    pass
def __iter__(self): return self.data.__iter__()
def size (self): return self.size
```

Implement the functions add and insert. The add function places the new element at the end of the collection, while insert places the new element at a specific point. Both functions need to check that the size does not exceed the capacity before placing the value. If it does, the size of the array stored in self.data should be doubled and the capacity modified appropriately. The remove method should delete an element at the given location. This reduces the size, but not the capacity. The test method should see if the value is held in the collection.

5. Chapter 11 described how operators in Python can be overloaded by defining functions with special built-in names. To overload the indexing operators, the two methods are __getitem__(*self, index*) and __setitem(*self, index, value*). The first provides the meaning when a *value* is indexed, while the second is used to implement the assignment to an indexed value. Provide implementations of these for your vector class, and demonstrate that the new class understands the Python index syntax.

6. Complete the implementation of the LinkedList abstraction by providing methods for testing to determine whether a value is held in the collection and to remove a value. Of the two, testing is easiest, while removing is tricky because you need to modify the previous link, or the first link if you remove the initial value.

7. The problem of removal described in question 6 is mitigated if links maintain references to both the next and the previous link. This is called a *double-linked list*. However, adding to a double-linked list is more complicated. Modify the LinkedList and Link classes to use the double-linked list idea.

8. Provide implementations of the methods __getitem__(*self, index*) and __setitem__(*self, index, value*) used in the execution of the indexing operators. Are these more or less efficient than those you implemented for the vector class?

9. A binary search tree is formed using two classes: a class for each node in the tree and a class that represents the tree itself. These were described in this chapter. Using these classes, implement the method for adding a new element to a collection. The add method first examines the root. If the root is None, then the collection is empty, and a new node is created and assigned to the root. Otherwise, the value being inserted is compared to the value of the root. If it is smaller and no left child exists, a new node is created and becomes the left child. Otherwise, if the element is larger and no right child exists, a new node is created and becomes the right child. If a child node exists, the same process

is repeated to insert the value into the child node. Note that values are always therefore being inserted at the leaves of the tree.

10. What happens if the previous algorithm and elements are inserted in order—for example, the values 1 to 10, in order smallest to largest? What sort of tree do you get? Various algorithms can be used to rebalance the tree, but they are beyond the scope of this book.

11. Have Python compute the hash values for 1, 1.4, 'a,' and ('a,' 'b'). Is the hash value of a long integer related to the value of the integer?

12. What happens if you give a mutable value, such as a list, to the function hash?

13. Finish the implementation of the method that is used to add a new key and value pair into a hash table. The function hash is guaranteed to return only an integer value. How do you convert this into an index in the table? Once you have an index, how do you add the element to the collection?

14. Extend the hash table you started in question 13 by adding methods to test whether a key is found in the collection and to remove the association with a given key from the collection.

15. Chapter 11 discussed how operators are implemented internally using methods with special names. Provide implementations for the methods __getitem__(self, key) and __setitem__(self, key, value) and demonstrate that your hash table will now work with the index syntax. That is, a value can be accessed as table[key] and a new value inserted into the table using table[key] = value.

16. Chapter 11 discussed the iterator protocol, which is used internally to perform the actions required by the *for* statement. Implement an iterator for your hash table.

17. A useful internal method to overload is __cmp__(self, object). This is invoked by the relational operators, such as < and >=. The cmp function should return a negative value if the first object is less than the second, zero if they are equal, and a positive value if the first is larger than the second. Add this operation to the class Association so that two Association classes are compared based on the comparisons of their keys.

18. Having defined in question 17 the comparison between associations based on keys, now provide an implementation of a priority queue data structure. The priority queue, like a dictionary, holds key and value pairs. However, the elements are sorted based on their keys. You can use a simple sorted list for this purpose. This allows the value with the smallest key (called the *value* with *highest priority*) to be quickly accessed and removed.

19. With a little bit of experimentation, you can determine the size of the hash table that is actually used by the Python Interpreter to implement a dictionary. Try executing the following statements. Looking at the result, how big do you think the hash table used by a dictionary is initially?

```
d = {}
d[1] = 1
for i in range(2,50):
    d[i] = i
    print d.keys()
    del d[i]
```

Brief Python Reference

Any printed document represents only a snapshot of a moment in time. Python is an evolving language, and you can and should expect that future versions of the language will add new features or alter the meaning of existing features. Because of Python's dynamic nature, the most reliable references are those found online, which will always be updated to reflect the current language definition. The most reliable source for all things Python is www.python.org.

The easiest source of information regarding Python execution is provided by the Python system itself. Most built-in functions and modules in the standard library are documented with docstrings (see Chapter 11). You can view this information by typing the __doc__ attribute:

```
>>> print range._ _doc_ _
range([start,] stop[, step]) -> list of integers
Return a list containing an arithmetic progression of integers.
range(i, j) returns [i, i+1, i+2, . . . , j-1]; start (!) defaults to 0.
When step is given, it specifies the increment (or decrement).
For example, range(4) returns [0, 1, 2, 3]. The end point is omitted!
These are exactly the valid indices for a list of 4 elements.
>>>
```

Slightly more extensive information can be obtained using the online help system. From inside an interactive Python session, type the command **help()**. This will produce a new prompt. If you type the name of a module or of a file within a module, it will produce helpful documentation:

```
>>> help()
help> random.randint
Help on method randint in random:
random.randint = randint(self, a, b) method of random.Random instance
Return random integer in range [a, b], including both end points.
help>
```

Type control-D, or the command quit to exit the on-line help system.

TYPES IN PYTHON

Approximately two dozen types are built into the Python Interpreter. These can be divided into a smaller number of categories, as shown in the following table.

Null type	The null object has type `NoneType`. There is precisely one null object, written `None`. This value has no attributes or operations, and it evaluates to false in an expression.
Numerics	Numbers are represented by a variety of types, such as `IntType`, `LongType`, `FloatType`, and `ComplexType`. They each recognize a variety of numeric operations.
Sequences	Sequences include strings (`StringType`), lists (`ListType`), tuples (`TupleType`), and ranges. A variety of operations are used to access or modify the values held in the collection.
Mappings	The dictionary (`DictType`) allows values to be referenced by key.
Callable	Callable types recognize the function `call` syntax. Types in this category include the `BuiltInFunctionType`, `BuiltInMethodType`, `ClassType`, `FunctionType` (for user defined functions), and `MethodType`.
Modules	`ModuleType` is the type associated with a module that has been imported into a running program.
Classes	A class definition creates a value of `ClassType`.
Files	Opening a file creates a value of `FileType`.
Internal	Various other internal types are created in the Python system, such as `CodeType`, which represented a compiled Python function.

Numeric Types

Integers are internally represented by two types. A value of `IntType` has a limited range, typically -2^{31} to 2^{31}. A value of `LongType` has arbitrary precision. However, the user is normally unaware of this distinction, as both types support the same set of operations and an `IntType` is implicitly converted to a `LongType` when necessary. Complex numbers are represented by a pair of floating-point numbers. The real and imaginary parts of a complex number z are accessed as `z.real` and `z.imag`.

The following operator tokens are recognized:

+	Addition
–	Subtraction
*	Multiplication
**	Exponentiation
/	Division

//	Integer division
%	Remainder for numeric types
<<	Left shift (integer only)
>>	Right shift (integer only)
&	Bitwise and of integer values
|	Bitwise or of integer values
^	Bitwise exclusive or of integer values
~	Bitwise negation of integer value
<	Less than comparison
>	Greater than comparison
<=	Less than or equal comparison
>=	Greater than or equal comparison
==	Equality comparison
!=	Inequality comparison
<>	Alternative form for Inequality comparison
abs(x)	Absolute value of x
divmod(x,y)	Return tuple (int (x/u), x % y)
row(x, y, m)	Returns (x ** y) % m
round(x)	Rounds floating value x to nearest integer

The only unary operators are unary negation and the unary plus operator.

The division operator returns a true division, hence 5/2 returns 2.5. The operator // can be used to produce an integer division.

For floating-point values, the modular division operator x % y is defined to be x-int(x/y) * y.

Comparisons can be chained. An expression such as x < y < z is interpreted as (x < y) and (y < z). An expression such as x < y > z is legal, but confusing.

Operations involving values of different types may result in values being coerced. Integers are converted to float, floating values to complex. If no coercion can be applied to permit values to be of the same type, an error is reported.

Some operators are overloaded with alternative meanings when applied to non-numeric arguments. For example, the + operator is used for sequence catenation, the % operator for string formatting, and the * operator for sequence repetition.

It is sometimes necessary to convert a value from one type to another. The following are some common functions for this purpose:

int(x)	Convert x into an integer
long(x)	Convert x into a long integer
float(x)	Convert x into a floating-point number
complex(r, i)	Convert into a complex number with real part r and imaginary part i
str(x)	Convert x into a string

repr(x)	Convert x into an expression string
eval(str)	Evaluate string as expression and return result
tuple(s)	Convert a sequence s into a tuple
list(s)	Convert sequence s into a list
chr(x)	Convert integer into a character
ord(x)	Convert a single character into its integer (ordinal) value
hex(x)	Convert integer into a hexadecimal string
oct(x)	Convert integer into an octal string

Boolean Types

The constants True and False are representatives of the Boolean type. Operators such as the relational operators (<, >, <=, >=, ==, !=, and <>) as well as the logical operators and, or, and not will return a Boolean type. However, any Python object can also be used as a Boolean value in situations for which a true/false value is required. Examples of such situations include the conditionals in an *if* or *while* statement, or as argument to a logical operator such as and, or or not. Rules for converting a value into a Boolean include the following:

- Any nonzero integer is considered to be true. Zero is considered to be false.
- Any nonempty string, list, tuple, or dictionary is considered to be true. An empty value is considered to be false.
- The special value None is considered to be false.

Sequence Types (Strings, Lists, and Tuples)

A *sequence* is an ordered set of values indexed by position. This general category includes strings, lists, and tuples. Strings are sequences of characters, while lists and tuples can contain any legal Python object. Strings and tuples are *immutable*—once created, they cannot be modified. Lists allow insertion, deletion, and substitution of elements.

The following table lists operations that are common to all sequences:

s[i]	Return element i in sequence s.
s[i:j]	Return slice starting at position i extending to position j. Omitting first argument indicates the start of the sequence. Omitting second argument indicates end of sequence.
len(s)	Return number of elements in sequence.
min(s)	Minimum value in s.
max(s)	Maximum value in s.
s.count(x)	Count occurrences of x in s.
s.index(x)	Return the smallest position i where s[i] equals x.

Because lists can be dynamically modified, they support a number of additional functions shown in the following table:

`list(s)`	Convert sequence s into a list
`s.append(x)`	Append new element x to end of s
`s.extend(l)`	Extend list with new list l (append all elements)
`s.insert(I, x)`	Insert x at indicated position
`s.pop()`	Return last element and remove it from the list
`s.pop(i)`	Return element i and remove it from the list
`s.remove(x)`	Search for x and remove it from s
`s.reverse()`	Reverse items of s in place
`s.sort()`	Sort items of s in place
`s.sort(comp)`	Sort items using `comp` as comparison function

A large number of higher-level operations are particular to strings. Since strings are immutable, these do not actually alter the leftmost value, but instead return a new value in which the transformation has been applied.

`s.capitalize()`	Return a string in which the first letter has been made uppercase
`s.center(n)`	Return a string in which s is centered in a string of width n
`s.endswith(e)`	Return true if s ends with the string e
`s.isalnum()`	Return true if s is all alphabetic or numeric
`s.isalpha()`	Return true if s is all alphabetic
`s.isdigit()`	Return true if s is all digit characters
`s.islower()`	Return true if s is all lowercase
`s.isspace()`	Return true if s is all space, tab, or newlines
`s.isupper()`	Return true if s is all uppercase
`s.join(seq)`	Join elements of `seq` together, placing a copy of s between each
`s.ljust(w)`	Place s to the left of a new string of width w
`s.lower()`	Return string in which all characters are lowercase
`s.lstring()`	Strip any spaces from the left of the string
`s.replace(o,n)`	Replace all occurrences of o with n
`s.rjust(w)`	Place s to the right of a new string of width w
`s.rstring()`	Strip any spaces or newlines from s
`s.split(sep)`	Return list of s that is split by occurrences of sep
`s.startswith(p)`	Return true if s begins with prefix p
`s.strip()`	Strip whitespace from both start and end of s
`s.swapcase()`	Turn uppercase letters to lowercase, and vice versa
`s.upper()`	Make all letters uppercase

In older versions of Python, the string functions described above were imported from the `string` module, and the value to the left of the dot was written as the first argument. That is, instead of writing

```
s.split(' ')
```

the programmer would write

```
import string
string.split(s, ' ')
```

You are still likely to see strings used in this way in older Python programs.

String Formatting

As noted, the % operator is overloaded to perform string formatting. The left argument is a string that may contain formatting directives. If only one directive is in the formatting string, the argument argument is the value to be printed. Otherwise, the right argument must be a tuple containing the appropriate number of values. The formatting directives are as follows:

%d or %i	Decimal integer
%u	Unsigned integer
%o	Octal integer
%x	Hexidecimal integer
%f or %e	Floating point
%s	String
%c	Single character from integer
%%	Literal %

Here are a few examples:

```
>>> 'Value is %d' % (42)
Value is 42
```

Mapping Types (Dictionaries)

A *mapping type* is a collection that uses keys to locate values. Unlike sequences, the keys do not represent positions, but are instead Python values. Items used as a key must be immutable. Typically strings are used as a key, and less frequently numbers or tuples are used. Keys must also be unique; only one value can be stored for any particular key.

The following table lists methods and operations that can be applied to mapping types:

len(m)	Return number of items in m
m[k]	Return the item of m with key k
m[k] = v	Set the value associated with key k to v
del m[k]	Delete item with key k from m
m.clear()	Remove all items from m
m.copy()	Return a copy of m
m.has _ key(k)	Return true if m has a value stored with key k

m.items()	Return a list of (key, value) pairs
m.keys()	Return a list of key values
m.update(b)	Add all objects from b to m
m.values()	Return a list of all values in m
m.get(k, d)	If k is a valid key, return m[k], otherwise return d

Using an invalid key will raise a `KeyError` exception. The programmer can either use `has_key(k)` to test whether a map has a given key before access or use the `get` method, which will return a default value if the key is not legal.

BUILT-IN FUNCTIONS

Certain functions are designated as *built-in*, meaning that they do not need to be imported from any module before they can be used. (More accurately, the built-in module is automatically imported by the Python interpreter at the start of execution.) Being built-in does not mean that the names are reserved. The programmer can override any name with a new definition, although such actions should be taken with care. The following table lists the more common built-in functions.

abs(x)	Return the absolute value of x.
apply(f, a)	Perform function call on f using arguments a.
callable(o)	Return true if o is a callable object.
chr(i)	Convert an integer between 0 and 255 into a one character string
cmp(x, y)	Compare x and y and return a negative value if x < y, a zero if x is equal to y, and a positive value if x > 0. Any two objects can be compared, although the result may not be meaningful except for numbers.
coerce(x, y)	Return a tuple in which x and y are converted into a common type.
complex(r, i)	Return a complex number with real part r and imaginary part i.
eval(str)	Evaluate string `str` and return result.
filter(f, s)	Return a list consisting of the objects from sequence s in which the function f returns true.
float(x)	Return floating-point equivalent to x.
getattr(o, a)	Return attribute a from object o, same as o.a.
globals()	Return dictionary of global name space.
hasattr(o, a)	Return true if o has an attribute named a.
hash(o)	Return an integer hash value for immutable object o.
hex(x)	Return a string containing hex value of x.
input(str)	Same as eval(raw _ input(str)).

`isinstance(o, c)`	Return true if o is an instance of class c.
`issubclass(c, c2)`	Return true if c is a subclass of class c2.
`len(s)`	Return number of items contained in s.
`list(s)`	Return list containing elements from sequence s.
`locals()`	Return dictionaries of local name space.
`long(x)`	Convert number or string x into a long intger.
`map(f, s)`	Apply function f to each item of sequence s, return new sequence.
`max(s)`	Return maximim value from sequence s.
`min(s)`	Return minimum value from sequence s.
`oct(x)`	Convert integer x into an octal string.
`open(n, m)`	Open file n and return file object. m should be 'r,' 'w.'.
`ord(x)`	Return the integer value (ordinal) for single character c.
`pow(x, y, m)`	Return (x ** y) % m.
`range(s, t, m)`	Return list of integers from s to t step m. If m is omitted default is 1.
`raw _ input(s)`	Print prompt s and return user response as string.
`reduce(f, s, i)`	Apply binary function f to sequence s cumulatively. Value i is identity used with first value. If i is omitted it is default to zero.
`repr(x)`	Return a string representation of x.
`round(x)`	Round floating-point value x.
`setattr(o, a, x)`	Set attribute a in object o to x, same as o.a = x.
`str(x)`	Return string representation of x.
`tuple(s)`	Convert sequence s into a tuple.
`type(x)`	Return the type of x.

PYTHON SYNTAX

Comments

A hash mark (#) indicates the start of a comment. Any text following the hash mark until the end of the current line is ignored by the Python Interpreter.

Expressions

Integers consist of one or more digits. Floating-point numbers have an embedded decimal point and/or an optional signed exponent. The exponent is indicated by the letter *e* or *E*, followed by an optionally signed integer. Various examples are shown at left on the following page. Integers can also be written in *octal* or *hexadecimal*. A number beginning with 0 and containing only the digits 0 through 7 is interpreted as an octal constant. A number beginning with the literal 0x or 0X, followed by the

```
0
123
12.34
.4
12.
4.3e3
4.3e-3
042
0xFACE
12+4i
```

digits 0 through 9 and the letters A through F is interpreted as a hexadecimal number. A complex number is written as a pair of numbers *realpart+imaginarypart*, where the *imginarypart* is followed by the letter *j* or *J*.

Valid operators for numbers and other built-in types were described in the earlier discussion on types.

Expression Statements

In interactive execution, an expression that is typed at the prompt is evaluated and the result printed. The variable named by an underscore character maintains the value of the last expression printed.

Assignment Statements

```
a = 8
a, b = 4, 2
a, b = (4, 2)
x = (4, 2)
a, b = x
a, b = b, a
a = b = 7
```

An assignment statement is written as a series of one or more comma-separated targets, the assignment operator, and an equal number of comma-separated expressions, or a tuple that contains the correct number of values. Several targets can be assigned at the same time. Various examples are shown at left.

Conditional (*if*) Statements

A conditional statement is indicated by the keyword `if`. This is followed by an expression that is interpreted as a Boolean value. Following the expression is a colon. A single statement can follow the colon and will be executed if the expression is true. Otherwise, a block of statements can be written on succeeding lines, indented one more tab stop than the *if* statement. The entire block will be executed if the expression is true and ignored if it is not.

Regardless of which form is used, an *if* statement can be followed by an *else* part. The *else* statement will be executed only if the *if* statement was not. The keyword `elif` can be used to combine an `else` and a following `if`.

```
if a < min: min = a
if x < y:
  print 'smaller value is ' , x
  min = x
if x < y:
  print 'smaller value is x', x
  min = x
else:
  print 'smaller value is y', y
  min = y
if x < y:
  min = x
elif z < x:
  min = z
```

Pass Statement

The *pass* statement is a null operation. It has no effect whatsoever. A *pass* statement is normally used in the body of a conditional when an alternative action is being performed by the else part.

```
if x < y:
   pass
else:
   min = x
```

Loops

The simplest type of loop is a *while* loop, which is written as a keyword `while`, followed by a Boolean expression. The statements in the loop will be executed as long as the expression evaluates true. A *break* statement contained within the body of the loop will immediately halt the loop. A *continue* statement will force execution back to the conditional test for the loop. An optional *else* statement following the loop will be executed as long as the loop executed normally, without the benefit of a *break* statement.

```
while x < y:
   x = x + 1
   if (x > 20): break
else:
   print 'did not reach 20'
```

A *for* loop assigns to a target a succession of elements from a list or other collection. A *range* statement can simplify the creation of a list of values from an arithmetic progreassion. The arguments to `range` are a starting value, termination test (which is not part of the collection), and step size. For example, `range(1, 7, 3)` would produce the list containing the elements 1 and 4. If the argument to a *for* statement is a dictionary, the list of keys are used. If the argument is a file, a list consisting of each line of the file is used. *Break*, *continue*, and *else* statements can be used with a *for*, with the same meaning as when used with a *while* statement.

```
for x in range(1, 7, 3): pass
```

Function Definitions

A function definition is indicated using the `def` keyword. This is followed by the function name, a parenthesized list of arguments, and a colon. The body of the function is indented one tab space, similar to the looping statements described earlier. A *return* statement within the body of the function halts execution and returns the indicated value.

```
def smallest(x, y):
   if x < y:
```

```
        return x
  else:
        return y
```

If a function reaches the end of the statement list without encountering a *return* statement, the value None is implicitly returned. Although normally functions are defined at the top level, they are actually an executable statement, and can be embedded in an *if* conditional.

```
if x < y:
  def minValue():
        return x
else:
  def minValue():
        return y
```

Functions that do not return an explicit value are often called *procedures*. Such functions can be invoked as statements, without using the results. Functions defined inside of class definitions are called *methods*.

An alternative method for defining short functions is the lambda operator. A lambda function consists of the keyword lambda, a list of arguments, a colon, and an expression that is the body of the function. Notice that lambda functions do not have a name and consist of only a single expression. These functions are normally used as arguments to other function calls.

```
aList = map(bList, lambda x: x + 1)
```

Class Definitions

A class is indicated by the keyword class, followed by the class name, and a parenthesized list of parent classes. Variables and methods defined in parent classes automatically become part of the new class. The built-in class object can be used as a parent class in the absence of any other obvious choice.

Earlier versions of Python allowed the parent class list to be omitted. However, such usage should now be avoided, as the introduction of the newer-style classes also fixed a number of subtle problems with the class definition mechanism.

```
class Stack(object):
  def __init__(self):
        self.storage = [ ]
  def push (self, newValue)
        self.storage.append(newValue)
  def pop (self)
        return self.storage.pop()
```

Within a class description, function definitions, called *methods*, must have a first argument that represents the class object. Conventionally, this argument is named self. Data fields can be created simply by assigning to an attribute of this object. A method named __init__ (two underscores before and after the name) is invoked as part of the process of creating a new instance of the class. This function, called a *constructor*, is used to perform any necessary initialization for the class.

The Import Statement

Statements beginning with the keyword `import` specify that a library of Python statements, called an *import library*, should be included in the current program. A suffix, typically *.py*, is appended to the name that follows the `import` to form a file name. The indicated file is interpreted and executed, and the resulting local name space is stored in a variable using the import name. Thereafter, features defined by this file can be accessed using the import name as the base for a qualified name.

```
import string
spring.split('abc def ghi', '')
```

The *from* statement is a variation of an *import* statement. It imports the indicated library, and then places the indicated names into the current local name space. The imported features can then be used just as if they were defined in the current file. This results in simpler names and can also produce faster execution since there is one less dynamic lookup needed to determine the meaning of a name.

MODULES IN THE STANDARD LIBRARY

The standard library distributed with every Python Interpreter contains a large number of modules. The following sections describe only the most common functions found in the most commonly used modules. Much more complete documentation and descriptions of other modules can be found in the online documentation at the python.org web site.

sys

The `sys` module contains variables and functions that pertain to the operation of the operator and the underlying operating system.

`argv`	The list of command-line options passed to the program
`maxint`	Largest integer supported by `IntType`
`modules`	Dictionary for mapping module names to loaded modules
`platform`	String describing current platform
`ps1`	String containing text for primary prompt, normally >>>
`ps2`	String for secondary prompt, normally . . .
`stdin`	File object for standard input
`stdout`	File object for standard output
`stderr`	File object for error output
`exit(n)`	Exit function by raising `SystemExit` exeption

types

The `types` module defines names for all the built-in object types. This is useful in conjunction with the built-in `isinstance()` function. The following illustrates this use:

```
import types
if isinstance (s, types.ListType):
   print 's is a list'
else:
   print 's is not a list'
```

Names defined by the types module include the following:

BuiltinFunctionType	CodeType	ComplexType	ClassType
DictType	DictionaryType	FileType	FloatType
FrameType	FunctionType	InstanceType	IntType
LambdaType	ListType	LongType	MethodType
ModuleType	NoneType	SinceType	StringType
TupleType	TypeType		

math

The `math` module defines standard mathematical functions. These functions work with integers and floats, but not with complex numbers. Constants include `math.pi` and `math.e`. Functions include `acos`, `asin`, `atan`, `ceil`, `cos`, `exp`, `fabs`, `floor`, `log`, `log10`, `sin`, `sqrt`, and `tan`.

random

The `random` module provides the ability to generate random numbers or select a random element from a sequence.

`choice(s)`	Select an element in random from s.
`randint(a, b)`	Return a random integer greater than or equal to a and less than or equal to b.
`random()`	Return a random number between 0 and 1.
`randrange(a, b)`	Return a random value from a range. Like the `range` function, the upper limit is not included in the collection.

shelve

The `shelve` module provides a simple way to save and restore the value of objects across several different executions. The *open* statement opens a file, called a *shelf*, that will be used to store the values. Thereafter the shelf can be used just like a dictionary. Values assigned to the shelf are stored in the file. When a value is read from the shelf, the associated value is accessed from the dictionary. A *close* statement should always be used with a shelf to ensure that all remaining values are copied to the associated file.

db = Open(filename)	Open or create a shelf
db['key']	Access value in shelf with given key
db['key'] = x	Store value x in shelf with given key
db.close()	Close the associated shelf

time

Time in Python is measured as the number of seconds since the "epoch." The epoch is January 1, 1970, on Unix and Windows systems, and January 1, 1900, on the Macintosh.

time()	Return seconds since the epoch.
gmtime(seconds)	Convert time into a tuple representing (year, month, day, hour, minute, second, weekday, day, dst). The latter is 1 if daylight savings is in effect, 0 if not, and -1 if no information is available. Typically invokes as gmtime(time()).
localtime(seconds)	Same format as gmtime, but for local time zone.
mktime(tuple)	Takes a tuple in the format of gmtime() and returns a number representing seconds in the format time().
asctime(tuple)	Takes a tuple in the format of gmtime() and converts to string of form 'Tue June 11 20:45:22 2006'.
clock()	Return the current CPU time in seconds as a floating-point number.
strftime(format, tuple)	Produce a string representation of a time represented as a tuple as produced by gmtime according to the format described by the first argument. Formatting string described below.
strptime(string, format)	Read a string representing a time described by the format, and return a tuple similar to gmtime.

The formatting commands used by strftime and strptime can include the following:

%a	Abbreviated weekday name
%A	Full weekday name
%b	Abbreviated month name
%B	Full month name
%c	Appropriate date and time representation
%d	Day of the month as a decimal number
%H	Hour (24-hour clock) as a number
%I	Hour (12-hour clock) as a number

`%%j`	Day of the year as a number
`%m`	Month as a decimal number
`%M`	Minute as a decimal number
`%p`	AM or PM
`%S`	Seconds as a decimal number
`%U`	Week number (0–53) of the year
`%w`	Weekday as a decimal number
`%x`	Appropriate date representation
`%X`	Locals appropriate time representation
`%y`	Year without century as a decimal number (0–99)
`%Y`	Year with century as a decimal number
`%Z`	Timezone name
`%%`	The % character

re

This module provides support for searching using regular expressions. The concept of regular expressions is described in Chapter 11. The following table lists the more common patterns for forming regular expressions:

Text	Matches literal
`^`	Start of string
`$`	End of string
`( ... )*`	Zero or more occurrences
`( ... )+`	One or more occurrences
`( ... )?`	Optional (zero or one)
`[chars]`	One character from range
`[^chars]`	One character not from range
`Pat	pat`	Alternative (one or the other)
`( ... )`	Group
`.`	Any character except newline

Regular expressions are first compiled into a regular expression object (or pattern).

```
pat = re.compile(str)
```

The pattern is then used in a variety of different searches. A search returns a match object. The operations supported by a regular expression object include the following:

`mo = pat.searc( text)`	Search text for pattern, return match object
`mo = pat.match(text)`	Search anchored at start of string

`lst = pat.Split(text)`	Break text by occurrences of patterns. Returns a list of strings
`lst = pat.Findall(text)`	Returns a list of matches of pattern
`pat.Sub(rep, text)`	Substitutes first occurrences of pattern with rep

A match object supports the following operations:

`m.start()`	Start of matched text
`m.end()`	End of matched text
`m.span()`	Tuple of start and end

In addition, a match object can be used where a Boolean is expected, such as in an *if* or *while* statement. The value is considered to be true if the match was successful, and false otherwise.

os

This module provides an interface to common operating system services. Among the services provided by this module are the following:

`environ`	A mapping object representing the current environment variables
`name`	The name of the current operating system
`mkdir(path)`	Make a directory
`unlink(path)`	Unlink (deletes) a file
`rename(src, dst)`	Rename a file

Many more functions are provided in this module; however, the use of these facilities is complex and beyond the scope of this book.

tempfile

This module provides functions useful for creating temporary files that are used only while a program is executing; then they are discarded.

`mktemp()`	Return a unique temporary file name
`mktemp(suffix)`	Return a unique temporary file name with given suffix
`temporaryfile(mode)`	Create a temporary file with the given mode

glob

The `glob` function in the module of the same name will return a list containing all file names in a directory that match a pattern. The pattern can be specified using notation similar to that employed by the regular expression matcher. For example, `glob.glob("*.html")` will return a list of files with the html suffix. The function `os.chdir` in the `os` module can be used to change the working directory prior to calling `glob`.

Tkinter

The Tkinter module is used to create graphical user interfaces using the Tkinter library. Like most GUI libraries, the Tkinter facility is based around the idea of windows, frames, menus, and buttons and other graphical widgets. Because the Tkinter library defines a large number of symbolic names and values, it is usually simply included as part of the local name space using the following command:

```
from Tkinter import *
```

The root window for the Tkinter application is accessed using the function Tk(). Among the commands the root window understands are the following:

title ("string")	Set the title for the main window.
geometry ("size")	Set the size of the window in pixels. The size is specified as widthxheight.
mainloop()	Start the main loop for the GUI system. The program will wait for user interaction, or until the main window is closed.

In addition, the root window is used as the parent window when creating graphical widgets. Widgets are graphical items that occupy space in a window. Example widgets include buttons, canvas, scroll bars, and the like. The first argument in the constructor for each widget is always the parent window, which is initially the root window. Subsequent arguments are normally specified in keyword format, rather than positional form.

widget(parent, options)	Constructor. Parent is parent window.
width=n	Set width of widget. Unit is either characters or pixels.
height=n	Set height of widget.
fb=str	Set foreground color of widget. Example strings include "Red," "Blue".
bg=str	Set background color of widget.
bind(selection, function)	Bind a callback function to an event on the widget. Events include <Button-1>, <ButtonRelease-1>, <Enter>, <Leave>, <B1-Motion>, <KeyPress>, <KeyRelease>.

Widgets also understand the following layout directives:

pack(options)	Place the widget following the previous. Options include side=LEFT (or RIGHT, TOP, or BOTTOM), fil=YES (or NO)
grid(row=n, column=n, options)	Place widget into a grid. Options include rowspan=n, columnspan=n.
place(relx=n.n, rely=n.n, options) place(x=n, y=n, options)	Place a widget in a location relative to the upper-left corner of parent. The values are between 0.0 and 1.0. Location can also be specified as an absolute x,y position.

Widgets include `Frame`, `Label`, `Entry`, `Text`, `button`, `Checkbutton`, `Radiobutton`, `Menu`, `Canvas`, `Scale`, `Listbox`, `Scrollbar`, and `Menubutton`.

Button and keypress events cause the callback function to be invoked with an argument of type `event`. The `event` object holds a number of different data fields, including the following:

X, y	The coordinates the event occurred
Char	The character pressed

A `Frame` is a general-purpose container for other widgets. Frames do not implement any additional methods beyond those common to all widgets.

A `Label` is a simple widget for displaying text of an image. In addition to the options common to all widgets (`height`, `width`, `fg`, `bg`) a label supports the following:

`text="str"`	Set text for label
`font=("name," size)`	Set font for text
`justify=loc`	Location is LEFT, RIGHT, or CENTER
`bitmap=map`	A bitmap to be used in place of the text
`image=img`	An image to be used in place of text
`relief=c`	C is either FLAT, SUNKEN, RAISED, GROOVE, or RIDGE. Borderwidth must be nonzero
`borderwidth=n`	Width of border (in pixels)
`anchor=c`	C is N, NE, E, SE, S, SW, W, NW, or CENTER (default)
`cursor=c`	Cursor to show when mouse is moved over the label
`textvariable=v`	Track image on label according to the value of `StringVar` v.

The `textvariable` option can be used to change the image on a label dynamically by changing the value held in a variable of type `StringVar`. This mechanism is common to many widgets.

```
s = StringVar()

s.set("one")
lab = Label(root, textvariable=s) # text is initially "one"
s.set("two") # now text on label is "two"
```

An `entry` is used to retrieve a single line of text from the user. It understands the following options:

`textvariable=v`	Track value of entry with string variable
`show=c`	Show character c instead of typed character (used for reading passwords, for example)

The value of an entry can be returned using the method `get`. Text can also be manipulated using `insert(index, text)` or `delete(from, to)`, which changes the value of the string at the given locations.

A `text` allows multi-line textual input. Locations in a `Text` are specified as a string with the format *line.column*. Lines begin with 1 and columns with 0 (zero), so that the initial location is "1.0." The symbolic constant END refers to the end of a text object. Text objects understand methods to insert and delete values at a given location.

A button is an object that can be pressed (clicked). When pressed, the callback function specified as an option to the constructor for the button is invoked. Options that a button understands include the following:

text=str	Text displayed on button
bitmap=b	Bitmap displayed on button
command=fun	Function invoked when pressed
font=f	Font used in button
padx=n, pady=n	Padding used between text and button border
relief=c	C is SUNKEN, RAISED, GROOVE, RIDGE, or FLAT
state=n	N is NORMAL (default), ACTIVE, or DISABLED
testvariable=v	Take text of button from string variable
borderwidth=n	Width of border for button

A checkbutton is similar, but it must specify an instance of IntVar or StringVar as the "variable" option. This variable is set to 1 if the button is selected, and 0 otherwise. You can change the value of this variable using the options ovalue and offvalue. A Radiobutton is similar, but it uses the option value=n to specify the value to be assigned to the variable when the button is selected.

A canvas is a widget that supports a number of commands that can be used to draw graphical images. These include the following:

create _ line(x1, y1, x2, y2, . . . xn, yn)	Create lines connecting the points
create _ arc(x1, y1, x2, y2)	Create an arc in the bounded box
create _ oval(x1, y1, x2, y2)	Create an oval in the bounded box
create _ rectangle(x1, y2, x2, y2)	Create a rectangle in the bounded box
create _ text(x, y, text=str)	Print text at given position

How to Learn a Second (or Third) Programming Language

This is *not* a book about how to write computer programs. It *is* a book on how to write computer programs in Python. As I noted in the Preface, Python is an excellent first programming language, because it's a wonderful vehicle for helping you learn programming concepts. Ideas such as variables, types, functions, and classes are found in many languages, and the knowledge you gain by learning Python can be a foundation upon which you can build your programming skills.

Programming languages have an interesting relationship with the study of computer science. Languages come and go with surprising rapidity. In almost no other engineering discipline do people change their fundamental tools with such frequency. This being the case, you can expect that over the course of your career you will, from time to time, be called upon to acquire new skills. This naturally leads to the question: How should I approach this task? You might be wondering how you should go about learning a new programming language. Fortunately, the following simple hints can make this job easier. These are summarized in Figure 1.

HINT 1: LEARN THE BASIC SYNTAX

Syntax is an essential first step in understanding a language, but learning syntax should never be confused with learning a language. By emphasizing certain aspects and hiding others, languages embody a style of thought, a perspective, what we call a *paradigm*. Ultimately, it is internalizing this style of thought that is most important. But to reach that point, you must first be able to read and write simple statements in the language.

Find out how to write the language to create features with which you are familiar. How do you write a comment? How do you write a conditional? An assignment? A simple arithmetic expression? A loop?

For comments, Python uses a pound sign (#). Anything following the pound sign to the end of line is considered to be a comment. The following is a simple assignment:

Hint 1: Learn the basic syntax
Hint 2: Study the primitive data types
Hint 3: Study the basic data structures
Hint 4: Examine the built-in operations
Hint 5: Become familiar with the programming environment
Hint 6: Determine the class of problems the language was designed to solve
Hint 7: See if there are useful libraries
Hint 8: Emulate, Copy and Steal
Hint 9: Experiment, Evolve and Redo
Hint 10: Have fun.

Figure 1: Hints for Learning a New Language

```
max = 100 # set the maximum value in the search range
```

Unlike many languages (such as Java and C), indentation is very important in Python. The body of a conditional statement is indented, as in the following example:

```
# compute the smaller of a and b
if a < b:
  m = a
else:
  m = b
```

Rather than using brackets or curly braces, all adjacent statements at the same level of indentation are considered to be a *block*. The block ends when the indentation returns to the previous level. The following *while* loop illustrates this technique:

```
# find first Fibonacci number larger than 100
a = 1
b = 1
while b < 100:
  c = a + b
  a = b
  b = c
print b # will print the number we seek
```

An interesting feature of Python is the multiple assignment feature, which allows several expressions to be evaluated at once, and then assigned to several targets. Use of this feature often eliminates the need for temporary variables. The preceding bit of code could be written in a more Python-esque fashion as follows:

```
# find first Fibonacci number larger than 100
a, b = 1, 1
while b < 100:
  a, b = b, a + b
print b # will print the number we seek
```

The result is shorter and eliminates the unnecessary temporary variable c.
Indentation can be repeated to multiple levels, as in the following:

```
# compute the smaller of a, b and c
if a < b:
  if c < a:
      m = c
  else
      m = a
else:
  if c < b:
      m = c
  else:
      m = b
```

Notice the *if* statement following the else in the code fragment above. This combination occurs in many problems. If extended to three or more levels, it can become unwieldy, as in the following:

```
# perform the operation OP on a and b
if op == '+':
  r = a + b
else:
  if op == '-':
      r = a—b
  else:
      if op == '*':
          r = a * b
```

To handle this situation, Python provides an *elif* statement, which is a combination of an else and an if:

```
if op == '+':
  r = a + b
elif op == '-':
  r = a—b
elif op == '*':
  r = a * b
```

Functions are defined using the keyword def. The body of the function is indented. The function definition halts when the indentation returns to the previous level:

```
def remainder(a, b):
  q = a/b
  r = a—q*b
  return r
```

Although many other aspects of syntax may eventually become important (scoping rules, how to create classes, modules, and the like), the simple ability to read assignments and control flow statements will allow you to get started in the exploration of the language and is sufficient at the start.

HINT 2: STUDY THE BASIC DATA TYPES

A programming language is a complex tool, built out of more fundamental tools. The most basic tools in the programming language are the *primitive types*. Almost all languages provide simple integers, but what about long or short integers? Signed and unsigned? Enumerated types? Characters? Strings? Does the language support floating-point values, and if so, for what ranges? If you are going to be doing numerical programming, it might be useful to be able to use complex numbers. Are they provided? If your problem requires you to use a data type that is not supported by the language, you might find it easier to use a different language rather than trying to build the facilities you need in an inappropriate language.

As a language, Python provides a small but surprisingly flexible set of primitive types. The language is dynamically typed (more on that topic in Hint 4) and so blurs the distinction between integers and floating-point. Since variables are not given declared types, the only type characterization of a variable is the value it currently holds. A variable can at one point be an integer, and later be transformed into a non-integer value:

```
numValue = 5 # an integer
numValue = numValue / 2.0 # numValue is now 2.5
```

Most languages impose a size restriction on integers. For example, in Java an integer is stored in 32 bits, meaning the largest integer is $2^{31}-1$, or 2,147,483,647. Python makes no such restriction. Integer values can be as large as necessary. This can be illustrated by the following loop, which will print various powers of 2 up to 2^{100}.

```
n = 10
while n <= 100:
  print 2 ** n
  n = n + 10
```

Strings are formed using *either* single or double quotes. Python makes no distinction between single character values and strings.

```
name = "fred"
middleInitial = 'e'
```

By letting you use both single and double quotes, Python makes it easy for you to embed a quotation mark in the middle of a string:

```
message = 'ann said: "is my painting dry yet?" '
reply = "no, it's not"
```

Many useful operations can be performed on the string types. A summary of operations used with primitive data types can be found in Appendix A.

HINT 3: STUDY THE BASIC DATA STRUCTURES

Basic data structures refers to the primitive data structures provided as part of the language itself, and not to any higher-level data abstractions formed using the primitive mechanisms. (Those are covered in Hint 7.)

Almost all languages provide arrays. Many provide strings, and a few offer even more. A language such as APL provides *linear homogeneous arrays*, Lisp makes it easy to write list structures, and SNOBOL provides generous support for strings. (If you have never heard of any of these languages, don't worry!) Perl provides tables (indexed dictionary-like structures) as a basic tool. C provides structures, C++ adds classes, and Java supports both classes and interfaces. Any problem you envision solving must ultimately be expressed in the data types provided by the language, so a basic understanding of the implications of the choices you have is a foundation upon which everything else is built.

Start by asking yourself how the features in the new language you are learning are different from those in languages you have previously encountered. Consider, for example, an array. In most programming languages, you declare a variable as an array type. You may also need to declare the size (that is, the number of elements) in the array as part of the declaration. Since Python is dynamically typed, you do neither. The concept of an array has been generalized to a mechanism known as the *list*. To create a list, you simply assign a variable a list value. You can create an array-like list expression as follows:

```
names = ["john", "paul", "george", "ringo"]
```

Lists are indexed by integers starting with 0. The indexing operation can be used either to access or modify an individual member of a list:

```
a = names[2]        # sets a to "george"
names[3] = "fred"   # changes last element to fred
```

You can extract or reassign a portion of a list using the slicing operation. A *slice* is a generalization of a subscript. Instead of a single index expression, a colon and a second integer representing a size follow the expression:

```
print names[1:2] # prints "paul" and "george"
```

If the second argument is omitted, the slice refers to the remainder of the list:

```
print names[1:] # prints "paul", "george" and "fred"
```

A slice can be used as a target of an assignment. The value being assigned need not have the same number of elements as the slice. The array is expanded or reduced to fit.

```
names[1:2] = ["sally", "ann", "alice"]
# list is now john, sally, ann, alice, and fred
```

Since the language is dynamically typed, lists can contain values of different types. Lists can even contain other lists, as in the following:

```
# name, age, children's names
info = ['fred smith', 43, ['george', 'alice'] ]
```

The slicing operation can also be applied to strings.

A *tuple* in Python is closely related to a list. A tuple is formed by enclosing a group of comma-separated values inside parentheses. Tuples support most of the same operations as lists, such as indexing and slicing. The only difference is that you cannot modify the contents of a tuple once it has been created.

```
info = ('fred smith', 43, ('george', 'alice'))
name = info[0] # access is allowed
info[0] = 'sam smith' # error, modification is not allowed
```

A form of assignment called a *multiple assignment* breaks a tuple into individual components and assigns each part to a separate variable:

```
name, age, children = info
print name # will print 'fred smith'
```

This feature is useful when a function needs to return multiple values. The function simply wraps the values into a tuple. After the call, the function result is unwrapped into the individual pieces.

A *dictionary* generalizes the list in yet another direction. A dictionary is an *associative array*, in which elements are stored as key/value pairs. Rather than using integer offsets, elements in a dictionary are accessed using the key. Strings are the most common type for the key; however, the language permits any immutable Python value to be used. Curly braces are used to create a dictionary. Any initial keys and values are provided as pairs separated by a colon:

```
# create a dictionary of names and ages
ageDict = { "fred" : 42 , "sally" : 39, "ann" : 28}
```

To access or modify members of a dictionary, the key is used as an index:

```
annAge = ageDict["ann"]
ageDict["fred"] = 43 # fred got one year older
ageDict["sam"] = 12 # new elements added just by assigning to them
```

Appendix A provides a summary of the operations that can be used with the primitive data types.

Do not be surprised if it takes a while for the true power of a data structure to sink in. Whether conscious of it or not, a programmer will always approach a problem using the tools he or she knows best. If you have a background in object-oriented languages, such as Java or C++, when faced with a new data type your first impulse will be to create a new class. In Python, the vast majority of the time this will be wrong, and rather than creating a new class, you should look for a way to use the existing data structures (lists and dictionaries) to store your information.

Python also supports classes and modules, but these are discussed in Chapter 7.

HINT 4: EXAMINE THE BUILT-IN OPERATIONS

Inasmuch as built-in data structures bring their own set of operations with them, this hint is largely combined with Hint 3. As you learn about strings, you can notice that the + operator is also used to perform string concatenation. As you have seen, the ** operator is used for exponentiation. The append method can be used to attach a new element to a list. The method has_key can be used to determine whether a particular key is valid for a given dictionary. As noted previously, these operations are summarized in Appendix A.

However, operations may exist that are not associated with any particular data structure. An example we have seen already is the *print* statement. This statement converts the text that follows into a string and places the string on an area called the *standard output* (typically a window set aside for that purpose). Commas can separate multiple arguments:

```
print "the minimum of a and b is " , r
```

A *for* statement can be used to examine each element in a string, list, or tuple:

```
names = ("john", "paul", "george", "ringo")
for name in names:
  print "member of the band: " , name
```

A special form called a range can be used to create arithmetic sequences. The function creates a list of integers:

```
a = range(5) # a is [0, 1, 2, 3, 4]
b = range(1, 8) # b is [1, 2, 3, 4, 5, 6, 7, 8]
c = range(1, 8, 3) # c is [1, 4, 7]
d = range(8, 1, -3) # d is [8, 5, 2]
```

A range is commonly combined with a *for* statement to create a loop that runs over an arithmetic progression:

```
for a in range(5, 100, 5):
  print "2 raised to ", a, " is ", 2**a
```

To loop over the elements of a dictionary, first form the list of keys:

```
for name in names.keys():
  print "age of ", name, " is ", ageDict[name]
```

HINT 5: BECOME FAMILIAR WITH THE PROGRAMMING ENVIRONMENT

The programming environment for a new language may be very different from the environment you are accustomed to. If your first language is C or Java, for example, you might think in terms of the steps edit, compile, execute, debug, and edit again. You might have even used an Integrated Development Environment (IDE) that helps reduce the time between each of these steps.

Python is an interpreted programming language. Coding in Python reduces the time between program entry and execution. Statements can be typed directly at the keyboard and are executed immediately. This feature is extremely useful during the initial stages of learning, when you are exploring the basic data types and the effect of operations performed on those data types.

The Python Interpreter can be used in two different ways. When used in interactive mode, expressions are typed directly at the keyboard and are immediately examined and executed. An example session is shown in Figure 2. This style of programming is useful when you are first learning the language, as you can experiment with different expressions and examine the result.

The alternative technique is to place an entire Python program into a file with the extension *.py*. This file can be imported into an interactive session during development. Once developed, the program can then be executed simply by the user clicking the program icon.

Some of the features of the programming environment (such as how to indicate the execution of a Python program stored in a file) will be specific to the operating system you are using. However, no matter what operating system is used, Python includes the idea of the standard input, output, and error output. Most often the standard input corresponds to keyboard input, and the standard and error output are displayed in windows. However, these can be changed depending on the operating system in use.

```
$ python
Python 2.3 (#1, Sep 13 2003, 00:49:11)
[GCC 3.3 20030304 (Apple Computer, Inc. build 1495)] on darwin
Type "help", "copyright", "credits" or "license" for more information.
>>> num = 5
>>> num = num / 2.0
>>> print num
2.5
>>> n = 10
>>> while n <= 100:
...    print 2 ** n
...    n = n + 10
...
1024
1048576
1073741824
1099511627776
1125899906842624
1152921504606846976
1180591620717411303424
1208925819614629174706176
1237940039285380274899124224
1267650600228229401496703205376
```

Figure 2: An Example Interactive Python Session

Python is a *dynamically typed* language, which is different from many programming languages, which are termed *statically typed*. In a statically typed language, the idea of a variable type is tied to a variable name, usually by means of a declaration statement. For example, the following statement in Java declares the variable names to be an array of String values. The only value this variable can maintain is an array of string.

```
String [ ] names;
```

In a dynamically typed language, on the other hand, types are associated not with names but with values. A variable can be said to be currently holding a list of strings, but nothing prevents the same variable from later being assigned a different type of value.

```
info = ['fred', 'sam', 'alice'] # variable holding a list of strings
info = 42 # now holding an integer
```

As you gain experience with Python, you will learn both the advantages of dynamic typing (flexibility, ease of use, speed) and some of the disadvantages (it is easy to pass the wrong type of value to a function, and this error will not be detected until the value is used).

HINT 6: DETERMINE THE CLASS OF PROBLEMS THE LANGUAGE WAS DESIGNED TO SOLVE

Languages do not develop in isolation; they are created for a reason, usually to solve a specific type of problem. Study the type of problems the language is being used to address. Try to understand what features of the language make this type of problem easier to deal with, and why those same features might make other types of problems difficult.

Python is described as a *general-purpose programming language*. However, the very same features on the positive side that contribute to rapid code development and ease of use are also the features that can consume a lot of execution time. These features include dynamic typing, infinite precision integers, and high-level data structures such as lists and dictionaries. In the vast majority of cases, machines nowadays are so fast that the user will not notice the execution time cost, and the benefits will outweigh the drawbacks. But in some situations, such as complex numerical simulations, where every execution cycle must be counted, an interpreted language would not be appropriate.

The case studies presented in this book offer a good indication of the types of problems for which Python can be used.

HINT 7: LOOK FOR USEFUL LIBRARIES

The programming language you use is only the first tool in your toolkit. Libraries of useful extensions that the programming language designer or others have developed can also be extremely useful. Smalltalk, for example, comes with a massive library of existing code. The standard template library in C++ is a large collection of common data structures. Java has an extensive collection of libraries for many different problem domains. Why reinvent the wheel when the majority of work for a problem may already have been developed? Use the Internet or other search tools to discover useful resources.

Libraries of existing Python code can be included in a new program using by the `import` statement:

```
import string # loads the string module
```

Most implementations of Python come with an extensive library of resources useful for mathematics, string handling, database management, network programming, and other tasks. The standard libraries are summarized in Appendix B. Many more have been developed by other programmers and are accessible via the Internet.

HINT 8: EMULATE, COPY, AND STEAL

A good place to start is with existing and working copies of programs. Download a moderately complex program. Make certain you can get it to execute correctly on your system, which may be slightly different from the system on which it was developed. Study these existing programs to figure out how they work and how the different language features are being used.

The case studies presented in this book are a good place to begin your examination of Python programs. Computer programs can, and should, be considered a form of literature. Learn how to read a program to understand what it does and how it works. You will find that in your programming career, you will spend far more time reading programs that have been developed by others than you will writing your own code.

HINT 9: EXPERIMENT, EVOLVE, AND REDO

Once you have explored a few working programs, experiment by making changes. Can you evolve a working program to make it solve a slightly different problem? Can you take one small part of a program and change how it addresses whatever problem it is solving? Try recoding a program you wrote in another language. Don't make a statement-for-statement copy, but think about how the language features of the new language can best be put to use in the rewritten version. Note carefully if some things are easier to do in the new language, and what things are harder.

When you are faced with a new problem, think carefully about previous problems that you have seen that possess features in common with the new problem. Then reexamine the programs you created. Practice experimentation, emulation, and evolution.

HINT 10: HAVE FUN

Developing computer programs can be an extremely difficult task, but it is also one of the most satisfying when a program finally works as you want it to. Most computer scientists first become interested in the field due to the sheer joy of programming. Try not to make the task drudgery. Experiment with projects that are whimsical and fun. Knowledge with pleasant associations is likely to be retained.

INDEX